Mastering AI App Development with MERN Stack

Step into the Future of App Development by Building Intelligent AI-Powered Applications with MERN Stack and TensorFlow.js for Seamless User Experiences

Anik Acharjee

www.orangeava.com

First Published: November 2024
Published By: Orange Education Pvt Ltd, AVA®
Address: 9, Daryaganj, Delhi, 110002, India

275 New North Road Islington Suite 1314 London,
N1 7AA, United Kingdom

ISBN (PBK): 978-93-48107-68-8
ISBN (E-BOOK): 978-93-48107-37-4

Scan the QR code to explore our entire catalogue

www.orangeava.com

Dedicated To

My beloved Parents:

Mr. C.R. Acharjee
Mrs. Tandra Acharjee

and

My wife Shampa and my daughter Anisha

About the Author

Anik Acharjee is a seasoned technology professional with a strong background in software development, particularly in building MERN Stack applications with AI integration. His journey in the tech industry is a testament to his dedication and passion for innovation.

With a solid educational foundation in Computer Science and Engineering, Anik has consistently expanded his skill set through self-education and hands-on experience. His professional career spans multiple roles, including software developer, technical lead, and consultant, accumulating over 8 years of valuable industry experience.

Anik's proficiency extends to a wide range of technologies, including MongoDB, Express.js, React.js, Node.js, and AI frameworks, enabling him to create robust and scalable applications. He has successfully conceptualized, developed, and deployed numerous projects across various domains, including web development, mobile applications, and AI-powered solutions. He is also the author of *Learn Web Technologies From Scratch*, a book that reflects his expertise and passion for modern web applications.

As the author of this book, Anik has had the privilege of delving deeper into the intersection of MERN Stack development and AI technologies. This book reflects his passion for integrating AI into modern web applications and his commitment to helping others unlock their full potential in this rapidly evolving field.

Through comprehensive insights and practical guidance, Anik aims to empower both aspiring and experienced developers to harness the power of MERN Stack and AI, navigating the ever-evolving landscape of web development. His motivation derives from an unwavering passion for innovation and a deep commitment to crafting applications that not only meet but exceed user expectations.

Anik's journey has taught him that continuous learning and self-education are powerful tools, and he is eager to inspire and empower others to embark on their learning journeys and achieve their aspirations in the dynamic world of MERN Stack and AI development.

About the Technical Reviewers

Krishna is a seasoned full-stack developer with over 6 years of experience, delivering robust and scalable applications for various industries, including banking and agritech. With extensive expertise in both frontend and backend technologies, Krishna is proficient in JavaScript frameworks like React and Node.js, and has a deep understanding of database management, cloud computing, and microservices architecture.

Beyond his technical skills, Krishna actively contributes to the open-source community and is passionate about sharing his knowledge with fellow developers. He regularly creates educational content, such as technical articles, to simplify complex programming concepts for others.

Always at the forefront of technological trends, Krishna is dedicated to learning, innovating, and delivering high-performance solutions that meet the evolving needs of modern digital ecosystems.

Alpna Patel is a Senior Software Engineer with over four years of experience in frontend development, specializing in React JS. Her passion for AI and machine learning emerged during her Master's studies, where she gained foundational knowledge in neural networks. Her research in sentiment analysis further enhanced her expertise in AI/ML applications.

Currently working in the IT domain, Alpna is driven by her enthusiasm for new technologies like generative AI and their potential to create innovative solutions. She is dedicated to staying at the forefront of the tech industry, constantly learning and applying her skills to build impactful applications.

Acknowledgements

There are a few people I would like to thank for their continued and ongoing support during the writing of this book. First and foremost, I would like to thank my parents for continuously encouraging me to write the book – this book would not have been possible without their support.

I am grateful to the course and the companies that supported me throughout the learning process of integrating MERN Stack with AI, as well as learning the tools and technologies related to MERN Stack. Thank you for all the hidden support provided.

I gratefully acknowledge Krishna Agrawal and Alpna Patel for their kind technical scrutiny of this book.

My gratitude also goes to the team at Orange AVA for their generous support in providing me ample time to complete the book.

Preface

Welcome to *Mastering AI App Development with MERN Stack*, a comprehensive guide designed to help you navigate the exciting world of artificial intelligence and full-stack web development using the MERN (MongoDB, Express, React, Node.js) stack. This book is structured to provide a deep dive into the core principles and practical applications of AI in web development, leveraging the MERN stack. In this book, we explore the foundational concepts of AI and how they can be integrated into web applications using the MERN stack.

We delve into the importance of automation and real-time data processing, which are crucial in today's fast-paced digital landscape. Through practical examples and real-world case studies, we demonstrate how AI can enhance web applications, making them more responsive and user-friendly. The book is divided into 15 chapters, each designed to build upon the previous one, providing a gradual learning curve. We start with the basics of the MERN stack and AI fundamentals, then move on to more advanced topics. Our approach is practical and hands-on, with numerous examples and projects that you can follow along with. By the end of this book, you will have a solid understanding of how to build AI-powered web applications using the MERN stack, and you will be equipped with the skills to tackle complex projects and contribute to the ever-evolving field of AI in web development. Whether you are a beginner looking to break into AI and web development or a seasoned developer seeking to expand your skill set, this book is designed to be your guide. Let's embark on this journey together and explore the exciting possibilities of building AI apps with the MERN stack.

Chapter 1 lays the foundational concepts of AI, including its history, core principles, and its transformative impact on technology and society. Readers will explore the components of the MERN stack – MongoDB for database management, Express.js for server-side operations, React for dynamic user interfaces, and Node.js for scalable server-side scripting. The chapter emphasizes the importance of JavaScript as the unifying programming language across the MERN stack, enabling seamless integration and development.

Chapter 2 delves into the specifics of installing and setting up the core technologies that comprise the MERN stack: MongoDB for database management, Express.js for server-side logic, React for the front-end interface, and Node.js for the backend environment. It emphasizes the importance of JavaScript as the primary programming language that ties these technologies together, enabling seamless development across the stack.

Chapter 3 introduces the reader to the exciting world of machine learning, providing a solid foundation in the concepts of supervised and unsupervised learning, neural networks, and deep learning. It emphasizes the versatility of JavaScript as a language not just for web development but also for implementing complex AI algorithms. The chapter explores TensorFlow.js, a powerful library that brings machine learning to JavaScript, enabling the training and deployment of models directly in the browser or on Node.js. Readers will learn about the TensorFlow.js ecosystem, including how to work with pre-trained models and how to train their own models from scratch.

Chapter 4 bridges the gap between theoretical machine learning concepts and their real-world application, focusing on the integration of AI functionalities within the server side of the MERN stack. Readers will explore how to leverage TensorFlow.js—a powerful and flexible library for machine learning in JavaScript—to develop, train, and deploy machine learning models directly in Node.js.

Chapter 5 explores how to infuse AI-driven interactivity and personalization into React components, enhancing the user experience with smart features such as predictive text, real-time recommendations, and adaptive content layouts. Readers will learn about the core concepts of React, including components, state, and props, and how to integrate these with AI models to create interfaces that respond intelligently to user input and behavior. The chapter will cover the use of React hooks for managing state in functional components, context for managing global data, and higher-order components for reusing logic across the application.

Chapter 6 introduces MongoDB's flexible document model, which is particularly well-suited for storing unstructured data, a common requirement for AI applications. Readers will learn how to use MongoDB in conjunction with Mongoose, an Object Data Modeling (ODM) library for MongoDB and Node.js, to create schemas that reflect the data needs of AI models and ensure data integrity.

Chapter 7 introduces the concept of middleware in web development, explaining how it operates within the request-response cycle in Express.js applications. It covers the creation of custom middleware functions that can perform tasks such as user authentication, data validation, and error handling, which are essential for AI-driven applications. Additionally, the chapter explores the integration of TensorFlow.js and other AI libraries within Express.js middleware, enabling the execution of machine learning models directly within the web server environment.

Chapter 8 introduces key concepts in chatbot development, including intent recognition, entity extraction, and conversation flow management. It delves into the use of Dialogflow and Microsoft Bot Framework as powerful tools for creating sophisticated chatbot experiences, highlighting their capabilities in processing and understanding user inputs. Additionally, the chapter covers the integration of these chatbots into web applications built with MongoDB, Express.js, React, and Node.js, ensuring a seamless user experience.

Chapter 9 introduces powerful libraries such as TensorFlow.js for image recognition and Web Speech API for voice recognition, demonstrating how to leverage these tools within a Node.js environment. It covers the process of training models to recognize images and speech patterns, as well as the integration of pre-trained models for quick feature deployment.

Chapter 10 explores the use of machine learning libraries such as TensorFlow.js to develop the algorithms that power recommendation systems. It also discusses the role of MongoDB in storing user data and interaction logs, which are crucial for generating accurate recommendations. Readers will learn how to leverage Node.js and Express.js to build the server-side logic that processes data and serves personalized content.

Chapter 11 introduces key concepts such as continuous integration and continuous deployment (CI/CD), which streamline the development lifecycle, and containerization with Docker, which simplifies deployment and scaling. Readers will learn how to use platforms like Heroku for hosting and how to configure cloud services such as AWS or Google Cloud for more complex deployments that require robust infrastructure and scalability.

Chapter 12 discusses the implementation of security measures such as JSON Web Tokens (JWT) for secure user authentication, OAuth for third-party authorization, and HTTPS protocols for encrypted data transmission. It also covers the use of security-focused middleware in Express.js, such as helmet and rate-limiting, to protect against common web attacks like cross-site scripting (XSS) and denial-of-service (DoS) attacks.

Chapter 13 introduces Kubernetes and Docker as essential tools for containerization and orchestration, allowing for the deployment of scalable applications across multiple servers. It also discusses the use of cloud services like AWS Elastic Beanstalk and Google Cloud Platform's App Engine, which provide managed environments that automatically scale applications based on demand.

Chapter 14 delves into the evolution of machine learning libraries beyond TensorFlow.js, introducing readers to newer, more specialized libraries that offer advanced capabilities for specific AI tasks. It also discusses the growing importance of ethical AI and responsible development practices, emphasizing the need for transparency, fairness, and privacy in AI applications.

Chapter 15 includes different case studies. The first case study will explore a dynamic e-commerce platform that leverages AI for personalized product recommendations, using technologies such as MongoDB for data storage, Express. js for server-side logic, React for building a responsive UI, and Node.js for backend development. It will highlight the use of TensorFlow.js for developing the machine learning models that drive the recommendation engine.

Downloading the code bundles and colored images

Please follow the links or scan the QR codes to download the
Code Bundles and Images of the book:

https://github.com/ava-orange-education/Mastering-AI-App-Development-with-MERN-Stack

The code bundles and images of the book are also hosted on
https://rebrand.ly/27b88a

In case there's an update to the code, it will be updated on the existing
GitHub repository.

Errata

We take immense pride in our work at **Orange Education Pvt Ltd,** and follow best practices to ensure the accuracy of our content to provide an indulging reading experience to our subscribers. Our readers are our mirrors, and we use their inputs to reflect and improve upon human errors, if any, that may have occurred during the publishing processes involved. To let us maintain the quality and help us reach out to any readers who might be having difficulties due to any unforeseen errors, please write to us at :

errata@orangeava.com

Your support, suggestions, and feedback are highly appreciated.

DID YOU KNOW

Did you know that Orange Education Pvt Ltd offers eBook versions of every book published, with PDF and ePub files available? You can upgrade to the eBook version at **www.orangeava.com** and as a print book customer, you are entitled to a discount on the eBook copy. Get in touch with us at: **info@orangeava.com** for more details.

At **www.orangeava.com**, you can also read a collection of free technical articles, sign up for a range of free newsletters, and receive exclusive discounts and offers on AVA® Books and eBooks.

PIRACY

If you come across any illegal copies of our works in any form on the internet, we would be grateful if you would provide us with the location address or website name. Please contact us at **info@orangeava.com** with a link to the material.

ARE YOU INTERESTED IN AUTHORING WITH US?

If there is a topic that you have expertise in, and you are interested in either writing or contributing to a book, please write to us at **business@orangeava.com**. We are on a journey to help developers and tech professionals to gain insights on the present technological advancements and innovations happening across the globe and build a community that believes Knowledge is best acquired by sharing and learning with others. Please reach out to us to learn what our audience demands and how you can be part of this educational reform. We also welcome ideas from tech experts and help them build learning and development content for their domains.

REVIEWS

Please leave a review. Once you have read and used this book, why not leave a review on the site that you purchased it from? Potential readers can then see and use your unbiased opinion to make purchase decisions. We at Orange Education would love to know what you think about our products, and our authors can learn from your feedback. Thank you!

For more information about Orange Education, please visit **www.orangeava.com**.

Table of Contents

CHAPTER 1

Introduction to AI and the MERN Ecosystem

Introduction

Introduction to AI and the MERN Ecosystem serves as the gateway to understanding the synergy between Artificial Intelligence (AI) and the MERN stack, setting the stage for a journey into sophisticated web development. This opening chapter lays the foundational concepts of AI, including its history, core principles, and its transformative impact on technology and society. Readers will explore the components of the MERN stack – MongoDB for database management, Express.js for server-side operations, React for dynamic user interfaces, and Node.js for scalable server-side scripting. The chapter emphasizes the importance of JavaScript as the unifying programming language across the MERN stack, enabling seamless integration and development. By highlighting the potential of AI within this modern web development framework, the chapter prepares readers to harness the combined power of MERN technologies and AI to build intelligent, responsive web applications that are at the forefront of the industry.

Structure

In this chapter, we will cover the following topics:

- Overview of Artificial Intelligence
- Introduction to the MERN Stack
- The Synergy Between AI and the MERN Stack
- Essential Tools and Technologies
- Setting the Stage for AI Integration

Overview of Artificial Intelligence

Artificial Intelligence (AI) is a branch of computer science dedicated to creating systems that can perform tasks that would typically require human intelligence. These tasks include learning, reasoning, problem-solving, perception, and understanding language. AI is not just about programming a computer to drive a car by obeying traffic signals, but it's about imbuing machines with the ability to think, learn from experience, and make decisions in complex environments.

The roots of AI can be traced back to ancient myths and stories of artificial beings endowed with intelligence or consciousness by master craftsmen; however, the formal foundation of the field began in the mid-20th century. Pioneers like Alan Turing, and later, researchers like John McCarthy and Marvin Minsky, played crucial roles in developing the theories and technologies that shape AI today. Turing's famous question, "Can machines think?", and his subsequent development of the Turing Test were instrumental in framing the discussion about what constitutes true intelligence.

AI has grown to encompass a variety of techniques and disciplines, including but not limited to machine learning, natural language processing (NLP), computer vision, and robotics. Machine learning itself has become a cornerstone of AI, with algorithms that can analyze and interpret vast amounts of data more quickly and accurately than humans. These algorithms improve over time through a process known as training, where they adjust their parameters to minimize errors in their predictions or decisions based on feedback.

The development of AI has been propelled by the increasing availability of large datasets, improvements in computing power, and the creation of more sophisticated algorithms. Deep learning, in particular, has been a game-changer, enabling the development of models that can automatically learn high-level abstractions from data. This has led to significant breakthroughs in image and speech recognition, language translation, and even game playing, with AI systems now able to defeat human champions in complex games like Go and chess.

Natural language processing enables machines to understand and respond to text or voice data in a way that is natural for humans. This technology underpins the functionality of chatbots and virtual assistants, which are becoming increasingly sophisticated and capable of handling a wide range of tasks, from customer service inquiries to providing personalized recommendations. Computer vision, another critical area of AI, allows machines to interpret and make decisions based on visual data, leading to advancements in fields such as medical imaging, autonomous vehicles, and surveillance systems.

Despite these advancements, AI is not without its challenges. The field grapples with issues such as bias in data and algorithms, the interpretability of AI models (often referred to as the "black box" problem), and the ethical implications of autonomous systems making decisions that affect human lives. As AI continues to advance and become more integrated into everyday technology, addressing these challenges is crucial to ensure that AI systems are fair, transparent, and aligned with human values.

AI technologies have evolved through various stages, from the creation of basic algorithms and the Turing Test to the development of machine learning, deep learning, and neural networks. Machine learning, a subset of AI, involves the development of algorithms that allow computers to learn from and make predictions based on data. Deep learning, a further subset of machine learning, uses large neural networks with many layers of processing units, taking advantage of advances in computing power and improved training techniques to learn complex patterns in large amounts of data.

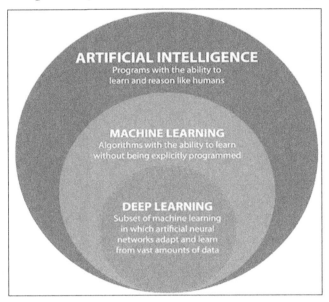

Figure 1.1: *Overview of Artificial Intelligence*
Source: *https://www.researchgate.net/publication/354348678/figure/fig1/AS:11431281187572961*
@1694283946559/Comprehensive-overview-of-artificial-intelligence
-AI-and-its-subfields-from.tif

AI's impact on society is profound and ever-expanding. It powers web search engines, enables voice-activated assistants like Siri and Alexa, enhances personalization in social media feeds, and facilitates more predictive responses in healthcare diagnostics. The technology has also raised important ethical and social issues, such as privacy concerns, the potential for job displacement, and the need for regulations to manage AI applications.

In the context of web development, AI's potential is vast. It can be used to create more personalized user experiences, automate repetitive tasks, and analyze user data to glean insights that can drive business strategy. The MERN stack, with its JavaScript-based framework, is particularly well-suited to integrating AI, as JavaScript's ubiquity across both client and server-side development allows for a seamless incorporation of AI features. As we continue to explore the MERN ecosystem, we will see how AI can be woven into the fabric of modern web applications, creating more intelligent, efficient, and user-centric experiences.

In summary, AI represents a dynamic and rapidly evolving field that stands at the confluence of computer science, cognitive science, and robotics. Its development continues to push the boundaries of what machines can do, often in ways that can mimic and sometimes exceed human capabilities. As we delve deeper into the MERN stack's role in web development, understanding AI's foundational concepts and its potential for integration will be crucial for harnessing its full potential in modern applications.

Introduction to the MERN Stack

The MERN stack is a powerful, modern web development framework that stands for MongoDB, Express.js, React, and Node.js. Each of these technologies plays a crucial role in web application development, making the MERN stack a popular choice for developers looking to build dynamic, scalable, and high-performance web applications.

Evolution of the MERN Stack

The MERN stack's evolution is a testament to the web development community's continuous search for more efficient and integrated ways to build applications. Initially, developers often had to work with disparate technologies for the frontend and backend, leading to a steeper learning curve and more complex codebases. The advent of Node.js was a turning point, allowing JavaScript, traditionally a client-side language, to be used on the server side. This innovation laid the groundwork for full-stack JavaScript development, where both the client and server could be written in a single language.

As Node.js gained popularity, frameworks like Express.js emerged to streamline server-side development, offering a robust set of features for web and mobile applications. On the frontend, React's introduction revolutionized UI development with its component-based architecture, improving reusability and the ability to manage state more effectively.

MongoDB's non-relational approach to database management addressed the need for more flexible data storage solutions that could handle the variety and velocity of data in modern web applications. Its document model aligned well with the JSON data structures commonly used in JavaScript, further smoothing the development process.

MongoDB is a document-oriented NoSQL database that is used to store application data. Unlike traditional relational databases, MongoDB uses a flexible document-based approach, which allows it to store complex hierarchical relationships and scale easily. This flexibility makes it particularly well-suited for handling the large and unstructured datasets often required in modern web applications.

Express.js is a lightweight and flexible Node.js web application framework that provides a robust set of features for building single and multi-page web applications.

It is designed to make the process of building server-side logic more straightforward and manageable. Express.js simplifies the server-side management of routes, requests, and responses, and integrates seamlessly with other components of the MERN stack.

React is a declarative, efficient, and flexible JavaScript library for building user interfaces. Developed and maintained by Facebook, React allows developers to create large web applications that can change data without reloading the page. Its key feature is the ability to build components, which are encapsulated components that manage their own state and can be composed to make complex UIs. React's component-based architecture makes it easy to develop and maintain the quality of the user interface of web applications.

Node.js is a JavaScript runtime built on Chrome's V8 JavaScript engine. It enables developers to execute JavaScript on the server side. Node.js uses an event-driven, non-blocking I/O model, making it lightweight and efficient, particularly for data-intensive real-time applications that run across distributed devices. Its use in the MERN stack allows for the use of a single programming language, JavaScript, across both client and server sides, simplifying development and reducing the potential for errors.

MERN Stack Architecture

The MERN stack architecture is a structured framework that outlines how the four core technologies—MongoDB, Express.js, React, and Node.js—interact with each other to create a seamless, end-to-end development experience. This architecture is designed to facilitate the development of dynamic web applications by leveraging a single language, JavaScript, across both the client and server sides.

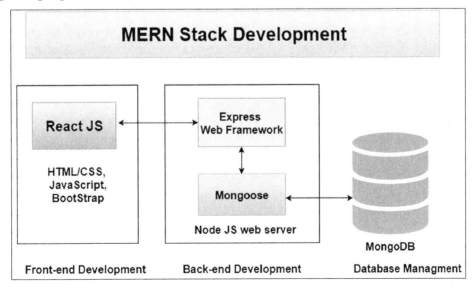

Figure 1.2: *MERN Architecture*
Source: https://www.bocasay.com/wp-content/uploads/2020/03/MERN-stack-1.png

How the Components Interact:

- **Client Side (Frontend) - React.js**: React is responsible for the user interface of the MERN application. It runs in the user's browser and presents the application's UI as a collection of components. React's virtual DOM efficiently updates the browser's DOM as the user interacts with the application, leading to a smooth and responsive experience.

- **Server Side (Backend) - Node.js and Express.js**: Node.js is the JavaScript runtime environment that runs the server-side code. Express.js is a framework that runs on top of Node.js, simplifying the creation of server-side logic and APIs. It handles routing, middleware, and server-side logic, such as user authentication and data processing.

- **Database - MongoDB**: MongoDB is the database layer in the MERN stack. It stores the application's data in a flexible, JSON-like format, which aligns well with JavaScript's object-oriented approach. MongoDB's NoSQL nature allows for scalable and flexible data storage, which is essential for modern web applications that handle large amounts of unstructured data.

Flow of Data in a MERN Application:

1. **User Interaction**: The process begins when a user interacts with the React-based frontend interface, such as submitting a form or requesting data.

2. **React to Express**: React sends these requests to the Express.js server, typically as HTTP requests. This communication is facilitated by the fetch API or libraries like Axios.

3. **Express to MongoDB**: Express.js processes the request, which may involve querying or updating data in the MongoDB database. Express uses Mongoose, an Object Data Modeling (ODM) library, to interact with MongoDB, allowing for easier data schema validation and query handling.

4. **MongoDB to Express**: Once the database operation is complete, MongoDB returns the data to Express.js, which then processes the results.

5. **Express to React**: Express sends a response back to the React frontend. This could be the requested data, a confirmation of a successful operation, or an error message.

6. **React Updates UI**: Upon receiving the response, React updates the UI accordingly, providing the user with feedback or new data.

   This architecture ensures that the entire application is JavaScript-centric, with JSON as the primary data exchange format, making the development process more streamlined and efficient. The MERN stack's architecture is particularly beneficial for applications that require real-time data updates, complex user interactions, and scalability to handle growth.

Reasons to Use MERN Stack

The MERN stack's unified JavaScript development experience is one of its most compelling advantages. It simplifies the development process by allowing teams to use a single language across the entire application, reducing context switching and making it easier to maintain a consistent coding style and best practices.

The stack's components are open-source and backed by strong communities, ensuring a wealth of resources, libraries, and tools are available to developers. This support system not only aids in resolving issues but also in keeping the technologies up-to-date with the latest web standards and practices.

Moreover, the MERN stack is designed for building dynamic, high-performance applications. React's virtual DOM minimizes costly DOM manipulations, while Node.js's non-blocking I/O model allows for handling numerous concurrent connections efficiently, making the stack suitable for real-time applications like chat apps and online gaming.

Importance of the MERN Stack

The MERN stack is important because it represents a modern approach to web development that aligns with the needs of today's dynamic web applications. It supports the rapid development of high-quality applications and provides scalability to grow with the user base. The stack's architecture is conducive to agile development practices, allowing for iterative development and continuous deployment, which are crucial in today's fast-paced software development environment.

Together, these technologies provide a cohesive environment for developers to work within, offering both the client-side and server-side environments necessary to develop full-fledged web applications. The MERN stack's unified JavaScript-based architecture streamlines development processes, enhances performance, and facilitates the maintenance and scalability of applications. It supports the rapid development of prototypes as well as full-scale applications, making it an ideal choice for startups and large enterprises alike.

By leveraging the MERN stack, developers can enjoy a more integrated development experience, reduce the time and complexity associated with managing multiple languages and frameworks, and build applications that are both powerful and efficient. The popularity of the MERN stack continues to grow as it proves to be an effective solution for modern web development challenges, combining flexibility, ease of use, and a robust community of developers and resources to support its implementation.

Today's Demand in the Market

In today's market, the demand for full-stack developers proficient in the MERN stack is high. Startups and enterprises alike seek developers who can build and maintain scalable, responsive, and feature-rich applications. The MERN stack's ability to streamline development workflows and reduce time-to-market makes it a valuable skill set for developers.

The stack's technologies are frequently updated with new features and improvements, reflecting their strong adoption and ongoing relevance in the industry. As businesses continue to emphasize digital presence and user experience, the MERN stack's role in web development is not only sustained but growing, with its comprehensive ecosystem and community support making it a go-to choice for modern web application development.

Integration and Compatibility with Other Technologies

The MERN stack is not only self-sufficient but also designed to be highly compatible with a variety of other technologies and tools that can further enhance its capabilities. This section will explore how the MERN stack integrates with various APIs, libraries, and frameworks to extend its functionality. It would cover:

- **Third-Party APIs**: How to incorporate external services and APIs, such as payment gateways, social media integrations, and cloud services, into MERN applications.

- **State Management Tools**: The use of state management libraries like Redux or MobX with React to handle complex application states.

- **Development and Debugging Tools**: Tools like Chrome DevTools, React Developer Tools, and Node.js Inspector that aid in development and debugging.

- **Testing Frameworks**: Integration with testing frameworks and libraries, such as Jest, Mocha, and Chai, for unit and integration testing of MERN applications.

- **DevOps and Deployment Tools**: How the MERN stack fits into modern DevOps practices with tools like Docker, Kubernetes, and CI/CD pipelines for efficient deployment and scaling.

- **Search Engine Optimization (SEO)**: Techniques and tools to enhance the SEO of MERN stack applications, considering that single-page applications (SPAs) can present challenges for search engine crawlers.

- **Mobile Development:** Utilizing technologies like React Native for building mobile applications that can share logic with web applications built on the MERN stack.

The Synergy Between AI and the MERN Stack

The synergy between Artificial Intelligence (AI) and the MERN stack represents a convergence of two powerful forces in modern web development. AI brings the power of machine learning, natural language processing, and predictive analytics to applications, while the MERN stack provides a full-stack JavaScript framework for building scalable and performant web applications. Together, they create a potent combination that can drive innovation and deliver sophisticated solutions.

- **Enhanced User Experience with AI**: AI technologies can analyze user data and behavior to deliver personalized experiences. When integrated with the MERN stack, developers can leverage React's dynamic UI capabilities to reflect these personalized experiences in real-time, offering recommendations, content, and interactions tailored to individual users.

- **Streamlined Development Process**: The MERN stack's use of JavaScript across both the frontend and backend simplifies the development process, allowing for a more streamlined workflow. This is particularly beneficial when incorporating AI features, as developers can work within a single language ecosystem, reducing the complexity and potential for errors when connecting AI services with web applications.

- **Real-Time Data Processing**: Node.js and Express.js facilitate real-time data processing and API management, which is crucial for AI functionalities that require immediate data analysis and response. This enables the creation of features such as chatbots, real-time analytics, and interactive dashboards that can process and display AI-generated insights without delay.

- **Scalable Data Management**: MongoDB's flexible, document-oriented database structure is ideal for handling the varied and voluminous data that AI algorithms need to function. Its scalability ensures that as an application grows and the amount of data increases, the database can handle the load, which is essential for AI models that continuously learn and evolve.

- **Cost-Effectiveness and Community Support**: The MERN stack, being open-source, benefits from a large community of developers who contribute to its continuous improvement. This community support extends to the integration of AI, where developers share tools, best practices, and libraries that make AI integration more accessible and cost-effective.

- **Rapid Prototyping and Iteration**: The combination of MERN and AI facilitates rapid prototyping and iterative development. React's component-based architecture allows for quick UI changes, while Node.js and Express.js enable fast backend updates, essential for testing and refining AI-driven features.

- **Market Demand and Future-Proofing**: As the demand for intelligent web applications grows, the synergy between AI and the MERN stack positions developers to meet this demand. By mastering these technologies, developers can future-proof their skills and create applications that are both cutting-edge and highly marketable.

Need for Synergy

The synergy between AI and the MERN stack is not just beneficial; it's becoming increasingly necessary as web applications grow more complex and user expectations rise. AI and the MERN stack complement each other in several key ways that address the challenges of modern web development:

- **Personalization and User Engagement**: Modern users expect a personalized experience when they interact with web applications. AI can analyze user data and behavior to deliver such personalized content, and when integrated with the MERN stack, this personalization can be reflected in real-time through React's dynamic UIs. This synergy allows for the creation of applications that adapt to user preferences, improving engagement and satisfaction.

- **Efficiency and Productivity**: The MERN stack's unified JavaScript development environment streamlines the process of building web applications. By incorporating AI, developers can automate routine tasks, such as data entry and analysis, content generation, and even complex decision-making processes. This automation frees developers to focus on more creative and strategic aspects of development, enhancing productivity.

- **Scalability and Performance**: As web applications scale, they must handle increasing amounts of data and traffic without compromising performance. AI can optimize resource allocation and load balancing, while the MERN stack's scalable architecture ensures that the application can grow. MongoDB's flexible schema and Node.js's non-blocking I/O are particularly well-suited to the data-intensive demands of AI applications.

- **Real-Time Interactions**: AI can process large volumes of data in real-time, which is essential for features like chatbots, instant recommendations, and live data visualization. The MERN stack, with its real-time capabilities powered by Node.js and Express.js, provides the necessary infrastructure to support these AI-driven interactions without latency, delivering a seamless user experience.

Examples of Challenges Addressed by AI within the MERN Stack:

- **Complex Data Analysis**: Web applications often need to process and interpret complex data sets to provide insights to users. AI, with its advanced algorithms for data analysis, can uncover patterns and insights from data that would be difficult or impossible for humans to discern. Within the MERN stack, this processed data can be efficiently managed by MongoDB and served to the user through a responsive React frontend.

- **Content Generation and Management**: Managing and generating content can be a significant challenge for web applications, especially those with large amounts of user-generated content. AI can assist in content moderation, automated tagging, and even generating content based on user interactions.

The MERN stack facilitates the storage, retrieval, and display of this content, ensuring that it is relevant and engaging for users.

- **User Behavior Prediction**: Understanding and predicting user behavior is crucial for applications that aim to provide anticipatory services or products. AI models can predict user actions based on historical data, and the MERN stack can respond to these predictions by dynamically updating the UI or preloading resources, thus enhancing the overall user experience.

AI Applications in MongoDB

MongoDB, as a flexible NoSQL database, is well-suited for AI applications that require the storage and processing of large, unstructured datasets. The database's dynamic schema allows for the easy accommodation of the varied data types that AI and machine learning models often work with. MongoDB's recent advancements, such as the introduction of MongoDB Atlas Vector Search, enable developers to perform vector embedding directly on data stored in MongoDB. This feature is particularly useful for generative AI applications, as it allows for the efficient development of features like semantic search and personalized recommendation systems.

MongoDB's AI Innovators Program is another initiative that supports the development of AI applications by providing credits, technical expertise, and co-marketing opportunities. This program aims to reduce the unique burdens of developing AI applications, such as the need for multiple iterations of model training and the associated development costs.

AI Applications in Express.js

Express.js, a web application framework for Node.js, serves as the backend component of the MERN stack and plays a crucial role in AI applications by managing server-side logic, API endpoints, and routing. It can be used to build RESTful APIs that AI-powered frontend applications can consume. For instance, Express.js can handle requests from a React-based chatbot interface, process them using AI models, and send back intelligent responses.

Express.js's lightweight and middleware-centric architecture makes it ideal for integrating various AI functionalities, such as natural language processing (NLP) and image recognition services, into web applications. It can also serve as a bridge between the frontend and AI services hosted on external platforms or within the same application stack.

AI Applications in React.js

React.js is a powerful library for building dynamic user interfaces and is increasingly being used to create AI-powered web applications. React's component-based architecture and virtual DOM make it an excellent choice for applications that require real-time updates based on AI-generated data, such as live data visualization and interactive dashboards.

Developers can integrate AI and machine learning directly into React applications, leveraging libraries like TensorFlow.js for in-browser machine learning or connecting to external AI services via API calls. React's state management and reactivity systems allow for seamless updates to the UI when AI models generate new insights or predictions.

AI Applications in Node.js

Node.js is a JavaScript runtime that enables server-side scripting and is essential for building scalable network applications within the MERN stack. Its non-blocking I/O model and event-driven architecture are well-suited for AI applications that require real-time data processing and high concurrency.

Node.js can be used to implement various AI and machine learning functionalities, such as training models, performing data analysis, and running predictive algorithms. Libraries like TensorFlow.js have been adapted for Node.js, allowing developers to execute machine learning models on the server side. Additionally, Node.js can interact with other AI services and libraries, providing a versatile environment for AI application development.

In conclusion, the synergy between AI and the MERN stack opens up a world of possibilities for developers and businesses alike. It allows for the creation of web applications that are not only intelligent and responsive but also scalable and efficient. As AI continues to advance, its integration with the MERN stack will likely become more seamless, further enhancing the capabilities of web applications and the experiences they provide.

Essential Tools and Technologies

In the realm of AI and the MERN ecosystem, a suite of essential tools and technologies plays a pivotal role in enhancing development efficiency and application performance. For AI, frameworks like TensorFlow and PyTorch offer robust libraries for building and training complex machine learning models, while tools like NLTK and spaCy support advanced natural language processing capabilities. Platforms such as Google AI Platform and AWS SageMaker streamline the deployment and scaling of AI models. In the MERN stack, Visual Studio Code is a preferred editor due to its extensive JavaScript support. MongoDB Compass facilitates direct interaction with the database, and Postman is invaluable for API testing. React Developer Tools aid in debugging React applications, and npm manages package installations and dependencies efficiently. Together, these tools not only empower developers to create sophisticated AI-driven applications but also ensure that these applications are scalable, maintainable, and ready for deployment in a fast-paced digital environment.

Essential Tools and Technologies in AI

Artificial Intelligence (AI) relies on a variety of tools and technologies that enable the development, training, and deployment of AI models. These tools are essential for handling the complexities of AI processes and enhancing the capabilities of AI systems:

- **Machine Learning Frameworks**: Tools like TensorFlow, PyTorch, and Keras are fundamental for developing and training machine learning models. They provide comprehensive libraries and APIs for designing and training complex neural networks.

- **Natural Language Processing (NLP) Tools**: Libraries such as NLTK, spaCy, and GPT (Generative Pre-trained Transformer) models facilitate the processing and understanding of human language, essential for applications like chatbots and language translation.

- **AI Development Platforms**: Google AI Platform, Microsoft Azure Machine Learning, and AWS SageMaker provide integrated environments for training, tuning, and deploying machine learning models at scale.

- **Data Processing and Visualization Tools**: Pandas for data manipulation, Matplotlib and Seaborn for data visualization, and Scikit-learn for implementing standard machine learning algorithms are crucial for analyzing and understanding data effectively.

- **AI Optimization Tools**: AutoML tools like Google's AutoML and H2O AutoML help automate the selection and tuning of machine learning models, making AI accessible to non-experts and improving efficiency in model development.

Essential Tools and Technologies in the MERN Ecosystem

The MERN stack, comprising MongoDB, Express.js, React, and Node.js, utilizes a range of tools and technologies that streamline the development of full-stack web applications:

- **Code Editors**: Visual Studio Code is widely favored for MERN development due to its extensive range of extensions, integrated Git control, and support for JavaScript and Node.js debugging.

- **Database Management**: MongoDB Compass is the official GUI for MongoDB. It allows developers to manage their database, run queries, and visualize their data structure easily.

- **API Testing and Development Tools**: Postman is extensively used for developing and testing APIs. It allows developers to create, share, test, and document APIs efficiently.

- **Frontend Development Tools**: React Developer Tools is a Chrome DevTools extension for debugging React applications. It allows developers to inspect the React component hierarchies in the Chrome Developer Tools.

- **Backend Frameworks**: Express.js serves as the backend framework running on Node.js. It simplifies the routing and middleware setup, making API creation straightforward.

- **Real-time Collaboration Tools**: Tools like GitHub and Bitbucket support version control and collaboration, essential for team-based projects and source code management.

- **Package Managers**: Node Package Manager (npm) is crucial for managing third-party packages in Node.js, allowing developers to install, update, and manage dependencies efficiently.

- **Build and Deployment Tools**: Webpack is used for bundling JavaScript files for usage in a browser, while tools like Docker help in containerizing the MERN applications for consistent deployment across different environments.

These tools and technologies not only facilitate the development process but also enhance the performance, scalability, and maintainability of AI and MERN stack applications, ensuring developers can build robust, efficient, and effective solutions.

Setting the Stage for AI Integration

Integrating AI into the MERN ecosystem involves several key considerations that ensure the success and sustainability of the development process and the final product. These considerations span technical, ethical, and operational domains.

- **Data Quality and Availability**
  - **Quality**: AI models are only as good as the data they are trained on. Ensuring high-quality data that is accurate, complete, and representative is crucial. Poor data quality can lead to biased or inaccurate model predictions.
  - **Availability**: Sufficient data is required to train robust AI models. In the MERN ecosystem, MongoDB can handle large volumes of structured and unstructured data, but considerations around data collection, storage, and management are vital. Ensuring data is readily accessible and efficiently processed in MongoDB impacts the performance of AI applications.

- **Scalability and Performance**
  - **Scalability**: As AI applications grow, the underlying infrastructure must scale accordingly. This includes scaling MongoDB databases to handle larger datasets and ensuring that Node.js servers can manage increased load from AI computations.
  - **Performance**: Integrating AI should not compromise the application's

performance. Techniques such as optimizing database queries in MongoDB, efficient data handling in Node.js, and minimizing the computational load on the client side with React are essential. Additionally, leveraging Node.js for asynchronous operations can help maintain a responsive application.

- **Ethical and Regulatory Considerations**
  - o **Ethical Implications**: AI applications can have significant ethical implications, particularly in areas like privacy, consent, and transparency. Decisions made by AI systems should be fair and not result in discriminatory outcomes. Developers must design AI integrations with ethical considerations in mind, ensuring that AI behaves in a manner aligned with societal values.
  - o **Regulatory Compliance**: Depending on the region and industry, AI applications may be subject to specific regulations. For instance, applications handling personal data must comply with GDPR in Europe or CCPA in California. Understanding and integrating these regulatory requirements from the outset is crucial for legal compliance and user trust.

- **Technical Expertise and Resources**
  - o **Expertise**: Integrating AI into the MERN stack requires a blend of skills in web development, database management, and AI model development and training. Teams may need to invest in training or hire specialists with experience in AI and machine learning.
  - o **Resources**: AI integration can be resource-intensive, requiring advanced computational power and storage. Organizations must ensure they have the necessary hardware or cloud infrastructure to support the development and deployment of AI models. Tools like TensorFlow.js are optimized for various environments, but leveraging them effectively still requires careful resource management.

In summary, integrating AI into the MERN ecosystem requires careful consideration of data quality and availability, scalability and performance of the system, adherence to ethical standards and regulatory requirements, and sufficient technical expertise and resources. Addressing these considerations thoughtfully will lead to the successful implementation of AI functionalities that enhance the capabilities of MERN-based applications, making them more intelligent, efficient, and user-centric.

Preparing Data for AI Integration

Integrating AI into the MERN ecosystem requires meticulous data preparation, which is a critical step in the development of effective AI models. Proper data preparation not only enhances the performance of AI models but also ensures their reliability and accuracy in making predictions or decisions.

Importance of Data Preparation for AI Integration

Data preparation is fundamental because AI models learn and make inferences from the data they are trained on. The quality and format of this data directly impact the model's ability to learn effectively and perform accurately. Inadequate or poor-quality data can lead to models that are biased, inaccurate, or ineffective, which can have serious implications, especially in applications that require high levels of precision and reliability.

Steps Involved in Preparing Data for AI Models:

1. **Data Collection and Acquisition**

   a. **Sourcing Data**: The first step involves gathering the necessary data from various sources. This could include internal data from the application's MongoDB database, external datasets, or real-time data collected through user interactions and sensors.

   b. **Data Integration**: Integrating data from multiple sources often requires alignment on format and structure. This step ensures that the collected data can be effectively used in a cohesive manner, which often involves transforming disparate data into a unified format that can be easily processed and analyzed.

2. **Data Cleaning and Preprocessing**

   a. **Handling Missing Values**: AI models require complete data sets to function correctly. Missing data must be handled either by imputation (filling missing values with statistical methods) or by removing the rows or columns with missing values, depending on the scenario and the amount of missing data.

   b. **Removing Outliers**: Outliers can skew the results of AI models. Identifying and removing outliers or processing them to reduce their impact is crucial for maintaining the integrity of the model's predictions.

   c. **Normalization and Scaling**: Many machine learning algorithms perform better when numerical input data is scaled or normalized. Techniques like Min-Max scaling or Z-score normalization are commonly used to ensure that the data fits within a specific scale.

3. **Feature Engineering and Selection**

   a. **Feature Engineering**: This involves creating new features from the existing data that can help improve the performance of AI models. It might include aggregating data over time to create historical averages or combining multiple data fields to create new composite attributes.

b. **Feature Selection**: Not all features are equally important for making predictions. Feature selection involves identifying the most relevant features to use in training the model. This reduces the complexity of the model, speeds up the training process, and can improve model performance by eliminating irrelevant or redundant data.

By meticulously preparing data through these steps, developers can significantly enhance the effectiveness and accuracy of AI models integrated into MERN applications. This preparation not only supports the technical needs of AI but also aligns with the strategic goals of the application, ensuring that the AI components act as powerful, efficient, and reliable enhancers of the application's capabilities.

Future Trends in AI Integration in the MERN Ecosystem

As technology continues to evolve, the integration of AI within the MERN ecosystem is poised to transform web development further. Emerging trends and innovations are shaping the future of how developers build, deploy, and manage AI-powered applications. Here are some key trends and predictions for the future of web development with AI-powered MERN applications:

- **Increased Adoption of AI for Enhanced User Experiences**

  AI is increasingly being used to create more personalized and engaging user experiences. In the MERN ecosystem, this can mean more sophisticated AI-driven features such as personalized content delivery, predictive search functionalities, and smarter user interface adaptations based on user behavior. React's dynamic rendering capabilities make it an ideal platform for these kinds of real-time, AI-driven updates.

- **Automation of Development Processes**

  AI is set to play a significant role in automating many aspects of the development process itself. This includes everything from automated code generation and optimization to real-time bug detection and fixing. Tools like GitHub Copilot, which suggest code snippets and entire functions, are just the beginning. In the MERN stack, we can expect more integrated AI tools that help streamline development workflows, reduce manual coding, and improve code quality and performance.

- **Advancements in AI-Operated DevOps**

  AI is also transforming DevOps practices by automating operations and monitoring tasks. In the context of the MERN ecosystem, AI can be used to optimize application performance in real-time, predict system failures, and dynamically allocate resources based on traffic and usage patterns. This not only improves application reliability and performance but also reduces the cost and complexity of infrastructure management.

- **Growth of Edge AI**

  With the increasing focus on privacy and data security, as well as the need for low-latency applications, edge AI is becoming more prominent. In the MERN stack, this could involve deploying AI models directly on client devices using lightweight versions of libraries like TensorFlow.js. This approach minimizes data transfer to the server and speeds up AI processing, enabling more responsive AI features in web applications.

- **Ethical AI and Regulation Compliance**

  As AI becomes more integral to web applications, there will be a heightened focus on ethical AI practices and regulatory compliance. Developers will need to ensure that AI systems are transparent, fair, and unbiased, particularly in applications that make automated decisions affecting users. The MERN ecosystem will likely incorporate more tools and frameworks that help developers address these ethical considerations and comply with increasing regulations around AI and data privacy.

- **Hybrid AI Models**

  Future trends may also see a rise in hybrid AI models that combine different types of machine learning techniques to enhance the capabilities of MERN applications. For instance, integrating deep learning for image and voice recognition with reinforcement learning for decision-making processes can create more sophisticated and adaptive AI systems.

These emerging trends indicate a future where AI not only enhances the functionality of web applications but also revolutionizes how they are developed and maintained. As AI technologies continue to advance, the MERN ecosystem will evolve to provide developers with more powerful tools and frameworks to build innovative, efficient, and impactful web applications.

Conclusion

This chapter provides a comprehensive overview of how AI can be synergized with the MERN stack to create dynamic and intelligent web applications. This chapter sets the stage for developers to explore further into both fields, emphasizing the importance of JavaScript as a unifying language that facilitates this integration.

As we move forward, the subsequent chapters will delve deeper into practical implementations and case studies that highlight the transformative potential of combining AI with the MERN stack, paving the way for innovations in web development.

Multiple Choice Questions

1. What does AI stand for in the context of technology?

    a. Automated Instructions

    b. Artificial Intelligence

    c. Analog Information

    d. Automatic Integration

2. Which database is used in the MERN stack?

    a. MySQL

    b. Oracle

    c. MongoDB

    d. PostgreSQL

3. What is the primary programming language used across the MERN stack?

    a. Python

    b. Java

    c. C++

    d. JavaScript

4. Which framework in the MERN stack is used for server-side operations?

    a. Angular

    b. Express.js

    c. Django

    d. Flask

5. What is React used for in the MERN stack?

    a. Database management

    b. Building user interfaces

    c. Server-side scripting

    d. Machine learning algorithms

6. Node.js in the MERN stack is responsible for what?

    a. Creating databases

    b. Front-end development

    c. Scalable server-side scripting

    d. Styling web pages

7. Which of the following is a benefit of integrating AI into the MERN stack?

    a. Decreased application performance

    b. Personalization of user experiences

    c. Limited scalability

    d. Reduced development speed

8. Which AI library or tool can be used with the MERN stack for machine learning capabilities?

    a. Laravel

    b. TensorFlow.js

    c. Bootstrap

    d. jQuery

9. What is the role of Git in the context of MERN stack development?

    a. Database querying

    b. Front-end templating

    c. Version control

    d. AI model training

10. Which of the following is NOT a component of the MERN stack?

    a. MongoDB

    b. Express.js

    c. React

    d. Apache

Answers

1. b
2. c
3. d
4. b
5. b
6. c
7. b
8. b
9. c
10. d

CHAPTER 2
Setting Up the MERN Development Environment

Introduction

Setting Up the MERN Development Environment is a practical guide designed to walk readers through the initial steps of configuring their workspace for MERN stack development, with a focus on integrating AI capabilities. This chapter delves into the specifics of installing and setting up the core technologies that comprise the MERN stack: MongoDB for database management, Express.js for server-side logic, React for the front-end interface, and Node.js for the backend environment. It emphasizes the importance of JavaScript as the primary programming language that ties these technologies together, enabling seamless development across the stack.

Key tools and software such as Visual Studio Code (VS Code) for code editing, npm (Node Package Manager) for managing library dependencies, and Git for version control are introduced to establish a robust development workflow. This foundational chapter ensures that readers are well-prepared with a fully configured development environment, setting the stage for the exciting journey of building AI-powered web applications.

Structure

In this chapter, we will cover the following topics:

- Introduction to the Development Environment
- Installing Core Technologies
- JavaScript: The Lingua Franca of MERN
- Development Tools and Editors
- Version Control with Git and GitHub

Introduction to the Development Environment

The development environment is the foundational workspace where software and web applications are conceived, developed, tested, and maintained. It encompasses the tools, software, and configurations that developers use to write code and manage projects. For MERN stack development, the environment is tailored to facilitate the seamless integration of MongoDB, Express.js, React, and Node.js – technologies that collectively enable the creation of full-stack JavaScript applications.

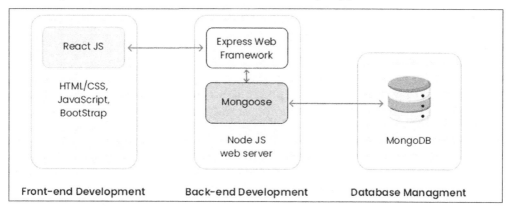

Figure 2.1: *Introduction to the Development Environment (Source: https://d2ms8rpfqc4h24. cloudfront.net/mern_stack_development_91bec79c96.jpg)*

A well-configured development environment is crucial for productivity and efficiency. It ensures that all necessary tools are available and properly set up, allowing developers to focus on coding rather than troubleshooting setup issues. For MERN stack development, this means having access to a reliable code editor, a JavaScript runtime environment, a document-based database, and a server framework, all orchestrated to work in harmony.

Visual Studio Code (VS Code) is a popular choice among developers for editing MERN stack applications. It is a powerful, open-source editor that supports JavaScript and Node.js natively and offers a vast ecosystem of extensions for other MERN stack technologies. VS Code's integrated terminal, debugging tools, and Git support make it an all-in-one solution for writing, testing, and version-controlling code.

npm (Node Package Manager) is another essential tool in the MERN stack developer's arsenal. It is used to manage the libraries and dependencies that a MERN application relies on. npm simplifies the process of installing, updating, and removing packages, and it ensures that the correct versions of each package are used across different development environments.

Git, a distributed version control system, is integral to managing the codebase of MERN applications. It allows multiple developers to work on the same project simultaneously without overwriting each other's changes. Git tracks every modification to the code, enabling developers to revert to previous versions if necessary and collaborate effectively, whether they are in the same room or across the globe.

Setting up the development environment also involves configuring MongoDB, the database layer of the MERN stack. MongoDB stores application data in a flexible, JSON-like format, which aligns well with the JavaScript-centric nature of the MERN stack. Tools like MongoDB Compass provide a graphical user interface to manage and interact with MongoDB databases, making it easier for developers to visualize and manipulate data.

Express.js and Node.js form the backend of the MERN stack, handling server-side logic and API requests. Express.js simplifies the creation of web servers and RESTful APIs, while Node.js provides the runtime environment to execute JavaScript on the server side. Together, they enable the development of scalable and high-performance server applications that can handle large volumes of traffic and data.

React.js completes the MERN stack by providing the frontend framework for building user interfaces. Its component-based architecture allows for the development of reusable UI elements, which can be dynamically updated in response to user interactions or data changes.

Creating a MERN Project Structure

When setting up a MERN development environment, one of the first steps is to establish a project structure that organizes the codebase in a logical and efficient manner. A typical MERN project structure separates the frontend and backend code into distinct directories, each with its own set of subdirectories and files that pertain to their respective responsibilities. This separation not only enhances maintainability but also aligns with the modular nature of the MERN stack.

Typical Folder Structure for a MERN Project

A standard MERN project structure might look like this:

```
/project-root
|-- /client
|    |-- /public
|    |-- /src
|         |-- /components
|         |-- /pages
|         |-- /services
|         |-- App.js
|
```

```
|          |-- index.js
|          |-- ...
|-- /server
|    |-- /config
|    |-- /controllers
|    |-- /models
|    |-- /routes
|    |-- server.js
|    |-- ...
|-- package.json
|-- .gitignore
|-- ...
```

Client Directory: The `client` directory houses the React frontend application. Inside, the `public` folder typically contains static assets like the `index.html` file, while the `src` folder contains the React source code, including components, pages, and services that interact with the backend API.

Server Directory: The `server` directory contains the Express.js backend application. It includes subdirectories such as `config` for configuration files, `controllers` for handling the business logic, `models` for database schemas, and `routes` for defining API endpoints. The `server.js` file is the entry point to the backend, where the Express application is configured and launched.

Organization of Backend and Frontend Code

The backend and frontend code are organized into separate directories to encapsulate their concerns. The backend code, residing in the `server` directory, is responsible for handling HTTP requests, interacting with the database, and serving API responses. The frontend code, located in the `client` directory, focuses on presenting data to the user, handling user interactions, and communicating with the backend via API calls.

Setting Up Directories for Server-Side and Client-Side Code

To set up the directories for server-side and client-side code, follow these steps:

1. **Initialize the Project**: Create a new directory for your project (`project-root`) and initialize it with a `package.json` file using `npm init`. This file will track both backend and frontend dependencies and scripts.

2. **Create Backend and Frontend Directories**: Inside the `project-root`, create two subdirectories: `client` for the frontend React application and `server` for the backend Express.js application.

3. **Configure Backend**: In the `server` directory, set up `server.js` and install backend dependencies like `express`, `mongoose`, and any middleware you plan to use. Define your models, routes, and controllers within their respective subdirectories.

4. **Configure Frontend**: In the `client` directory, you can use `create-react-app` to bootstrap the React application. Organize your React components, services, and other frontend assets within the `src` folder. Set up proxy settings in `package.json` to redirect API calls to the backend server during development.

5. **Version Control**: Create a `.gitignore` file to exclude `node_modules` and other non-essential files from your Git repository. This helps to keep your repository clean and avoids uploading unnecessary files.

By following these steps, you can create a well-organized MERN project structure that facilitates development and collaboration. This structure supports the modular nature of the MERN stack and provides a solid foundation for building scalable and maintainable web applications.

In summary, the development environment for MERN stack applications is a carefully orchestrated collection of tools and technologies that work together to enable efficient full-stack JavaScript development. By understanding and setting up this environment, developers can embark on the journey of building AI-powered web applications with confidence and ease.

Installing Core Technologies

Setting up the core technologies of the MERN stack is a critical step in preparing your development environment. This section will guide you through the installation of MongoDB, Express.js, React, and Node.js, ensuring that each component is correctly configured to work together seamlessly.

1. Installing Node.js and npm

Node.js is the runtime environment that allows you to run JavaScript on the server side, and npm is its package manager, essential for managing dependencies in Node.js applications.

- **Windows and macOS**: Download the installer from the official Node.js website - https://nodejs.org/. Run the installer, which includes npm, and follow the prompts to complete the installation. After installation, open a command prompt or terminal and type `node -v` and `npm -v` to verify that Node.js and npm are correctly installed.

- **Linux**: Installation methods can vary based on the distribution. For most Linux users, Node.js can be installed via package manager with commands like `sudo apt install nodejs` for Debian-based distributions or `sudo yum install nodejs` for Red Hat-based distributions. Ensure npm is installed by running `sudo apt install npm` or `sudo yum install npm`.

2. Installing MongoDB

MongoDB is a NoSQL database used to store the application's data.

- **Windows**: Download the MongoDB Community Server MSI installer from the MongoDB Download Center - https://www.mongodb.com/try/download/community. Run the installer and follow the setup wizard to install MongoDB. After installation, add MongoDB's `bin` directory to your system's PATH to run MongoDB from any command prompt.

- **macOS and Linux**: Use a package manager to install MongoDB. For macOS, you can use Homebrew with the command `brew install mongodb`, and for Ubuntu Linux, you can use `sudo apt-get install -y mongodb`. Ensure that MongoDB is running with `sudo service mongodb start`, once the installation is completed.

3. Installing Express.js

Express.js is a web application framework for Node.js, designed for building web applications and APIs.

- **All Operating Systems**: First, ensure Node.js and npm are installed. Create a new directory for your project and navigate into it via the command line. Initialize a new Node.js project with `npm init`. Install Express within your project by running `npm install express --save` to add it to your project's dependencies.

4. Installing React

React is a library for building user interfaces, primarily used for constructing the frontend of web applications.

- **All Operating Systems**: Ensure Node.js and npm are installed. You can create a new React application using Create React App, a comfortable setup script for React projects. Run `npx create-react-app my-app` in the command line, replacing `my-app` with your application's name. This command sets up a new React project with all necessary dependencies and build configurations.

Verification of Installation

After installing these core technologies, it's important to verify that everything is set up correctly in your project folder:

Technology	Command/Action	Purpose
Node.js	Run `node -v` in the command line	Checks the installed version of Node.js
npm	Run `npm -v` in the command line	Checks the installed version of npm
MongoDB	Run `mongo --version` in the command line	Verifies that MongoDB is installed and checks version
Express.js	Run `node app.js` in the command line	Starts the Express server and checks it is listening on the correct port
React	Navigate to your React application directory and run `npm start`	Opens the React application in a web browser

Figure 2.2: *Verification of Installation*

By following these steps, you will have successfully set up the core technologies of the MERN stack, creating a robust foundation for developing AI-powered web applications.

Additional Tools and Libraries in MERN Development

In addition to the core technologies of the MERN stack, several additional tools and libraries play crucial roles in enhancing the development workflow. These tools help streamline various aspects of development, from code editing and version control to testing and API management. Here's an overview of some essential tools and libraries commonly used in MERN development:

- **npm (Node Package Manager)**

  npm is the default package manager for Node.js and is essential for managing libraries and dependencies in MERN projects. It allows developers to install, update, and manage packages required for their applications. npm also handles version control and dependency conflicts, making it easier to maintain a stable development environment.

- **Yarn**

  Yarn is an alternative to npm that offers faster and more secure dependency management. It caches every package it downloads, so it never needs to download the same package again, and it executes operations in parallel to maximize resource utilization. Yarn's deterministic algorithm for installations ensures consistency across machines, which is crucial for collaborative projects.

- **Git**

  Git is a distributed version control system that is integral to managing the source code of MERN applications. It allows multiple developers to work on the same project without interfering with each other's changes. Git helps track changes, revert to previous versions, and manage branches for feature development and bug fixes. It is essential for coordinating team efforts and maintaining a history of project development.

- **Visual Studio Code (VS Code)**

  VS Code is a popular code editor among MERN developers due to its extensive support for JavaScript and built-in features like IntelliSense for code completion and debugging tools. It supports a wide range of extensions, such as ESLint for code linting, Prettier for code formatting, and GitLens for enhanced Git integration. VS Code's lightweight design and powerful features make it an ideal choice for MERN development.

- **Postman**

  Postman is a powerful tool for developing and testing APIs. In MERN projects, where Express.js is used to handle server-side logic and API responses, Postman can be used to test API endpoints quickly and efficiently. It provides a user-friendly interface to send requests to the server, check responses, and debug the API. Postman also supports automated testing, which can be integrated into the CI/CD pipeline.

- **Chrome Developer Tools**

  Chrome Developer Tools are essential for debugging and optimizing MERN applications, especially the React frontend. These tools allow developers to inspect HTML elements, debug JavaScript code in the browser, and analyze network activity. The performance tab helps identify bottlenecks in the application, while the console provides a direct way to log information and interact with the web page.

Let's organize the preceding content into a table format to enhance clarity and comprehension:

Tool/Library	Description
npm (Node Package Manager)	The default package manager for Node.js, essential for managing libraries and dependencies. It facilitates the installation, updating, and management of packages, and handles version control and dependency conflicts.
Yarn	An alternative to npm that provides faster and more secure dependency management. It caches downloaded packages for efficiency and uses a deterministic algorithm for installations to ensure consistency across environments.
Git	A distributed version control system crucial for managing the source code of MERN applications. It supports multiple developers working simultaneously without conflict, tracks changes, and manages branches for development.
Visual Studio Code (VS Code)	A popular code editor among MERN developers known for its extensive support for JavaScript, built-in IntelliSense for code completion, debugging tools, and a range of extensions like ESLint, Prettier, and GitLens.
Postman	A tool for developing and testing APIs, used extensively in MERN projects to test API endpoints. It offers a user-friendly interface for sending requests, checking responses, and debugging, along with support for automated testing.
Chrome Developer Tools	Essential for debugging and optimizing MERN applications, especially useful for the React frontend. These tools allow developers to inspect HTML elements, debug JavaScript, analyze network activity, and identify performance bottlenecks.

Figure 2.3: *Additional Tools and Libraries in MERN Development*

Each of these tools and libraries brings unique benefits to the MERN development process, enhancing productivity, improving code quality, and ensuring a smoother workflow. By leveraging these tools, developers can more effectively build, test, and deploy robust, high-performance web applications using the MERN stack.

JavaScript: The Lingua Franca of MERN

JavaScript stands at the core of the MERN stack, serving as the primary programming language that unifies the development process across both the client and server sides. This section explores why JavaScript is integral to the MERN ecosystem and how it enhances the development of modern web applications, particularly those powered by AI.

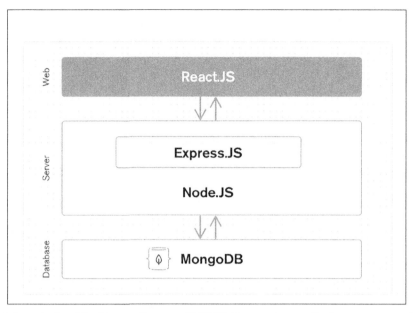

Figure 2.4: *JavaScript: The Lingua Franca of MERN (Source: https://webassets.mongodb.com/_com_assets/cms/mern-stack-b9q1kbudz0.png)*

Central Role in MERN

JavaScript's role as the lingua franca in the MERN stack cannot be overstated. Each component of the MERN stack is either written in or directly utilizes JavaScript:

- **MongoDB**: While MongoDB is a database that stores data in a format called BSON, which is similar to JavaScript Object Notation (JSON), it integrates smoothly with Node.js, allowing JavaScript to be used for database operations through libraries like Mongoose. This integration simplifies data handling and manipulation, making it more intuitive for JavaScript developers.

- **Express.js**: As a server framework for Node.js, Express.js is written in JavaScript. It handles HTTP requests and middleware with a simple and flexible API, making server-side scripting straightforward and efficient for developers familiar with JavaScript.

- **React**: React is a JavaScript library for building user interfaces. It allows developers to create reusable UI components that manage their state, enabling dynamic and interactive web applications. React's JSX syntax, which resembles HTML but allows JavaScript expressions, makes it a powerful tool for developing complex interfaces.

- **Node.js**: At the backend, Node.js executes JavaScript code on the server. It provides a non-blocking, event-driven environment, which is ideal for data-intensive real-time applications that run across distributed devices.

Enhancing AI Integration

JavaScript's ubiquity in the MERN stack also facilitates the integration of AI functionalities. Libraries like TensorFlow.js allow developers to implement machine learning directly in JavaScript, both in the browser and on the server. This accessibility makes it easier to deploy AI models and manage data flow between the client and server, enhancing applications with capabilities such as real-time data analysis, machine learning-driven recommendations, and more.

Benefits for Developers

The use of JavaScript across all layers of the MERN stack offers several benefits:

- **Unified Language**: Having a single programming language across the stack simplifies learning and reduces context switching for developers. This uniformity allows for a more cohesive development experience and reduces the likelihood of errors.

- **Community and Resources**: JavaScript's popularity ensures a vast community of developers and an extensive array of resources, libraries, and tools. This community support is invaluable for troubleshooting, learning, and staying updated with the latest in technology and best practices.

- **Flexibility and Speed**: JavaScript's event-driven nature and the non-blocking I/O model of Node.js enable the development of fast and scalable applications. This is particularly beneficial for applications that require handling numerous real-time interactions and large volumes of data, common in AI-driven applications.

Understanding the MERN Stack: The Role of JavaScript

The MERN stack is a powerful combination of technologies used to develop full-stack web applications. MERN stands for MongoDB, Express.js, React.js, and Node.js – four key technologies that provide an end-to-end framework for developers. What ties all these technologies together seamlessly is JavaScript, making it the backbone of the MERN stack. Here's how JavaScript integrates these components and the advantages of using it throughout the entire development stack.

Here is How JavaScript Ties the MERN Components Together:

- **MongoDB**: Although MongoDB is a NoSQL database that stores data in a format called BSON, it is heavily influenced by JavaScript. Queries in MongoDB are executed in a JavaScript-like syntax, which can be run directly in a JavaScript environment. This seamless integration simplifies the process of fetching and manipulating data for developers who are already familiar with JavaScript.

- **Express.js**: This is a web application framework for Node.js, designed to build web applications and APIs. It is minimal, flexible, and written entirely in JavaScript. Express streamlines the server-side logic and routing mechanisms, making it easier to write secure, modular, and fast applications.

- **React.js**: React is a JavaScript library for building user interfaces, particularly known for its efficient rendering of UI components. It uses JSX (JavaScript XML), which allows HTML to be written within JavaScript. This leads to a more intuitive and powerful interface development process, where logic and markup can be combined seamlessly.

- **Node.js**: At the core of the MERN stack's backend development is Node.js, a JavaScript runtime built on Chrome's V8 JavaScript engine. It executes JavaScript code server-side, allowing developers to use JavaScript for both client-side and server-side scripting. This unification provides a consistent developer experience across the full stack of the application.

Advantages of Using JavaScript Throughout the Entire Development Stack

- **Unified Language**: JavaScript across the full stack simplifies development. Developers need to know only one programming language for both client-side and server-side, reducing the learning curve and streamlining the development process.

- **Efficiency and Performance**: JavaScript facilitates non-blocking I/O operations in Node.js, which enhances the performance of web applications that perform a lot of disk or network operations. React's virtual DOM further optimizes the update process on the client side, making the user interface more responsive.

- **Community and Ecosystem**: JavaScript is one of the most popular programming languages with a vast ecosystem of libraries, frameworks, and tools. This extensive community support and wealth of resources make it easier to solve problems, find documentation, and recruit skilled developers.

- **Versatility**: JavaScript's flexibility allows developers to build a wide range of applications – from simple websites to complex enterprise-level solutions. The use of JavaScript also facilitates the integration of various other technologies and APIs, enhancing the functionality and scalability of applications.

- **Cost-Effective Development**: Using a single language across the stack can significantly reduce development time and costs. It simplifies the architecture and eliminates the need to context switch between different languages, which can lead to fewer bugs and faster development cycles.

JavaScript not only binds the MERN stack components together but also offers numerous advantages that enhance the development process. Its ability to run both client-side and server-side makes it an ideal choice for modern web application development, ensuring a cohesive and efficient development experience.

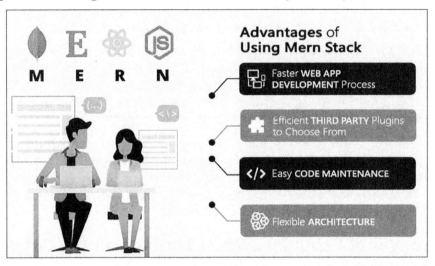

Figure 2.5: *Advantages of Using JavaScript Throughout the Entire Development Stack (Source: https://media.licdn.com/dms/image/D4D12AQFgYSO77epYCw/article-cover_image-shrink_60 0_2000/0/1699286305534?e=2147483647&t=QnzrYaJDlOpBKbq0T2D8Xc-KpiKg11nilGp03MlAB-ZQ&v=beta)*

In summary, JavaScript's role as the lingua franca of the MERN stack is foundational to its success and popularity. Its ability to unify the development process across the client and server sides, coupled with its support for modern AI technologies, makes it an ideal choice for developers looking to build advanced, efficient, and scalable web applications.

Development Tools and Editors

In the realm of MERN stack development, choosing the right development tools and editors is crucial for enhancing productivity, ensuring code quality, and facilitating collaboration. This section explores essential development tools and editors that are integral to building MERN stack applications, with a focus on their roles and benefits in the development process.

Introduction to Integrated Development Environments (IDEs)

An Integrated Development Environment (IDE) is a crucial tool in the arsenal of modern software developers. It combines several essential tools into a single graphical user interface (GUI) to streamline the entire development process. IDEs enhance productivity by integrating various aspects of software development, including writing, editing, testing, and debugging code. Here's an overview of the key features of IDEs that make them indispensable for developers:

Code Editing

At its core, an IDE offers an advanced code editor designed to facilitate the writing and editing of source code. This editor goes beyond simple text editing, providing features tailored to the needs of programmers:

- **Syntax Highlighting**: This feature displays source code in different colors and fonts according to the category of terms. This not only makes the code more readable but also helps in quickly identifying errors in syntax or logic.

- **Code Completion**: Often referred to as auto-completion or IntelliSense, this feature predicts what a developer is likely to type next and provides a drop-down list of suggestions. This speeds up the coding process and reduces typos and other common mistakes.

- **Code Navigation**: IDEs allow developers to jump to different parts of the code, such as declarations, implementations, and usages of a symbol. This is particularly useful in large codebases where navigating to references manually would be time-consuming.

Debugging

Debugging tools are integrated directly into IDEs, providing developers with powerful capabilities to test and debug their applications within the same environment where they write their code:

- **Breakpoints**: Developers can set breakpoints in the code where the execution will pause, allowing them to inspect the program state at that point. This is crucial for understanding the flow of execution and identifying where things go wrong.

- **Step Execution**: This feature allows developers to execute their program one step at a time, moving into functions or over them, which helps in closely monitoring the changes in program state across different stages of execution.

- **Variable Inspection**: During a debugging session, developers can inspect the current values of variables and expressions without having to add temporary code to print out data.

Version Control Integration

Modern IDEs often include built-in support for version control systems (VCS), such as Git, which are essential for managing changes to the codebase, especially in collaborative environments:

- **Source Control Management**: IDEs provide GUIs for common version control tasks, such as committing changes, branching, merging, and viewing history. This integration helps streamline workflow by reducing the need to switch between the IDE and a separate VCS tool.

- **Diff Tool**: Integrated diff tools highlight changes between different code versions, helping developers understand what has changed and aiding in the merge process.

Additional Features

Beyond these core functionalities, IDEs may also offer:

- **Build Automation**: Tools to automate the build process, making it easy to compile and deploy applications directly from the IDE.

- **Database Management**: Some IDEs include tools for managing databases, allowing developers to design, query, and manage databases without leaving the IDE.

- **Customizability**: IDEs often allow customization of the development environment, enabling developers to tailor the interface, tools, and behavior to their preferences and workflow.

Integrated Development Environments streamline the software development process by combining editing, debugging, and version control into a single interface. This integration not only boosts productivity but also enhances code quality and simplifies the complexities associated with modern software development.

Introduction to Text Editors

Text editors are essential tools in the toolkit of any developer, enabling the creation, modification, and management of plain text files. These tools are fundamental for writing and editing code, scripts, configurations, and any other tasks that involve direct manipulation of text. Unlike word processors, text editors are designed to work with raw text and often provide powerful features tailored for coding and programming.

Text Editor Features

Text editors are software applications designed for creating and editing plain text files. They vary widely in features and complexity, catering to different needs, from simple notetaking to advanced software development.

Syntax Highlighting

Syntax highlighting is one of the most crucial features of modern text editors, especially for developers. It involves the color-coding of text in the editor to reflect the syntax of different programming languages. This feature makes it easier to read code and quickly identify elements such as keywords, variables, operators, and comments. Syntax highlighting helps in reducing the cognitive load on the programmer and speeds up both coding and debugging by making errors more conspicuous.

Code Completion

Code completion, often referred to as IntelliSense in some editors, is a feature that speeds up the coding process by predicting and suggesting completions for partially typed words. These suggestions can be based on variable names, function names, or snippets within the scope of the project or the currently open files. This feature not only speeds up the coding process but also helps in reducing errors and learning more about the coding language and its libraries.

Customization Options

Customization is another significant feature offered by many text editors. This can range from simple modifications like changing the theme (dark or light), font size, and editor layout, to more advanced customizations such as defining custom syntax highlighting for lesser-known languages, adding or modifying keyboard shortcuts, and installing plugins that extend the editor's functionality. Customization allows developers to tailor their environment to their preferences, which can improve workflow efficiency and comfort.

Additional Features

- **Plugins and Extensions**: Many text editors support plugins or extensions that add new features or enhance existing ones. These can include integration with other tools, new language support, advanced code linting, and more.

- **Search and Replace**: Advanced search and replace functionalities, including support for regular expressions, allow developers to quickly make broad changes across multiple files.

- **Version Control Integration**: Integration with version control systems like Git directly within the text editor helps manage changes and collaboration more efficiently.

- **File Management**: Some text editors come with built-in file explorers and other tools to manage and navigate large projects with ease.

Text editors are indispensable for developers due to their flexibility, efficiency, and the powerful suite of features they offer. Whether you are coding in a high-level programming language, writing markup for a website, or scripting in a shell, a good text editor can significantly enhance your productivity and effectiveness.

Visual Studio Code (VS Code)

Visual Studio Code, commonly referred to as VS Code, is a highly popular code editor among MERN stack developers. Its appeal lies in its lightweight design, powerful features, and extensive support for JavaScript and related technologies. The official website link is: https://code.visualstudio.com/. The key features include:

- **IntelliSense**: Provides smart completions based on variable types, function definitions, and imported modules.

- **Debugging**: Built-in debugging tools allow developers to launch or attach to their running apps and debug with breakpoints, call stacks, and an interactive console.

- **Extensions**: A vast marketplace of extensions offers support for nearly every major programming language, framework, and tool, including those specific to the MERN stack such as ESLint for JavaScript linting, Prettier for code formatting, and extensions for Node.js and React development.

- **Integrated Terminal**: Developers can run shell commands directly within the editor, streamlining the workflow by eliminating the need to switch between tools.

Sublime Text

Sublime Text is another powerful editor known for its speed, performance, and user-friendly interface. While it may not be as feature-rich as VS Code in terms of MERN-specific extensions, it offers various functionality as follows. The official website link is: https://www.sublimetext.com/:

- **Goto Anything**: Quick navigation to files, symbols, or lines with simple keystrokes.

- **Multiple Selections**: Make many changes at the same time, renaming variables, and manipulating files faster.

- **Customizability**: Extensive customization options through JSON settings files, allowing developers to tailor the editor to their preferences.

Atom

Atom, developed by GitHub, is an open-source text editor designed for ease of use, customization, and collaboration. The official website link is: https://atom-editor.cc/. It stands out with features like:

- **Teletype**: Atom's Teletype feature enables developers to share their workspace with team members for real-time collaboration, making it an excellent choice for team projects.

- **Hackable**: Atom prides itself on being "a hackable text editor for the 21st Century," allowing developers to deeply customize the editor by adding packages or even directly modifying the code that runs the editor itself.

WebStorm

WebStorm is a powerful Integrated Development Environment (IDE) specifically designed for modern JavaScript development, including server-side with Node.js and frontend with React. The official website link is: https://www.jetbrains.com/webstorm/. It offers:

- **Full-fledged IDE**: WebStorm provides comprehensive coding assistance, navigation, error detection, and refactorings for JavaScript, complemented by powerful debugging, testing, and version control integration.
- **Built-in Tools**: Integrated tools for compiling, running, and debugging Node.js applications and managing other tasks like npm and Git make it a robust environment for MERN development.

Let's understand the preceding IDEs in a tabular format:

IDE Name	Features
VS Code	- IntelliSense for code completion and snippets - Debugging directly from the editor - Git integration for version control - Extensive extension marketplace - Integrated terminal - Customizable workspace with themes and settings
Sublime Text	- Goto Anything for quick navigation - Multiple Selections for simultaneous edits - Command Palette for fast access to functionality - Split Editing support - Highly customizable with simple JSON files - Package ecosystem for extending functionality

Atom	- Hackable to the core to customize anything
	- Integrated package manager
	- Smart autocompletion
	- File system browser
	- Multiple panes for comparing and editing code across files
	- Find and replace functionality
	- Supports teletype for collaborative coding
WebStorm	- Powerful navigation and refactoring tools
	- Built-in debugger for client-side code and Node.js
	- Test runner interface
	- Seamless tool integration (e.g., linters, build tools)
	- Version control system integration
	- Code quality tools
	- Advanced support for JavaScript, TypeScript, React, and more

Figure 2.6: *Different IDEs used for MERN Stack*

Choosing the Right Tool

The choice of development tools and editors is often subjective, influenced by personal preferences, project requirements, and team workflows. VS Code stands out for its versatility and extensive ecosystem, making it a top choice for MERN stack development. However, tools like Sublime Text, Atom, and WebStorm also offer unique advantages that may suit different development styles and needs.

In summary, the right development tool or editor enhances the MERN stack development experience by providing powerful coding assistance, efficient project management, and seamless integration with other technologies and tools used in the development process.

Version Control with Git and GitHub

Version control is an essential tool for modern software development, particularly when managing large projects with multiple contributors. Git, the most widely used version control system, allows multiple developers to work on the same project without conflicting changes. GitHub, a platform built around Git, enhances this functionality with online hosting, collaboration features, and more. This section will cover the basics of Git and GitHub, focusing on their roles in MERN stack development.

Understanding Version Control

Version control systems (VCS) track changes to a project over time. This allows developers to revert files back to their previous state, compare changes over time, and collaborate on software projects. Git, a distributed version control system, is particularly powerful for its branching and merging capabilities, which facilitate non-linear development workflows.

Introducing Git

Git is a free, open-source version control system designed to handle everything from small to very large projects with speed and efficiency. It enables things like local branching, convenient staging areas, and multiple workflows.

Basic Git Concepts

Here's a brief overview of basic Git terms:

- **Repository**: A directory that is being tracked by Git.
- **Clone**: A copy of a repository that lives on your computer.
- **Commit**: A snapshot of your repository at a particular point in time.
- **Branch**: A parallel version of the repository. It is contained within the repository but does not affect the primary or master branch, allowing you to work freely without disrupting the live project.
- **Merge**: A way to bring a branch's changes back into the main branch of the repository.
- **Pull**: It refers to receiving data from GitHub. It fetches and merges changes on the remote server to your working directory.
- **Push**: It refers to sending your committed changes to a remote repository on GitHub.

Setting Up Git

To start using Git, you need to install it on your system. This can typically be done through your operating system's package manager, or by downloading it from the Git website. Once installed, you should configure it with your username and email, which will be used to identify the changes you make.

Here's a detailed guide on how to download and install Git, particularly focusing on Windows systems, as well as how to configure it for first-time use.

Downloading and Installing Git on Windows

1. **Visit the Official Website**:

   To download Git, navigate to the official Git website at https://git-scm.com/downloads. This page automatically detects your operating system and suggests the appropriate version for download.

2. **Download the Installer**:

   Click on the download link for Windows. The site will start the download of the latest stable version of the Git installer. Save the executable file to a convenient location on your system.

3. **Run the Installation:**

   Once the download is complete, double-click the executable file to start the installation process. You will be greeted by the Git Setup wizard.

4. **Installation Steps:**

   a. **Select Components**: You can leave the default components selected or customize them according to your needs. Common components include Git Bash (a BASH emulation to run Git commands) and Git GUI.

   b. **Adjusting your PATH environment**: It's recommended to choose the option that allows Git to be used from the command line and also from third-party software.

   c. **Choosing the SSH executable**: Unless you have specific needs, you can stick with the bundled SSH executable provided by Git.

   d. **Configuring line-ending conversions**: For Windows, it's typically best to let Git convert LF to CRLF on checkout.

   e. **Configuring the terminal emulator to use with Git Bash**: The default option, MinTTY, is generally recommended for its better features.

   f. **Additional configuration**: Options like enabling file system caching and the credential manager can be left at their defaults for most users.

   g. **Install**: Click the **'Install'** button to proceed with the installation.

5. **Completing the Installation:**

   After completing the installation process, you can choose to view the Release Notes or launch Git Bash immediately to start using Git.

Configuring Git for the First Time

After installing Git, it's important to configure your user information, which will be used in every Git commit you do.

1. **Open Git Bash:**

   You can access Git Bash through the **Start** menu or by right-clicking in a folder while holding down the *Shift* key and selecting **"Open Git Bash here"**.

2. **Set Your Username:**

   Type the following command, replacing `**Your Name**` with your actual name:

   ```
   git config --global user.name "Your Name"
   ```

3. **Set Your Email Address:**

   Similarly, set your email address with the following command, replacing `**your.email@example.com**` with your actual email address:

   ```
   git config --global user.email "your.email@example.com"
   ```

4. **Check Your Configuration:**

   To verify that your configuration was successful, you can use:

   ```
   git config --list
   ```

This command displays all the settings Git can find at that point.

By following these steps, you will have Git installed and configured on your Windows machine, ready to manage your projects. Whether you are working on personal projects or collaborating in large teams, Git is a powerful tool that will help you maintain a clear history of your development work.

Git Workflow

The typical Git workflow involves:

Serial No	Step	Action
1	Cloning	Cloning a repository to get a local copy on your machine.
2	Making Changes	Making changes to your local copy by **editing, adding, and deleting** files.
3	Staging	Staging the changes, which prepares them to be committed.
4	Committing	Committing the changes, which takes a snapshot of the staged changes.
5	Pushing/Pulling	Pushing the changes to a remote repository, or pulling updates from the remote repository.

Figure 2.7: *Typical Git Workflow*

Collaborative Development with Git

Git supports collaborative development through branches and forks. Developers can branch out from the main project to experiment or develop features without affecting the main codebase. Changes can be merged back to the main project through pull requests, which others can review and discuss.

Introducing GitHub

GitHub is a cloud-based hosting service that lets you manage Git repositories. It provides a web-based graphical interface and access control, along with several collaboration features such as bug tracking, feature requests, task management, and wikis for every project.

GitHub Workflow

The GitHub workflow extends the Git workflow with features like fork and pull requests. A fork is a copy of a repository that you manage on your GitHub account. You can make changes in your fork and submit a pull request if you want your changes to be merged into the original repository.

Collaborative Development with GitHub

GitHub simplifies collaboration by providing tools to manage the sharing of code and review of changes. Teams can comment on code, track issues, and approve changes before they are merged. GitHub also integrates with various CI/CD tools, enhancing the automation of testing and deployment processes.

GitHub Features and Integrations

GitHub offers various features like GitHub Actions for automation, GitHub Pages for hosting, and extensive APIs for integration. It also supports integration with many third-party tools, enhancing its capabilities to fit into any development workflow.

In summary, Git and GitHub are indispensable tools for version control and collaboration in software development. They support the MERN stack development by enabling efficient code management, team collaboration, and integration with other tools and services.

Conclusion

This chapter has provided a comprehensive guide to setting up the MERN development environment, laying the groundwork for developers to embark on creating AI-powered web applications. By walking through the initial steps of configuring the workspace, readers have gained insights into the core technologies that define the MERN stack: MongoDB, Express.js, React, and Node.js. Each component plays a crucial role in the development process, from managing databases and server-side logic to crafting dynamic front-end interfaces and executing server-side JavaScript.

The importance of JavaScript as the unifying language across the MERN stack has been emphasized, showcasing its pivotal role in enabling seamless development and integration of AI capabilities. JavaScript's versatility and widespread support make it an ideal choice for modern web development, bridging the gap between client-side and server-side programming.

Key tools and software essential for a robust MERN development workflow have been introduced, including Visual Studio Code (VS Code) for code editing, npm (Node Package Manager) for managing library dependencies, and Git for version control. These tools not only enhance productivity but also ensure that developers can manage their codebase efficiently, collaborate with others, and maintain a high standard of code quality.

The chapter also delved into the significance of version control with Git and GitHub, highlighting how these platforms facilitate collaborative development and project management. By understanding how to leverage Git for versioning and GitHub for collaboration, developers can work more effectively in teams, contributing to the success of AI-powered projects.

In conclusion, setting up the MERN development environment is a foundational step for any developer looking to build scalable, efficient, and intelligent web applications. With the core technologies installed and configured, and essential tools at their disposal, developers are well-equipped to tackle the challenges of modern web development. The journey ahead promises exciting opportunities to innovate and create impactful applications using the MERN stack, enhanced by the integration of AI capabilities.

The upcoming chapter delves into the basics of Machine Learning using JavaScript, focusing on TensorFlow.js, a robust library that empowers JavaScript with machine learning capabilities.

Multiple Choice Questions

1. What does MERN stand for?

   a. MongoDB, Express.js, React.js, Node.js

   b. MySQL, Ember.js, Ruby, .NET

   c. MariaDB, Ember.js, Rails, Node.js

   d. MongoDB, Eclipse, Ruby, .NET

2. Which tool is used as a package manager for Node.js?

   a. Docker

   b. npm

    c.   Webpack

    d.   Gradle

3.   What is the primary use of Express.js in the MERN stack?

    a.   Database management

    b.   Frontend development

    c.   Server-side logic

    d.   Machine learning

4.   Which of the following is a popular code editor for MERN stack development?

    a.   Adobe Dreamweaver

    b.   Microsoft Word

    c.   Visual Studio Code

    d.   Notepad

5.   What feature of Git allows developers to save different versions of their code?

    a.   Push

    b.   Commit

    c.   Pull

    d.   Clone

6.   Which JavaScript library in the MERN stack is used primarily for building user interfaces?

    a.   jQuery

    b.   Angular

    c.   React

    d.   Vue.js

7.   What is MongoDB used for in the MERN stack?

    a.   Building user interfaces

    b.   Managing databases

    c.   Server-side programming

    d.   Version control

8. Which of the following is NOT a feature of modern IDEs like WebStorm?

    a. Syntax highlighting

    b. Code completion

    c. Spreadsheet management

    d. Debugging tools

9. What does npm stand for?

    a. Node Package Manager

    b. Network Protocol Manager

    c. New Programming Module

    d. Node Protocol Module

10. Which version control system is integrated with GitHub for managing MERN projects?

    a. SVN

    b. Mercurial

    c. Git

    d. CVS

Answers

1. a

2. b

3. c

4. c

5. b

6. c

7. b

8. c

9. a

10. c

CHAPTER 3

Fundamentals of Machine Learning with JavaScript

Introduction

Fundamentals of Machine Learning with JavaScript demystifies the core principles and algorithms that underpin machine learning, tailored specifically for JavaScript developers working within the MERN ecosystem. This chapter introduces the reader to the exciting world of machine learning, providing a solid foundation in the concepts of supervised and unsupervised learning, neural networks, and deep learning. It emphasizes the versatility of JavaScript as a language not just for web development but also for implementing complex AI algorithms.

The chapter explores TensorFlow.js, a powerful library that brings machine learning to JavaScript, enabling the training and deployment of models directly in the browser or on Node.js. Readers will learn about the TensorFlow.js ecosystem, including how to work with pre-trained models and how to train their own models from scratch. By the end of this chapter, readers will have a thorough understanding of the machine learning landscape in JavaScript and be prepared to start integrating these concepts into their MERN applications.

Structure

In this chapter, we will cover the following topics:

- Introduction to Machine Learning
- Machine Learning Concepts and Algorithms
- JavaScript and Machine Learning
- Getting Started with TensorFlow.js
- Building Your First Machine Learning Model with TensorFlow.js

Introduction to Machine Learning

Machine learning (ML) is a dynamic field of artificial intelligence (AI) that focuses on enabling algorithms to learn from and make predictions or decisions based on data. This technology allows systems to improve over time without being explicitly programmed to do so.

Figure 3.1: *Introduction to Machine Learning*

Machine learning is pivotal in various applications, from autonomous vehicles to personalized healthcare, and it's increasingly becoming integral in web development, particularly within the JavaScript ecosystem.

Defining Machine Learning

At its core, machine learning involves training a model using data. This model can then make predictions or decisions without human intervention. It's based on the idea that systems can learn from data, identify patterns, and make decisions with minimal human input.

Types of Machine Learning

Machine learning can be broadly classified into three types:

- **Supervised Learning**: This type involves training a model on a labeled dataset, which means that each input data point is paired with an output label. Supervised learning algorithms are designed to learn by example. After sufficient training, the model is evaluated on a test set to see how well it can predict new answers.

- **Unsupervised Learning**: Unlike supervised learning, unsupervised learning algorithms are used when the information used to train is neither classified nor labeled. Unsupervised learning studies how systems can infer a function to describe a hidden structure from unlabeled data. The system doesn't figure out the right output, but it explores the data and can draw inferences from datasets to describe hidden structures from unlabeled data.

- **Reinforcement Learning**: In reinforcement learning, an algorithm learns to perform a task simply by trying to maximize the rewards it receives for its actions. This type of learning has three primary components: the agent (the learner or decision-maker), the environment (everything the agent interacts with), and actions (what the agent can do).

The Machine Learning Process

Embarking on an ML project involves a series of systematic steps that guide the journey from raw data to a deployable ML model. This process is iterative and often cyclical, allowing for continuous improvement and refinement of the model based on feedback and performance metrics. Here's an overview of the typical steps involved in a machine learning project:

Data Collection and Preprocessing

- **Data Collection**: The foundation of any ML project is data. This step involves gathering data from various sources, which could include databases, files, sensors, or online repositories. The goal is to collect a diverse and representative dataset that reflects the real-world complexity of the problem you are trying to solve.

- **Data Preprocessing**: Raw data is often messy and incomplete. Preprocessing includes cleaning the data by handling missing values, removing outliers, and normalizing data. This step is crucial to ensure that the ML model learns from clean, high-quality data, which significantly impacts the model's accuracy and performance.

Feature Engineering

- **Creating Features**: Feature engineering is the process of using domain knowledge to extract relevant features from raw data. This involves transforming data into formats that are better suited for ML models, enabling the models to learn more effectively. Good features can improve model performance, while poor feature selection can hamper the model's ability to learn.

Model Selection and Training

- **Model Selection**: Choosing the right ML algorithm depends on the type of problem (classification, regression, clustering, and more), the size and type of data, and the computational resources available. Common algorithms include decision trees, support vector machines, neural networks, and ensemble methods like random forests.

- **Model Training**: With the selected algorithm, the next step is to train the model using the prepared dataset. This involves feeding the data into the model, allowing it to learn from the data's features and make predictions. The training process adjusts the model's parameters to minimize errors, optimizing its performance on the given task.

Evaluation

- **Testing the Model**: After training, the model is evaluated using a separate dataset not seen by the model during training. This step assesses the model's performance, typically using metrics such as accuracy, precision, recall, and F1 score for classification tasks, or mean squared error for regression tasks.

- **Identifying Biases**: It's also essential to evaluate the model for potential biases, ensuring that it performs well across different segments of the data and doesn't exhibit unfair biases towards any particular group.

Deployment and Monitoring

- **Deployment**: Once the model is trained and evaluated, it can be deployed into a production environment where it can start making predictions on new data. Deployment strategies can vary widely depending on the application, from embedding the model into a web application to deploying it on cloud-based ML platforms.

- **Monitoring**: After deployment, continuous monitoring is crucial to ensure the model performs as expected in the real world. Monitoring can help identify when the model's performance degrades over time due to changes in data patterns, necessitating retraining or model updates.

The machine learning process is iterative, with insights gained from each step feeding back into earlier stages to refine and improve the model. By following these steps, developers and data scientists can systematically approach ML projects, leading to more effective and impactful machine learning solutions.

Machine Learning and AI

Machine learning is a subset of artificial intelligence, which broadly refers to any technique that enables computers to mimic human behavior. The distinction between AI and machine learning arises with the tasks that are being performed. AI can perform tasks that typically require human intelligence, such as visual perception, speech recognition, and decision-making. Machine learning is a current application of AI based around the idea that we should be able to give machines access to data and let them learn for themselves.

Machine Learning in the JavaScript Ecosystem

JavaScript, traditionally known for its dominance in web development, is now making significant inroads into the domain of machine learning. Libraries such as TensorFlow. js have been developed to bring machine learning capabilities to JavaScript, allowing developers to implement models directly in the browser or on Node.js. This integration enables the development of AI-enhanced web applications directly within the JavaScript ecosystem, leveraging the widespread use and flexibility of JavaScript.

In summary, machine learning represents a significant advancement in how computers can automate decision-making processes and derive meaningful insights from vast datasets. As this technology continues to evolve, its integration into JavaScript through libraries like TensorFlow.js is making ML more accessible to web developers, thereby expanding the possibilities of what web applications can achieve. This foundational understanding sets the stage for deeper exploration into machine learning algorithms and their applications within the JavaScript environment.

Machine Learning Concepts and Algorithms

Machine learning is a vast field with a variety of concepts and algorithms designed to solve different types of problems. Understanding these concepts and the algorithms that underpin them is crucial for anyone looking to delve into machine learning with JavaScript. This section provides an overview of key machine learning concepts and algorithms, setting the stage for their application within the JavaScript ecosystem.

Machine Learning can be broadly categorized into four main types: Supervised Learning, Unsupervised Learning, Semi-supervised Learning, and Reinforcement Learning. Each type has its methodologies, algorithms, and use cases, making them suitable for different kinds of tasks and challenges in the field of artificial intelligence.

Type of Machine Learning	Description
Supervised Learning	Deals with labeled datasets and includes processes like classification and regression.
Unsupervised Learning	Uses unlabeled data with no specific idea of what results are expected; includes clustering and dimensionality reduction.
Semi-supervised Learning	Known as hybrid learning, it combines labeled and unlabeled data and lies between supervised and unsupervised learning.
Reinforcement Learning	Does not use training datasets; an example is playing games where the model learns through rewards and penalties.

Figure 3.2: *Types of Machine Learning*

Supervised Learning

Supervised learning is one of the most common types of machine learning. In this approach, the algorithm learns from a labeled dataset, meaning each example in the dataset is paired with the correct output. The goal is to learn mapping from inputs to outputs that can be used to make predictions on unseen data.

Definition

Supervised learning involves training a model on a labeled dataset, which means that each training example is paired with an output label. The model learns to predict the output from the input data during training, and its performance is evaluated on unseen data.

Key algorithms include:

Machine Learning Algorithm	Description
Linear Regression	Used for predicting a continuous value. For example, predicting house prices based on their characteristics.
Logistic Regression	Used for binary classification tasks, such as spam detection or diagnosing a disease as positive or negative.
Decision Trees and Random Forests	Versatile algorithms used for both classification and regression tasks. They are particularly useful for their interpretability and handling of non-linear data.
Support Vector Machines (SVM)	Effective in high-dimensional spaces, making them suitable for tasks like image classification and text categorization.

Figure 3.3: *Machine Learning Algorithms*

Examples

- Predicting house prices based on features like size and location (regression).
- Classifying emails as spam or not spam (classification).

Unsupervised Learning

In unsupervised learning, the algorithm is trained on data without labels. The goal is to discover inherent patterns or groupings in the data.

Definition

Unsupervised learning involves training a model on data that has not been labeled, categorized, or classified. The model attempts to understand the patterns and structure in the data without any explicit instructions on what to look for.

Examples

- Segmenting customers into groups with similar preferences (clustering).
- Reducing the dimensions of data to visualize it (dimensionality reduction).

Common unsupervised learning algorithms include:

Algorithm	Description
K-Means Clustering	A method to partition data into K distinct clusters based on distance to the centroid of a cluster.
Hierarchical Clustering	Builds a tree of clusters by iteratively merging or splitting existing clusters.
Principal Component Analysis (PCA)	A technique for reducing the dimensionality of datasets, increasing interpretability while minimizing information loss.

Figure 3.4: Common Unsupervised Learning Algorithms

Semi-Supervised Learning

Definition

Semi-supervised learning falls between supervised learning and unsupervised learning. In semi-supervised learning, the model is trained on a dataset that contains both labeled and unlabeled data. Generally, a small amount of data is labeled while a large amount of data is unlabeled.

Examples

- A photo archive where only some photos are tagged with labels, and the model learns to label new photos.
- Language translation models trained on a small set of sentences for which translations are known.

Reinforcement Learning

Reinforcement learning is a type of machine learning where an agent learns to make decisions by taking actions in an environment to achieve some objectives. The agent learns from the consequences of its actions, rather than from being taught explicitly. It is widely used in areas such as robotics, gaming, and navigation.

Definition

Reinforcement learning is a type of machine learning where an agent learns to make decisions by performing certain actions and receiving rewards or penalties in return. It is about taking suitable action to maximize reward in a particular situation.

Examples

- A chess game where the model learns to make moves that increase its chances of winning.
- Autonomous vehicles learning to navigate through traffic.

Common reinforcement learning algorithms include:

Algorithm	Description
Q-Learning	A model-free reinforcement learning algorithm that learns the value of an action in a particular state.
Deep Q-Networks (DQN)	Combines Q-Learning with deep neural networks, allowing the agent to evaluate the state of the environment directly from raw inputs such as pixels.

Figure 3.5: *Common Reinforcement Learning Algorithms*

Evaluation Metrics

Understanding how to evaluate the performance of machine learning models is crucial. Common metrics include accuracy, precision, recall, and F1 score for classification tasks, and mean squared error (MSE) for regression tasks.

Neural Networks and Deep Learning

Neural networks are a set of algorithms, modeled loosely after the human brain, designed to recognize patterns. They interpret sensory data through a kind of machine perception, labeling, or clustering raw input. Deep learning, a subset of neural networks, involves networks with a large number of layers that enable learning from vast amounts of data.

Key concepts include:

Machine Learning Concept	Description
Convolutional Neural Networks (CNNs)	Particularly effective for tasks involving images, such as image recognition and classification.
Recurrent Neural Networks (RNNs)	Suited for sequential data, such as time series analysis or natural language processing.
Transfer Learning	Involves taking a pre-trained model and fine-tuning it for a similar but different task, significantly reducing the need for large datasets and computational resources.

Figure 3.6: *Machine Learning Techniques*

Applications of Machine Learning

Machine learning has a wide array of applications across various industries, revolutionizing the way we approach problem-solving and decision-making.

Here are some of the key applications of machine learning:

Image Recognition and Classification

Definition: Image recognition is the process of identifying and detecting an object or feature in a digital image or video. Classification involves categorizing these objects into various classes.

Applications:
- Facial recognition systems for security and identification purposes.
- Medical imaging to assist in diagnosing diseases.
- Automated photo tagging on social media platforms.

Natural Language Processing (NLP)

Definition: NLP is a field of machine learning focused on enabling machines to understand and interpret human language.

Applications:

- Language translation services that convert text from one language to another.

- Sentiment analysis to gauge public opinion, customer sentiment, and so on.

- Chatbots and virtual assistants that can interact with users in natural language.

Predictive Analytics

Definition: Predictive analytics uses statistical algorithms and machine learning techniques to identify the likelihood of future outcomes based on historical data.

Applications:

- Forecasting consumer behavior and purchasing patterns.

- Predicting equipment failures in manufacturing through predictive maintenance.

- Anticipating market trends and movements in finance.

Recommender Systems

Definition: Recommender systems are algorithms that suggest relevant items to users based on their preferences and previous interactions.

Applications:

- E-commerce websites recommending products to customers.

- Streaming services recommended movies, TV shows, and music to users.

- Personalized content delivery on news feeds and social media platforms.

Autonomous Vehicles

Definition: Autonomous vehicles are equipped with ML algorithms that enable them to perceive their environment and make driving decisions with little or no human intervention.

Applications:

- Self-driving cars using computer vision, sensor fusion, and machine learning for navigation.

- Drones used for delivery, surveillance, and photography that autonomously navigate and avoid obstacles.

Healthcare Applications

Definition: Machine learning in healthcare involves the use of algorithms and models to improve medical diagnosis, treatment, and administrative processes.

Applications:

- Predictive diagnostics to identify disease risk factors and early symptoms.
- Personalized medicine tailored to individual genetic profiles.
- Drug discovery and development processes.

Financial Forecasting

Definition: Financial forecasting uses machine learning models to predict future financial conditions and market trends based on current and historical data.

Applications:

- Algorithmic trading strategies that make automated trading decisions.
- Credit scoring models to assess the risk of lending.
- Fraud detection systems that identify unusual patterns indicative of fraudulent activity.

Machine learning's versatility allows it to be applied to virtually any domain where data is available, making it a powerful tool for innovation and efficiency. As machine learning technology continues to advance, its applications are expected to expand, further integrating into the fabric of industry and everyday life.

JavaScript and Machine Learning

The intersection of JavaScript and machine learning represents a burgeoning field that extends the capabilities of web development into the realm of artificial intelligence. JavaScript, a language deeply entrenched in web development, is now being harnessed to implement complex AI algorithms, thanks to the advent of powerful libraries like TensorFlow.js. This section explores how JavaScript is being used in machine learning and the benefits it brings to the table.

Figure 3.7: *JavaScript and Machine Learning*

The Rise of Machine Learning in JavaScript

Traditionally, machine learning has been dominated by languages like Python due to their extensive libraries and frameworks. However, JavaScript has emerged as a strong contender, bringing machine learning to the browser and server side with Node.js. This shift is largely attributed to TensorFlow.js, which allows developers to define, train, and run machine learning models directly in the JavaScript environment.

Advantages of JavaScript for Machine Learning

Here are some key advantages of JavaScript for machine learning:

- **Ubiquity**: JavaScript's omnipresence in web development makes it a strategic choice for integrating machine learning into web applications. With JavaScript, developers can deploy machine learning models that run on the client side, reducing server load and providing faster and more interactive user experiences.

- **Familiarity**: A vast number of developers are proficient in JavaScript, and the language's syntax and constructs are well-known. This familiarity lowers the barrier to entry for web developers looking to venture into machine learning, allowing them to leverage their existing JavaScript skills.

- **Flexibility**: JavaScript's flexibility is a significant advantage. Machine learning models can be run on various devices and platforms, including browsers, servers, and mobile devices, thanks to JavaScript's cross-platform nature. This flexibility also extends to the development process, where JavaScript developers can easily integrate machine learning models with other web technologies.

- **Accessibility:** One of the most significant advantages of JavaScript is its ability to run natively in web browsers. This means that machine learning models can be deployed directly within web applications, making them accessible to a broad audience without the need for additional software installations. Users can interact with ML-powered features seamlessly as part of their web browsing experience.

- **Integration with Web Applications:** JavaScript is the cornerstone of web application development. By using JavaScript for machine learning, developers can integrate ML models directly into web-based systems and user interfaces. This integration is smooth and natural, as the same language is used for both the application and the embedded ML functionalities, leading to a more cohesive development process.

- **Community Support and Libraries:** The JavaScript ecosystem is rich with libraries and frameworks designed to facilitate machine learning. TensorFlow. js, for example, is a powerful library that brings machine learning to JavaScript, enabling the training and deployment of models in the browser or on Node.js. Other libraries like Brain.js provide simplified approaches to neural networks, making machine learning more approachable for JavaScript developers. The community support for these libraries continues to grow, providing extensive resources, documentation, and forums for collaboration.

Comparison with Other Programming Languages for Machine Learning

While Python and R have been the go-to languages for traditional machine learning tasks due to their extensive libraries and tools, JavaScript offers unique advantages. As the language of the web, JavaScript allows developers to build end-to-end solutions that incorporate machine learning without switching contexts. This holistic approach is particularly beneficial for applications that require real-time interaction and responsiveness, such as dynamic web interfaces and browser-based games.

JavaScript

- **Accessibility**: JavaScript runs natively in the browser, which makes it highly accessible for integrating machine learning into web applications without additional installations.

- **Community Support**: There is a growing number of machine learning libraries in JavaScript, such as TensorFlow.js and Brain.js, which provide developers with tools to create and deploy ML models.

- **Integration**: JavaScript is well-suited for integrating machine learning outputs into web dashboards and applications, although it may be less suited for computationally intensive tasks due to its basic mathematical functionality.

- **Versatility**: JavaScript can be used for both front-end and back-end development, making it a comprehensive language for full-stack development, including machine learning.

Python

- **Ecosystem**: Python has a rich ecosystem of machine learning libraries, such as NumPy, Pandas, Scikit-learn, and TensorFlow, making it a frontrunner for machine learning and data science.

- **Ease of Learning**: Python is known for its ease of learning and readability, which makes it beginner-friendly and a popular choice in academia and data science.

- **Performance**: While Python may be slower than some lower-level languages, it is widely used for prototyping and experimentation in machine learning.

R

- **Statistical Analysis**: R is a language designed for statistical analysis and visualization, making it another strong contender for machine learning, particularly in academia and research settings.

Java

- **Performance**: Java is known for its speed and scalability, making it suitable for high-performance machine learning applications, especially those that require fast execution.

- **Libraries**: Java has several machine learning libraries, such as JavaML and Deeplearning4J, which support popular machine learning algorithms and neural networks.

C++

- **Speed**: C++ offers high performance and control over system resources, which is critical for analyzing large datasets in machine learning.

- **Complexity**: The trade-off is that C++ is not as easy for quick prototyping and has a steeper learning curve compared to higher-level languages like JavaScript and Python.

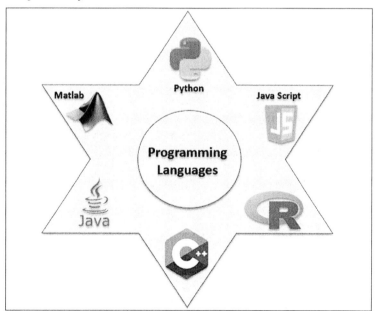

Figure 3.8: *Different programming languages used for Machine Learning (Source: https://cdn. educba.com/academy/wp-content/uploads/2019/11/Machine-Learning-Programming-Languages-2.png)*

In summary, while JavaScript is traditionally associated with web development, it is becoming increasingly viable for machine learning, especially with the development of libraries like TensorFlow.js. Python remains a dominant language for machine learning due to its extensive libraries and ease of use. The choice between JavaScript, Python, and other languages often depends on the specific requirements of the project, the developer's familiarity with the language, and the performance needs of the machine learning application. JavaScript's ubiquity, ease of integration with web technologies, growing community support, and the development of dedicated ML libraries make it an increasingly attractive option for machine learning projects. As the tools and frameworks continue to mature, JavaScript is poised to become an even more powerful language for building sophisticated, AI-driven web applications.

TensorFlow.js: A Gateway to Machine Learning in JavaScript

TensorFlow.js is a library that brings machine learning to JavaScript developers. It provides an accessible yet powerful platform for training and deploying machine learning models. With TensorFlow.js, developers can:

Capability	Description
Utilize pre-trained models	Developers can use pre-trained machine learning models in TensorFlow.js for a quick start in various tasks, without the need to train the models from scratch.
Train models from scratch	Developers can train machine learning models from the ground up using JavaScript, taking advantage of TensorFlow.js's intuitive API and hardware acceleration capabilities of modern browsers.
Perform complex tasks	With TensorFlow.js, developers can perform a wide range of complex tasks within the browser or Node.js environment, such as image and speech recognition, natural language processing, and more.

Figure 3.9: TensorFlow Capabilities

Practical Applications

The practical applications of machine learning in JavaScript are diverse and growing. Some examples include:

- Real-time image and video analysis directly in the browser, enabling applications like augmented reality and interactive gaming.
- On-the-fly language translation and sentiment analysis in web applications, enhancing user engagement and accessibility.

- Browser-based tools for data visualization and analysis, making machine learning insights more accessible to end-users.

Getting Started with TensorFlow.js

TensorFlow.js is a powerful and flexible library that brings machine learning to JavaScript, allowing developers to create, train, and deploy machine learning models directly in the browser or on Node.js. This section will guide you through the initial steps of getting started with TensorFlow.js, from setting up the environment to running your first machine learning model.

Introduction to TensorFlow.js

TensorFlow.js is an open-source web ML library that can run anywhere JavaScript can. It's based on the original TensorFlow library written in Python and aims to recreate this developer experience and set of APIs for the JavaScript ecosystem. TensorFlow.js enables you to run existing models, retrain existing models with your data, or develop ML models directly in JavaScript using flexible and intuitive APIs.

Advantages of Using TensorFlow.js

TensorFlow.js is a library that brings machine learning and deep learning to JavaScript, enabling developers to harness the power of TensorFlow in web environments. Here are some of the key advantages of using TensorFlow.js:

Accessibility

- **Runs in the Browser**: TensorFlow.js operates directly within the web browser, which means there is no need for users to install additional software or libraries. This accessibility allows for the rapid deployment and use of machine learning models, making it easier for end-users to benefit from AI without complex setup processes.

Integration with Web Applications

- **Seamless Integration**: With TensorFlow.js, machine learning models can be integrated seamlessly into web applications. This allows for the creation of interactive and intelligent web experiences, where machine learning models can process and analyze data in real-time, directly within the user interface.

Compatibility with Existing TensorFlow Models

- **Model Conversion**: TensorFlow.js provides the ability to convert pre-existing TensorFlow models (developed in Python) to be compatible with the JavaScript library. This compatibility ensures that the investment in developing TensorFlow models is preserved and that these models can be easily deployed in web environments.

Community Support and Resources

- **Robust Community**: TensorFlow.js benefits from the strong community support that surrounds TensorFlow. There is a wealth of resources available, including tutorials, documentation, and forums where developers can seek help and share their experiences. This community-driven support accelerates learning and problem-solving within the TensorFlow.js ecosystem.

Additional Advantages

- **Client-Side Processing**: Machine learning operations are performed on the client's machine, which can lead to faster response times and reduced server load. This client-side processing also enhances user privacy, as sensitive data does not need to be sent to a server for analysis.

- **Use of Sensors**: TensorFlow.js can take advantage of the various sensors available in modern devices, such as cameras and microphones, to create immersive and interactive applications that respond to user inputs in innovative ways.

- **Hardware Acceleration**: TensorFlow.js leverages WebGL for hardware acceleration, which can significantly improve the performance of machine learning models by utilizing the power of the GPU. This acceleration is particularly beneficial for complex models and large datasets.

- **Cross-Platform**: TensorFlow.js is not limited to the browser; it can also be used on the server side with Node.js, providing flexibility in how and where machine learning models are deployed and run.

In summary, TensorFlow.js stands out for its accessibility, ease of integration, compatibility with existing TensorFlow models, and strong community support. These advantages make TensorFlow.js a compelling choice for developers looking to incorporate machine learning into web applications, enhancing user experience and opening up new possibilities for AI-driven web functionality.

Key Components of TensorFlow.js

TensorFlow.js is a comprehensive library for machine learning in JavaScript, and it consists of several key components that enable developers to build and deploy ML models. Following is an overview of these components:

TensorFlow.js Core

- **Tensors**: Tensors are the core data structures in TensorFlow.js, analogous to multi-dimensional arrays. They are used to represent all data in TensorFlow.js, including inputs, outputs, and the model's internal state. Tensors can be manipulated and transformed through a variety of operations provided by the library.

- **Operations**: TensorFlow.js provides a wide array of operations that can be performed on tensors. These include basic mathematical operations like addition, subtraction, multiplication, and division, as well as more complex functions like reshaping, slicing, and concatenating tensors. These operations are essential for building and manipulating the data structures required for machine learning models.

- **Models**: In TensorFlow.js, models are constructs that define the structure of a machine learning algorithm. They can be built using predefined layers or custom operations. TensorFlow.js supports the training of models using data, allowing the models to learn and make predictions or decisions based on that data.

- **Layers**: TensorFlow.js offers a variety of pre-built layers that serve as the building blocks for neural network architectures. These include dense (fully connected) layers, convolutional layers for image data, recurrent layers for sequence data, and many others. Each layer type is designed to handle specific types of data and model complexity.

Let's summarize the preceding component in a tabular format:

Component	Description
Tensors	The fundamental data structure in TensorFlow.js, representing data as multi-dimensional arrays. Tensors can be created, manipulated, and operated on using TensorFlow.js.
Operations	TensorFlow.js provides a wide range of operations for tensor manipulation, including basic mathematical operations like addition, subtraction, multiplication, and more complex functions.
Models	TensorFlow.js allows developers to build and train machine learning models. Models are composed of layers and can be trained on data to learn patterns for making predictions.
Layers	TensorFlow.js offers various types of layers, such as dense (fully connected), convolutional, and recurrent layers, which are the building blocks for neural network architectures.

Figure 3.10: *TensorFlow.js Core Components*

TensorFlow.js Layers API

- **High-level API**: The Layers API in TensorFlow.js is a high-level API that simplifies the process of building neural network models. It provides an abstraction that allows developers to define models in a more intuitive and less error-prone way compared to using the lower-level Core API.

- **Pre-built Layers**: The Layers API comes with a set of pre-built layers that are commonly used in neural networks. These include layers for convolutional neural networks (CNNs), recurrent neural networks (RNNs), and others. These pre-built layers can be easily stacked to create complex models for a wide range of tasks.

Let's summarize the preceding component in a tabular format:

Component	Description
TensorFlow.js Layers API	A high-level, user-friendly API for building neural network models in TensorFlow.js. It simplifies the process of defining models by providing pre-built layers and easy-to-use functions.
Pre-built Layers	TensorFlow.js offers a variety of pre-built layers for common machine learning tasks, such as dense layers for fully connected neural networks, convolutional layers for image processing, and recurrent layers for sequence data.

Figure 3.11: *TensorFlow.js Layers API*

TensorFlow.js Converter

- **Conversion Tools**: The TensorFlow.js Converter is a set of tools that allows developers to import existing TensorFlow models, which are typically written in Python, into the TensorFlow.js format. This enables the use of a vast array of pre-trained models within the JavaScript environment, greatly accelerating the development process and allowing for the leveraging of TensorFlow's powerful ecosystem.

In summary, TensorFlow.js provides a robust set of tools and components that make it possible to perform machine learning in the JavaScript environment. From the fundamental tensors and operations to the high-level Layers API and model conversion tools, TensorFlow.js equips developers with everything they need to build, train, and deploy machine learning models in web applications.

Setting Up a Development Environment for TensorFlow

TensorFlow.js involves setting up your development environment, installing the necessary tools, and understanding how to use TensorFlow.js in both the browser and Node.js environments.

Here's a guide to help you begin your journey with TensorFlow.js:

- **Install Node.js**: Before you can use TensorFlow.js, you need to have Node.js installed on your system. Node.js is a JavaScript runtime that allows you to run JavaScript on the server side.

- **Code Editor**: Choose a code editor that you are comfortable with. Visual Studio Code is a popular choice among developers and comes with features that support JavaScript development.

- **Local Web Server**: If you are working with TensorFlow.js in the browser, you will need a local web server to serve your HTML and JavaScript files. This can be set up using Node.js or other server software.

Installation and Setup

- **Install TensorFlow.js**: You can install TensorFlow.js using npm (Node.js package manager) or yarn, which are tools for managing JavaScript packages. The installation command is as follows:

```
npm install @tensorflow/tfjs
```

Alternatively, you can include TensorFlow.js in your HTML file using a script tag for browser-based projects.

- **Import the Library**: After installation, import TensorFlow.js into your project to start using it. In Node.js, you can require the library at the beginning of your script. In the browser, you can use the script tag to include TensorFlow.js.

Using TensorFlow.js in the Browser

- **Client-Side ML**: TensorFlow.js allows you to build and run machine learning models directly in the browser. This enables interactive applications that can perform machine learning tasks without server-side processing.

- **Simple Example**: A simple TensorFlow.js script in the browser might involve creating a model, training it on some data, and then making predictions. This can be done entirely within an HTML file with script tags.

Using TensorFlow.js with Node.js

- **Server-Side ML**: TensorFlow.js can also be used on the server side with Node.js. This is useful for tasks that require more computational power or when you want to keep your machine learning models private.

- **Running Scripts**: With Node.js, you can write TensorFlow.js scripts that can be executed on the server. This allows for more complex machine learning tasks that can be integrated with web services.

Creating and Running a Simple TensorFlow.js Script

Creating the Script: A basic TensorFlow.js script involves defining a model, compiling it with an optimizer and loss function, and then training the model with data. Here's a simple example:

```
const tf = require('@tensorflow/tfjs');

const model = tf.sequential();
model.add(tf.layers.dense({units: 1, inputShape: [1]}));

model.compile({loss: 'meanSquaredError', optimizer: 'sgd'});

const xs = tf.tensor2d([1, 2, 3, 4], [4, 1]);
const ys = tf.tensor2d([1, 3, 5, 7], [4, 1]);

model.fit(xs, ys, {epochs: 10}).then(() => {
  model.predict(tf.tensor2d([5], [1, 1])).print();
});
```

Running the Script: Once you have written your TensorFlow.js script, you can run it using Node.js by executing the following command in your terminal:

```
node your-script.js
```

This will train the model and output the prediction for the new data point.

By following these steps, you will have a solid foundation to start exploring the capabilities of TensorFlow.js for machine learning in JavaScript. Whether you are working in the browser or on the server with Node.js, TensorFlow.js provides the tools you need to build and deploy ML models.

Code Explanation

1. **Import TensorFlow.js:**

```
const tf = require('@tensorflow/tfjs');
```

This line imports the TensorFlow.js library into your Node.js script, making the TensorFlow.js functions available for use.

2. **Define a Sequential Model**:

```
const model = tf.sequential();
```

A sequential model is created, which is a linear stack of layers. It's the simplest kind of model in TensorFlow.js, where you can add layers in sequence.

3. **Add a Dense Layer**:

```
model.add(tf.layers.dense({units: 1, inputShape: [1]}));
```

A dense (fully connected) layer is added to the model with one unit (neuron). The `inputShape` of `[1]` indicates that the input to this layer is a one-dimensional array.

4. **Compile the Model**:

```
model.compile({loss: 'meanSquaredError', optimizer: 'sgd'});
```

The model is compiled, which is a necessary step before training. Here, the loss function is set to **'meanSquaredError'**, which is common for regression problems. The optimizer **'sgd'** stands for stochastic gradient descent, a method to update the model's weights during training.

5. **Generate Synthetic Data**:

```
const xs = tf.tensor2d([1, 2, 3, 4], [4, 1]);
const ys = tf.tensor2d([1, 3, 5, 7], [4, 1]);
```

Synthetic data is generated for training the model. `xs` are the input features, and `ys` are the labels. Both are created as 2D tensors, with the shape `[1]`, indicating four data points with one feature each.

6. **Train the Model**:

```
model.fit(xs, ys, {epochs: 10});
```

The model is trained using the `fit` method with the input features `xs` and labels `ys`. The model will train for 10 epochs, which means it will go through the training data ten times.

7. **Make a Prediction**:

```
model.predict(tf.tensor2d([5], [1, 1])).print();
```

After training, the model makes a prediction on a new data point that it hasn't seen before. The input is wrapped in a 2D tensor to match the model's expected input shape. The prediction result is printed to the console.

Steps to Run the Code

1. **Set Up Your Environment:**

   a. Ensure that Node.js is installed on your system.

   b. Create a new directory for your project and navigate into it.

2. **Initialize a New Node.js Project:**

   a. Run `npm init` in your terminal and follow the prompts to create a `package.json` file.

3. **Install TensorFlow.js:**

   a. Run `npm install @tensorflow/tfjs` to install TensorFlow.js as a dependency.

4. **Create a JavaScript File:**

   a. Create a new file, for example, `linear-regression.js`, and paste the provided code into this file.

5. **Run the Script:**

   a. Execute the script by running `node linear-regression.js` in your terminal.

   b. The script will train the model and output the prediction to the console.

By following these steps, you can run the provided TensorFlow.js code to create a simple linear regression model, train it on synthetic data, and make a prediction.

Building Your First Machine Learning Model with TensorFlow.js

We are diving into TensorFlow.js to craft our inaugural machine learning model. We will start by delving into either regression or classification to grasp their nuances.

Building Your First Regression Model with TensorFlow.js

When starting with machine learning in TensorFlow.js, a regression model is often the first step for many developers. Regression models are used to predict continuous numerical values based on input variables. For instance, you might predict housing prices based on features like square footage, location, and the number of bedrooms. To build a regression model in TensorFlow.js, you begin by defining the architecture of your model using the sequential API, which allows you to stack layers in a linear fashion. A typical regression model might include a dense layer with a single output unit, as the goal is to output a single continuous value.

The next step involves compiling the model with a loss function and an optimizer. For regression, the mean squared error loss function is commonly used, and an optimizer like **'adam'** or stochastic gradient descent (SGD) helps to minimize this loss. With your model architecture in place, you will prepare your dataset, often involving normalization or standardization of your input features to help the model learn more effectively. After preprocessing your data, you will use the `fit` method to train your model, passing in your input features and corresponding target values. Training might take several epochs, during which the model's weights are adjusted to minimize the loss function. Once trained, you can use the `predict` method to estimate values for new and unseen inputs.

To start, you will need to set up your environment by installing Node.js and TensorFlow. js, as described in previous instructions. Once your environment is ready, you can begin coding your model. For a regression model, you might use a simple neural network with one dense layer for starters, as it can approximate any continuous function given enough neurons and training data.

TensorFlow.js Regression Model Code

```
const tf = require('@tensorflow/tfjs');

const model = tf.sequential();
model.add(tf.layers.dense({units: 1, inputShape: [1]}));

model.compile({loss: 'meanSquaredError', optimizer: 'adam'});

const xs = tf.tensor2d([1, 2, 3, 4, 5, 6], [6, 1]);
const ys = tf.tensor2d([3, 6, 9, 12, 15, 18], [6, 1]);

model.fit(xs, ys, {epochs: 100}).then(() => {
  model.predict(tf.tensor2d([7], [1, 1])).print();
});
```

Code Explanation

- **Model Definition**: We define a sequential model, which is a stack of layers where each layer has exactly one input tensor and one output tensor. We add a dense layer with one unit, which is suitable for a single output regression.

- **Model Compilation**: We compile the model with the mean squared error loss function, which measures the average of the squares of the errors between predicted and actual values. The **'adam'** optimizer is an alternative to stochastic gradient descent that adjusts the learning rate throughout training.

- **Data Generation**: We create synthetic data (`xs` for input and `ys` for output) that follows a linear relationship (in this case, `y = 3x`). The data is shaped into two-dimensional tensors to match the model's expected input.

- **Model Training**: We train the model with the `fit` method using our synthetic data for 100 epochs, which should be sufficient for the model to learn the relationship between `xs` and `ys`.

- **Prediction**: After training, we use the `predict` method to estimate the output for a new input value of 7. We expect the model to predict a value close to 21 (since 7 * 3 = 21), given the linear relationship it has learned.

Running the Code

1. **Save the Code**: Copy the code into a file named `regression-model.js`.

2. **Execute the Script**: Run the script using Node.js by executing `node regression-model.js` in your terminal.

3. **View the Output**: The output will be printed to the console, showing the model's prediction for the input value of 7.

Building Your First Classification Model with TensorFlow.js

On the other hand, classification models in TensorFlow.js are designed to categorize input data into discrete classes. A common application is image classification, where the model might identify if a photograph contains a cat or a dog. Classification models differ from regression models primarily in the output layer and the loss function used. For a binary classification task, your model's final layer would use a **'sigmoid'** activation function to output a value between 0 and 1, representing the probability of the input being in one class or the other. For multi-class classification, a **'softmax'** activation function is used to output a probability distribution across multiple classes.

The model is compiled with a loss function appropriate for classification, such as binary cross-entropy for binary classification or categorical cross-entropy for multi-class problems. The optimizer remains an essential component in adjusting the weights to improve model accuracy. Training a classification model also involves using the `fit` method, but this time your target values will be categorical labels, which may require one-hot encoding for multi-class problems. After training, you can evaluate your model's performance using metrics like accuracy, precision, and recall, and make predictions on new data using the `predict` method. TensorFlow.js provides a flexible and powerful platform to build and deploy both regression and classification models, making machine learning more accessible to JavaScript developers.

Creating a classification model with TensorFlow.js involves using labeled datasets to train a model to categorize data into predefined classes. A typical example of a classification task is identifying whether an email is spam or not. TensorFlow.js enables you to perform such tasks in the browser or on Node.js, making machine learning models more accessible and interactive.

Before diving into the code, ensure you have Node.js installed and have initialized a new project with TensorFlow.js as a dependency. Once your environment is set up, you can start writing your classification model. For this example, we will build a simple binary classification model that learns to distinguish between two classes.

TensorFlow.js Classification Model Code

```
const tf = require('@tensorflow/tfjs');

const model = tf.sequential();
model.add(tf.layers.dense({units: 2, inputShape: [2], activation:
'softmax'}));

model.compile({loss: 'categoricalCrossentropy', optimizer:
'adam'});

const xs = tf.tensor2d([[0, 0], [0, 1], [1, 0], [1, 1]], [4, 2]);
const ys = tf.tensor2d([[1, 0], [0, 1], [0, 1], [1, 0]], [4, 2]);

model.fit(xs, ys, {epochs: 50}).then(() => {
  model.predict(tf.tensor2d([[0.5, 0.5]], [1, 2])).print();
});
```

Code Explanation

- **Model Definition**: We define a sequential model for binary classification, which is a stack of layers where each layer has exactly one input tensor and one output tensor. We add a dense layer with two units, which corresponds to the two possible classes.

- **Model Compilation**: We compile the model with the categorical cross-entropy loss function, which is suitable for binary classification problems. The **'adam'** optimizer is used for its efficiency in training.

- **Data Generation**: We create synthetic data (`xs` for input features and `ys` for output labels) that represent the two classes. The data is shaped into two-dimensional tensors to match the model's expected input.

- **Model Training**: We train the model using the `fit` method with our synthetic data for 50 epochs, which should allow the model to learn the distinction between the two classes.

- **Prediction**: After training, we use the `predict` method to estimate the class for a new input value `[0.5, 0.5]`. The output will be a probability distribution over the two classes, showing the model's confidence in each class.

Running the Code

1. **Save the Code**: Copy the code into a file named `classification-model.js`.

2. **Execute the Script**: Run the script using Node.js by executing `node classification-model.js` in your terminal.

3. **View the Output**: The output will be printed to the console, showing the model's probabilities for the input belonging to each of the two classes.

Conclusion

This chapter provides a comprehensive introduction to machine learning, tailored for JavaScript developers in the MERN ecosystem. It begins by explaining the essence of machine learning – a branch of artificial intelligence that focuses on enabling computers to learn from data and make decisions autonomously. The chapter emphasizes the importance of machine learning in today's technology landscape and sets the stage for a deeper exploration of its core principles and algorithms.

The chapter then delves into the specifics of machine learning, distinguishing between supervised learning, which uses labeled data for tasks like classification and regression, and unsupervised learning, which involves unlabeled data for clustering and dimensionality reduction. It also covers semi-supervised learning, which combines elements of both supervised and unsupervised learning, and reinforcement learning, where an agent learns to make decisions through trial and error to achieve a goal. These concepts are crucial for understanding the different approaches one can take when building machine learning models.

As the chapter progresses, it highlights the versatility of JavaScript as not just a language for web development but also a potent tool for implementing complex AI algorithms. It introduces TensorFlow.js, a powerful library that brings machine learning capabilities to JavaScript, enabling developers to train and deploy models directly in the browser or on Node.js. The chapter provides guidance on setting up TensorFlow.

js and explores its key features, including how to work with pre-trained models and train models from scratch.

In the next chapter, we will dive deep into the practical aspects of bringing artificial intelligence to life in web applications using the Node.js environment, powered by the TensorFlow.js library.

Multiple Choice Questions

1. What is machine learning primarily about?

    a. Programming computers to perform specific tasks

    b. Enabling computers to learn from data and improve over time

    c. Using complex algorithms to perform calculations

    d. Building web applications using JavaScript

2. Which type of machine learning is characterized by the use of labeled datasets?

    a. Supervised learning

    b. Unsupervised learning

    c. Semi-supervised learning

    d. Reinforcement learning

3. Why is JavaScript considered a versatile language for machine learning?

    a. It can only be used for web development

    b. It is the only language that supports TensorFlow.js

    c. It allows for the integration of machine learning in web applications

    d. It is faster than all other programming languages

4. What is TensorFlow.js?

    a. A database management system

    b. A library that brings machine learning to JavaScript

    c. A version control system

    d. A web server

5. What is the first step in building a machine learning model with TensorFlow.js?

    a. Defining a model architecture

    b. Compiling the model

    c. Training the model on a dataset

    d. Deploying the model to a server

6. What is unsupervised learning best suited for?

    a. Tasks with labeled data

    b. Clustering and dimensionality reduction

    c. Regression tasks

    d. Classification tasks

7. Which algorithm is commonly used for dimensionality reduction?

    a. Linear Regression

    b. Decision Trees

    c. Principal Component Analysis (PCA)

    d. Q-Learning

8. Which library allows JavaScript developers to work with pre-trained machine learning models?

    a. jQuery

    b. React

    c. TensorFlow.js

    d. Node.js

9. How can you install TensorFlow.js for use in a Node.js project?

    a. Using the `install` command in the browser

    b. Downloading it as a ZIP file

    c. Using npm or yarn package managers

    d. Copying and pasting the TensorFlow.js source code

10. After training a TensorFlow.js model, what method is used to evaluate its performance on new data?

    a. `model.evaluate()`

    b. `model.compile()`

    c. `model.predict()`

    d. `model.fit()`

Answers

1. b

2. a

3. c

4. b

5. a

6. b

7. c

8. c

9. c

10. c

CHAPTER 4

Implementing AI with Node.js and TensorFlow.js

Introduction

Implementing AI with Node.js and TensorFlow.js dives deep into the practical aspects of bringing artificial intelligence to life in web applications using the Node.js environment, powered by the TensorFlow.js library. This chapter is designed to bridge the gap between theoretical machine learning concepts and their real-world application, focusing on the integration of AI functionalities within the server-side of the MERN stack. Readers will explore how to leverage TensorFlow.js—a powerful and flexible library for machine learning in JavaScript—to develop, train, and deploy machine learning models directly in Node.js.

The chapter covers a range of topics, from setting up TensorFlow.js in a Node.js environment to creating and training custom machine learning models that can analyze and predict data patterns. It also introduces essential techniques for working with datasets, including data collection, preprocessing, and augmentation, to ensure models are trained on high-quality data. Additionally, readers will learn about deploying trained models for inference, enabling AI-driven features such as personalized content recommendations, predictive analytics, and more, in their MERN applications.

By the end of this chapter, readers will be equipped with the knowledge and skills to implement sophisticated AI features in their web applications, using Node.js and TensorFlow.js, enhancing the user experience and functionality of their projects.

Structure

In this chapter, we will cover the following topics:

- Setting Up TensorFlow.js in Node.js

- Understanding TensorFlow.js Core Concepts
- Designing Machine Learning Models
- Data Handling and Preprocessing
- Training Machine Learning Models
- Model Evaluation and Validation
- Fine-Tuning and Optimization
- Deploying Models for Inference

Setting Up TensorFlow.js in Node.js

To begin implementing AI with Node.js and TensorFlow.js, you first need to set up TensorFlow.js in your Node.js environment. TensorFlow.js is a powerful library that allows you to run machine learning models and deep learning neural networks in the browser or on the server with Node.js. This setup will enable you to develop, train, and deploy machine learning models directly within your Node.js applications.

Installation Steps

Follow these steps to install TensorFlow.js in Node.js:

1. **Install Node.js**: Ensure that Node.js is installed on your system. You can download it from the Node.js official website: https://nodejs.org/

2. **Initialize Your Project**: Create a new directory for your project and initialize it with `npm` to create a `package.json` file that will manage your project's dependencies.

   ```
   mkdir my-tfjs-project
     cd my-tfjs-project
     npm init -y
   ```

3. **Install TensorFlow.js**: Install the TensorFlow.js package for Node.js using `npm` or `yarn`. This will add TensorFlow.js to your project's dependencies.

   ```
   npm install @tensorflow/tfjs
     # Or, if you have a GPU and want to leverage it:
     npm install @tensorflow/tfjs-node-gpu
   ```

Sample Code to Verify Installation

Once TensorFlow.js is installed, you can write a simple script to verify that it is working correctly. Create a file named `index.js` and add the following code:

```
const tf = require('@tensorflow/tfjs');

const tensor = tf.tensor([1, 2, 3, 4]);
tensor.print();

const squaredTensor = tensor.square();
squaredTensor.print();
```

Running the Code

To run the code, use the following command in your terminal:

```
node index.js
```

Code Explanation

1. The first line imports the TensorFlow.js library for Node.js, which is necessary to access TensorFlow.js functions and classes.

2. A tensor is created using `tf.tensor()`, which is a central unit of data in TensorFlow.js. The tensor contains the numbers 1, 2, 3, and 4.

3. The `print()` method is called on the tensor to output its values to the console.

4. A new tensor is created by squaring the values of the original tensor using the `square()` method.

5. The squared tensor is then printed to the console, showing the result of the operation.

By following these steps, you will have successfully set up TensorFlow.js in your Node.js environment, allowing you to proceed with building and training machine learning models. This setup is the first step towards integrating AI capabilities into your MERN stack applications, leveraging the power of TensorFlow.js for server-side machine learning.

Configuring TensorFlow.js for Node.js: Choosing Between CPU and GPU Acceleration

When setting up TensorFlow.js in a Node.js environment, one of the key decisions you will need to make is whether to use CPU or GPU acceleration. This choice can significantly impact the performance of your machine learning models, especially for computationally intensive tasks.

CPU Acceleration

Let us understand the advantages of using CPU Acceleration when setting up TensorFlow.js in a Node.js environment.

Advantages:

Criteria	Information
Simplicity	CPU acceleration is generally easier to set up and requires no additional hardware or software configuration beyond installing TensorFlow.js.
Compatibility	All systems have a CPU, making this option universally compatible.
Cost-Effective	Using CPU acceleration does not incur additional costs associated with purchasing or maintaining GPU hardware.

Figure 4.1: *Advantages of CPU Acceleration*

Disadvantages:

- **Performance**: CPUs are generally slower than GPUs for the types of parallel computations required in machine learning. This can lead to longer training times and slower inference speeds, especially for large models or datasets.

Setup:

To use CPU acceleration with TensorFlow.js in Node.js, you simply need to install the `@tensorflow/tfjs` package:

```
npm install @tensorflow/tfjs
```

This package provides the necessary bindings to run TensorFlow.js on the CPU.

GPU Acceleration

Let us understand the advantages of using GPU Acceleration, when setting up TensorFlow.js in a Node.js environment.

Advantages:

Criteria	Information
Performance	GPUs are designed for parallel processing, making them significantly faster than CPUs for many machine learning tasks. This can result in much shorter training times and faster inference.
Efficiency	For large-scale models and datasets, GPUs can handle the computations more efficiently, making them ideal for deep learning applications.

Figure 4.2: *Advantages of GPU Acceleration*

Now, we will discuss the cons of the same:

Disadvantages:

Criteria	Information
Complexity	Setting up GPU acceleration requires additional steps, including installing the appropriate GPU drivers and TensorFlow.js GPU package.
Cost	GPUs are more expensive than CPUs, both in terms of initial purchase and ongoing operational costs. They also consume more power.

Figure 4.3: *Disadvantages of GPU Acceleration*

Setup:

To use GPU acceleration with TensorFlow.js in Node.js, you need to install the `@tensorflow/tfjs-node-gpu` package and ensure that your system has the necessary GPU drivers installed. Here are the steps:

1. **Install GPU Drivers**:

   a. For NVIDIA GPUs, you need to install the CUDA toolkit and cuDNN library. Follow the instructions on the NVIDIA website to install these components: https://developer.nvidia.com/cuda-downloads

2. **Install TensorFlow.js GPU Package**:

   ```
   npm install @tensorflow/tfjs-node-gpu
   ```

3. **Verify GPU Setup**:

   You can verify that TensorFlow.js is using the GPU by running the following code:

   ```
   const tf = require('@tensorflow/tfjs-node-gpu');
     console.log(tf.getBackend()); // Should print 'tensorflow'
   ```

Example Code

Here is a simple example to demonstrate the setup and usage of TensorFlow.js with GPU acceleration:

```
const tf = require('@tensorflow/tfjs-node-gpu');

// Define a simple tensor.
const tensor = tf.tensor([1, 2, 3, 4]);
tensor.print(); // This will print the tensor's values to the
console.

// Simple operation: square the values of the tensor.
const squaredTensor = tensor.square();
squaredTensor.print(); // This will print the squared values.
```

Running the Code

1. **Save the Code**: Copy the code into a file named `gpu-test.js`.

2. **Execute the Script**: Run the script using Node.js by executing `node gpu-test.js` in your terminal.

3. **View the Output**: The output will be printed to the console, showing the tensor's values and their squared values.

By choosing the appropriate acceleration method (CPU or GPU) based on your specific needs and resources, you can optimize the performance of your machine learning models in a Node.js environment using TensorFlow.js.

Understanding TensorFlow.js Core Concepts

To effectively implement AI with TensorFlow.js in a Node.js environment, it is crucial to understand the core concepts that underpin the TensorFlow.js library. These concepts form the foundation for building, training, and deploying machine learning models. Here, we will explore the fundamental building blocks of TensorFlow.js, including tensors, operations, models, and layers.

Tensors

Definition:

- A tensor is the central unit of data in TensorFlow.js, representing multi-dimensional arrays. Tensors are similar to arrays in JavaScript but come with additional capabilities for mathematical operations and machine learning tasks.

- Tensors can hold various types of data, including scalars (single numbers), vectors (one-dimensional arrays), matrices (two-dimensional arrays), and higher-dimensional data structures.

Creation and Manipulation:

- Tensors are created using the `tf.tensor()` function, which can take an array and an optional shape parameter.

```
const tf = require('@tensorflow/tfjs');
const tensor = tf.tensor([1, 2, 3, 4], [2, 2]);
tensor.print(); // Prints the tensor values
```

- TensorFlow.js provides a variety of methods to manipulate tensors, such as reshaping, slicing, and concatenating.

Operations

Mathematical Operations:

TensorFlow.js supports a wide range of mathematical operations that can be performed on tensors. These include basic arithmetic operations such as addition, subtraction, multiplication, and division, as well as more complex functions such as matrix multiplication and element-wise operations.

```
const a = tf.tensor([1, 2, 3]);
const b = tf.tensor([4, 5, 6]);
const sum = tf.add(a, b);
sum.print(); // Prints [5, 7, 9]
```

Element-wise Operations:

Element-wise operations are applied individually to each element of the tensors. These operations include functions such as `tf.add()`, `tf.sub()`, `tf.mul()`, and `tf.div()`.

```
const c = tf.tensor([1, 2, 3]);
const d = tf.tensor([4, 5, 6]);
const product = tf.mul(c, d);
product.print(); // Prints [4, 10, 18]
```

Models

Definition:

- In machine learning, a model is a function with learnable parameters that maps an input to an output. The optimal parameters are obtained by training the model on data.

- TensorFlow.js provides two main ways to create models: using the Layers API and the Core API.

Layers API:

The Layers API is a high-level API that simplifies the process of building neural network models. It allows you to stack layers to create a model.

```
const model = tf.sequential();
model.add(tf.layers.dense({units: 10, inputShape: [4],
activation: 'relu'}));
model.add(tf.layers.dense({units: 1, activation: 'sigmoid'}));
```

Core API:

The Core API provides lower-level operations for more fine-grained control over model creation. It involves manually defining the mathematical operations and parameters.

```
const w = tf.variable(tf.randomNormal([4, 10]));
const b = tf.variable(tf.zeros([10]));
const x = tf.tensor([1, 2, 3, 4]);
const y = tf.matMul(x, w).add(b).relu();
y.print();
```

Layers

Overview:

- Layers are the building blocks for constructing neural network models. Each layer performs a specific type of computation and has learnable parameters.
- Common types of layers include dense (fully connected) layers, convolutional layers, and recurrent layers.

Dense Layer:

A dense layer is a fully connected layer where each input node is connected to each output node.

```
const denseLayer = tf.layers.dense({units: 10, inputShape: [4],
activation: 'relu'});
```

Convolutional Layer:

Convolutional layers are used primarily for image data and apply convolution operations to the input.

```
const convLayer = tf.layers.conv2d({filters: 32, kernelSize: 3,
activation: 'relu', inputShape: [28, 28, 1]});
```

Recurrent Layer:

Recurrent layers are used for sequence data, such as time series or text, and include layers such as LSTM and GRU.

```
const lstmLayer = tf.layers.lstm({units: 50, returnSequences: true,
inputShape: [10, 20]});
```

By understanding these core concepts, you will be well-equipped to leverage TensorFlow.js for building, training, and deploying machine learning models in a Node.js environment. These foundational elements are crucial for implementing sophisticated AI features in your web applications, enhancing both functionality and user experience.

Designing Machine Learning Models

Designing machine learning models is a critical step in the development of AI-driven applications. This process involves selecting the appropriate model architecture, defining the layers and their configurations, and ensuring that the model is well-suited to the specific problem at hand. In the context of Node.js and TensorFlow.js, designing machine learning models leverages the flexibility and power of JavaScript to create robust and efficient models that can be trained and deployed within the server-side environment of the MERN stack.

Model Architecture

The architecture of a machine learning model defines how the model processes input data to produce output predictions. Common architectures include:

- **Sequential Models**: These models consist of a linear stack of layers, where each layer has exactly one input tensor and one output tensor. Sequential models are simple to implement and are suitable for many straightforward tasks.

  ```
  const model = tf.sequential();
  model.add(tf.layers.dense({units: 10, inputShape: [4],
  activation: 'relu'}));
  model.add(tf.layers.dense({units: 1, activation: 'sigmoid'}));
  ```

- **Functional Models**: These models allow for more complex architectures, including models with multiple inputs and outputs, shared layers, and non-linear topologies. The Functional API provides greater flexibility for designing sophisticated models.

  ```
  const input = tf.input({shape: [4]});
  const dense1 = tf.layers.dense({units: 10, activation:
  'relu'}).apply(input);
  ```

```
const output = tf.layers.dense({units: 1, activation:
'sigmoid'}).apply(dense1);
const model = tf.model({inputs: input, outputs: output});
```

Defining Layers

Layers are the building blocks of neural networks. Each layer performs a specific type of computation and has learnable parameters. Common types of layers include:

- **Dense (Fully Connected) Layers**: These layers are used in many types of neural networks and connect each input node to each output node.

  ```
  model.add(tf.layers.dense({units: 10, inputShape: [4],
  activation: 'relu'}));
  ```

- **Convolutional Layers**: These layers are primarily used for processing image data. They apply convolution operations to the input, which helps in detecting spatial hierarchies in images.

  ```
  model.add(tf.layers.conv2d({filters: 32, kernelSize: 3,
  activation: 'relu', inputShape: [28, 28, 1]}));
  ```

- **Recurrent Layers**: These layers are used for sequence data, such as time series or text. They include layers such as Long Short-Term Memory (LSTM) and Gated Recurrent Unit (GRU).

  ```
  model.add(tf.layers.lstm({units: 50, returnSequences: true,
  inputShape: [10, 20]}));
  ```

Activation Functions

Activation functions introduce non-linearity into the model, allowing it to learn complex patterns. Common activation functions include:

- **Rectified Linear Unit (ReLU)**: Often used in hidden layers to introduce non-linearity.

  ```
  tf.layers.dense({units: 10, activation: 'relu'});
  ```

- **Sigmoid**: Used in the output layer for binary classification tasks.

  ```
  tf.layers.dense({units: 1, activation: 'sigmoid'});
  ```

- **Softmax**: Used in the output layer for multi-class classification tasks.

  ```
  tf.layers.dense({units: 3, activation: 'softmax'});
  ```

Compiling the Model

Once the model architecture is defined, the next step is to compile the model. This involves specifying the loss function, optimizer, and metrics to evaluate the model's performance.

- **Loss Function**: The loss function measures how well the model's predictions match the actual data. Common loss functions include mean squared error for regression tasks and categorical cross-entropy for classification tasks.

```
model.compile({loss: 'meanSquaredError', optimizer: 'adam'});
```

- **Optimizer**: The optimizer updates the model's parameters to minimize the loss function. Popular optimizers include Stochastic Gradient Descent (SGD) and Adam.

```
model.compile({loss: 'categoricalCrossentropy', optimizer:
'adam', metrics: ['accuracy']});
```

- **Metrics**: Metrics are used to evaluate the model's performance. Accuracy is a common metric for classification tasks.

```
model.compile({loss: 'categoricalCrossentropy', optimizer:
'adam', metrics: ['accuracy']});
```

Example: Designing a Simple Classification Model

Here is an example of designing a simple classification model using TensorFlow.js in Node.js:

```
const tf = require('@tensorflow/tfjs');

const model = tf.sequential();

model.add(tf.layers.dense({units: 10, inputShape: [4],
activation: 'relu'}));

model.add(tf.layers.dense({units: 3, activation: 'softmax'}));

model.compile({
  loss: 'categoricalCrossentropy',
  optimizer: 'adam',
  metrics: ['accuracy']
});

model.summary();
```

This example demonstrates the process of designing a simple neural network for a classification task. By understanding and applying these core concepts, you can create more complex and tailored machine learning models to meet the specific needs of your applications. This foundational knowledge is essential for leveraging TensorFlow.js to build, train, and deploy machine learning models in a Node.js environment.

Code Explanation

The provided code snippet demonstrates how to define, compile, and summarize a simple neural network model using TensorFlow.js in a Node.js environment. Here is a detailed explanation of each part of the code:

1. **Import TensorFlow.js**:

   ```
   const tf = require('@tensorflow/tfjs');
   ```

   This line imports the TensorFlow.js library for Node.js, making its functions and classes available for use in the script.

2. **Define a Sequential Model**:

   ```
   const model = tf.sequential();
   ```

   A sequential model is created that is a linear stack of layers. This type of model is suitable for most neural network architectures where layers are added sequentially.

3. **Add a Dense Layer**:

   ```
   model.add(tf.layers.dense({units: 10, inputShape: [4],
   activation: 'relu'}));
   ```

   A dense (fully connected) layer with 10 units (neurons) is added to the model. The `inputShape: [4]` parameter specifies that the input data will have 4 features. The ReLU (Rectified Linear Unit) activation function is used to introduce non-linearity into the model.

4. **Add an Output Layer**:

   ```
   model.add(tf.layers.dense({units: 3, activation: 'softmax'}));
   ```

   An output layer with 3 units is added to the model. The **softmax** activation function is used, which is suitable for multi-class classification tasks. It outputs a probability distribution over the 3 classes.

5. **Compile the Model**:

   ```
   model.compile({
       loss: 'categoricalCrossentropy',
       optimizer: 'adam',
       metrics: ['accuracy']
   });
   ```

The model is compiled with the categorical cross-entropy loss function, which is appropriate for multi-class classification problems. The Adam optimizer is used for training, which is efficient and widely used in practice. The accuracy metric is specified to evaluate the model's performance during training.

6. **Print the Model Summary**:

```
model.summary();
```

The `summary()` method prints a summary of the model's architecture, including the layers, their output shapes, and the number of parameters.

Steps to Execute the Code

1. **Set Up Your Environment**:

   Ensure that Node.js is installed on your system. You can download it from the Node.js official website: https://nodejs.org/

2. **Create a Project Directory**:

   Create a new directory for your project and navigate into it using your command line interface.

```
mkdir my-tfjs-project
  cd my-tfjs-project
```

3. **Initialize a Node.js Project**:

   Run `npm init -y` to create a `package.json` file that will manage your project's dependencies.

```
npm init -y
```

4. **Install TensorFlow.js**:

   Install the TensorFlow.js package for Node.js using `npm`.

```
npm install @tensorflow/tfjs
```

5. **Create a JavaScript File**:

   Create a new JavaScript file in your project directory, for example, `model.js`, and paste the provided code into this file.

6. **Run the Script**:

   Execute the script using Node.js by running the following command in your terminal:

```
node model.js
```

7. **View the Output**:

The output will be printed to the console, showing the summary of the model's architecture, including the layers, their output shapes, and the number of parameters.

By following these steps, you will be able to define, compile, and summarize a simple neural network model using TensorFlow.js in a Node.js environment. This setup is the foundation for building more complex machine learning models and integrating AI capabilities into your Node.js applications.

Data Handling and Preprocessing

Data handling and preprocessing are critical steps in the machine learning pipeline. These steps ensure that the data fed into the machine learning models is clean, consistent, and suitable for training. In the context of Node.js and TensorFlow.js, data handling and preprocessing involve several key tasks, including data collection, cleaning, transformation, and augmentation. Proper data preprocessing can significantly enhance the performance and accuracy of machine learning models.

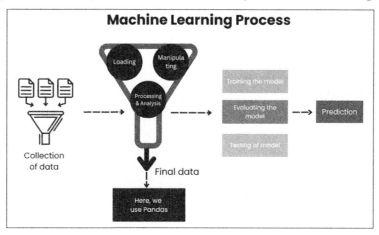

Figure 4.4: *Data Handling and Preprocessing in Machine Learning (Source: https://images.pris-mic.io/turing/65980bee531ac2845a27268b_ML_Process_6_11zon_48bf52c426.webp)*

Data Collection

Data collection in the machine learning process involves gathering and measuring information from various sources to create a dataset that is relevant to the project's goals. This step is crucial, as the quality and accuracy of the collected data directly impact the performance and effectiveness of the machine learning models. Proper data collection ensures that the models can identify patterns, make predictions, and generate insights based on reliable and relevant data.

Sources:

Data can be collected from various sources, such as databases, APIs, files, and web scraping. In a Node.js environment, you can use libraries such as `axios` for API calls, `fs` for file system operations, and `mongodb` for database interactions.

```javascript
const axios = require('axios');
const fs = require('fs');
const MongoClient = require('mongodb').MongoClient;

// Fetching data from an API
axios.get('https://api.example.com/data')
  .then(response => {
    const data = response.data;
    // Process the data
  })
  .catch(error => {
    console.error('Error fetching data:', error);
  });

// Reading data from a file
fs.readFile('data.json', 'utf8', (err, data) => {
  if (err) {
    console.error('Error reading file:', err);
    return;
  }
  const jsonData = JSON.parse(data);
  // Process the data
});

// Fetching data from a MongoDB database
MongoClient.connect('mongodb://localhost:27017', (err, client)
=> {
    if (err) {
      console.error('Error connecting to MongoDB:', err);
      return;
    }
    const db = client.db('mydatabase');
    db.collection('mycollection').find({}).toArray((err, data) =>
  {
```

```
      if (err) {
        console.error('Error fetching data from MongoDB:', err);
        return;
      }
    });
  });
```

Data Cleaning

Data cleaning in the machine learning process involves identifying and rectifying errors, inconsistencies, and inaccuracies in the dataset to ensure its quality and reliability. This step is crucial as it directly impacts the performance and accuracy of machine learning models, making it essential for effective data analysis and decision-making.

Handling Missing Values:

Missing values can be handled by removing rows with missing data or imputing missing values using techniques such as mean, median, or mode.

```
    const tf = require('@tensorflow/tfjs');


    // Imputing missing values with the mean
    const data = tf.tensor2d([[1, 2], [3, NaN], [5, 6]]);
    const cleanedData = data.where(data.isNaN(), data.mean());
    cleanedData.print();
```

Removing Duplicates:

Duplicate records can distort analyses and should be removed to maintain data integrity.

```
    const uniqueData = data.unique();
    uniqueData.print();
```

Data Transformation

Standardization and Normalization:

Standardizing and normalizing data ensures consistency in measurements and prevents certain features from dominating others.

```
    // Standardization: (value - mean) / standard deviation
    const standardizedData = data.sub(data.mean()).div(data.std());
    standardizedData.print();
```

```
// Normalization: (value - min) / (max - min)
const min = data.min();
const max = data.max();
const normalizedData = data.sub(min).div(max.sub(min));
normalizedData.print();
```

Encoding Categorical Variables:

Categorical variables need to be converted into numerical form using techniques such as one-hot encoding.

```
const categories = ['cat', 'dog', 'fish'];
const oneHotEncoded = tf.oneHot(tf.tensor1d([0, 1, 2],
'int32'), categories.length);
oneHotEncoded.print();
```

Data Augmentation

Techniques:

Data augmentation techniques artificially increase the size and diversity of the training dataset, which can help prevent overfitting and improve model generalization.

```
// Image augmentation using TensorFlow.js
const image = tf.node.decodeImage(fs.readFileSync('image.
jpg'));
const flippedImage = image.reverse(1); // Horizontal flip
const rotatedImage = image.rot90(); // 90-degree rotation
flippedImage.print();
rotatedImage.print();
```

Example: Preprocessing Pipeline

Here is an example of a complete preprocessing pipeline in TensorFlow.js:

```
const tf = require('@tensorflow/tfjs');
const fs = require('fs');

// Load data
const rawData = JSON.parse(fs.readFileSync('data.json', 'utf8'));

// Separate numerical and categorical data
const numericalData = rawData.map(row => row.slice(0, 3));
const categoricalData = rawData.map(row => row[3]);
```

```
// Convert numerical data to tensor
let numericalTensor = tf.tensor2d(numericalData);

// Handle missing values
numericalTensor = numericalTensor.where(numericalTensor.isNaN(),
numericalTensor.mean());

// Standardize numerical data
const { mean, variance } = tf.moments(numericalTensor, 0);
const std = tf.sqrt(variance);
numericalTensor = numericalTensor.sub(mean).div(std);

// One-hot encode categorical variables
const categories = ['cat', 'dog', 'fish'];
const categoricalLabels = categoricalData.map(label =>
categories.indexOf(label));
const categoricalTensor = tf.oneHot(tf.tensor1d(categorical
Labels, 'int32'), categories.length);

// Print the preprocessed data
numericalTensor.print();
categoricalTensor.print();
```

```
     data.json:-
            [
  [1, 2, 3, "cat"],
  [4, 5, 6, "dog"],
  [7, 8, 9, "fish"],
  [10, 11, 12, "cat"],
  [13, 14, 15, "dog"],
  [16, 17, 18, "fish"],
  [19, 20, 21, "cat"],
  [22, 23, 24, "dog"],
  [25, 26, 27, "fish"],
  [28, 29, 30, "cat"]
]
```

Running the Code

1. **Set Up Your Environment**:

    Ensure that Node.js is installed on your system. You can download it from the Node.js official website: https://nodejs.org/

2. **Create a Project Directory**:

   Create a new directory for your project and navigate into it using your command line interface.

   ```
   mkdir my-tfjs-project
     cd my-tfjs-project
   ```

3. **Initialize a Node.js Project**:

   Run `npm init -y` to create a `package.json` file that will manage your project's dependencies.

   ```
   npm init -y
   ```

4. **Install TensorFlow.js**:

   Install the TensorFlow.js package for Node.js using `npm`.

   ```
   npm install @tensorflow/tfjs
   ```

5. **Create a JavaScript File**:

   Create a new JavaScript file in your project directory, for example, `preprocessing.js`, and paste the provided code into this file.

6. **Run the Script**:

   Execute the script using Node.js by running the following command in your terminal:

   ```
   node preprocessing.js
   ```

7. **View the Output**:

   The output will be printed to the console, showing the preprocessed data.

   By following these steps, you will be able to handle and preprocess data effectively in a Node.js environment using TensorFlow.js. Proper data handling and preprocessing are essential for building robust and accurate machine learning models, ensuring that the data fed into the models is clean, consistent, and suitable for training.

Training Machine Learning Models

Training machine learning models is a crucial step in the development of AI applications. This process involves optimizing the model's parameters to minimize a specified loss function, thereby improving the model's ability to make accurate predictions. In the context of Node.js and TensorFlow.js, training models involve several key steps, including data preparation, model compilation, and the actual training process using the `fit` method. This section will guide you through these steps, providing code examples and explanations to help you effectively train machine learning models in a Node.js environment.

Data Preparation

Before training a model, it is essential to prepare the data. This involves converting raw data into a format suitable for training, such as tensors. Data preparation may include tasks such as normalization, shuffling, and splitting the data into training and validation sets.

```
const tf = require('@tensorflow/tfjs');

// Example data: features and labels
const features = tf.tensor2d([[1, 2], [2, 3], [3, 4], [4, 5]],
[4, 2]);
const labels = tf.tensor2d([[0], [1], [0], [1]], [4, 1]);

// Calculate the mean and variance
const { mean, variance } = tf.moments(features, 0);

// Calculate the standard deviation
const std = tf.sqrt(variance);

// Normalize the data
const normalizedFeatures = features.sub(mean).div(std);

// Print the normalized features
normalizedFeatures.print();
```

Model Compilation

Once the data is prepared, the next step is to compile the model. Compiling a model involves specifying the loss function, optimizer, and metrics. The loss function measures how well the model's predictions match the actual data, while the optimizer updates the model's parameters to minimize the loss function. Metrics are used to evaluate the model's performance during training.

```
// Define a simple sequential model
const model = tf.sequential();
model.add(tf.layers.dense({units: 10, inputShape: [2],
activation: 'relu'}));
model.add(tf.layers.dense({units: 1, activation: 'sigmoid'}));
```

```
// Compile the model
model.compile({
  loss: 'binaryCrossentropy',
  optimizer: 'adam',
  metrics: ['accuracy']
});
```

Training the Model

The actual training process involves using the `fit` method, which trains the model for a specified number of epochs. During each epoch, the model is presented with batches of training data, and its parameters are updated based on the gradients of the loss function. The `fit` method is asynchronous and returns a promise that resolves to a history object containing information about the training process.

```
// Train the model
async function trainModel() {
  const history = await model.fit(normalizedFeatures, labels, {
    epochs: 50,
    batchSize: 2,
    validationSplit: 0.2,
    callbacks: {
      onEpochEnd: (epoch, logs) => {
        console.log(`Epoch ${epoch + 1}: loss = ${logs.loss}, ac-
curacy = ${logs.acc}`);
      }
    }
  });
  console.log('Training complete');
  console.log(history.history);
}

trainModel();
```

Code Explanation

- **Data Preparation**: The example starts by creating tensors for the features and labels. The features are then normalized to have a mean of 0 and a standard deviation of 1, which helps improve the training process.

- **Model Compilation**: A simple sequential model is defined with two dense layers. The model is compiled with the binary cross-entropy loss function, the Adam optimizer, and accuracy as the evaluation metric.

- **Training the Model**: The `fit` method is used to train the model. The method takes the training data, the number of epochs, the batch size, and a validation split as arguments. It also includes callbacks to log the loss and accuracy at the end of each epoch.

Running the Code

1. **Set Up Your Environment**:

    Ensure that Node.js is installed on your system. You can download it from the Node.js official website: https://nodejs.org/

2. **Create a Project Directory**:

    Create a new directory for your project and navigate into it using your command line interface.

    ```
    mkdir my-tfjs-project
      cd my-tfjs-project
    ```

3. **Initialize a Node.js Project**:

    Run `npm init -y` to create a `package.json` file that will manage your project's dependencies.

    ```
    npm init -y
    ```

4. **Install TensorFlow.js**:

    Install the TensorFlow.js package for Node.js using `npm`.

    ```
    npm install @tensorflow/tfjs
    ```

5. **Create a JavaScript File**:

    Create a new JavaScript file in your project directory, for example, `train-model.js`, and paste the provided code into this file.

6. **Run the Script**:

    Execute the script using Node.js by running the following command in your terminal:

    ```
    node train-model.js
    ```

7. **View the Output:**

    The output will be printed to the console, showing the loss and accuracy for each epoch, as well as the final training history.

By following these steps, you will be able to train machine learning models effectively in a Node.js environment using TensorFlow.js. This process is essential for developing AI-driven features in your web applications, enabling you to build models that can analyze and predict data patterns with high accuracy.

Model Evaluation and Validation

Model evaluation and validation are critical steps in the machine learning pipeline. These processes ensure that the trained model performs well on unseen data and generalizes effectively to new, real-world scenarios. In the context of Node.js and TensorFlow.js, model evaluation and validation involve using various metrics and techniques to assess the model's performance and make necessary adjustments. This section will guide you through the key concepts and methods for evaluating and validating machine learning models.

Importance of Model Evaluation and Validation

Model evaluation and validation help to:

- **Assess Performance**: Determine how well the model performs on unseen data.
- **Identify Overfitting or Underfitting**: Ensure the model generalizes well and is not just memorizing the training data.
- **Optimize Model Parameters**: Fine-tune the model to improve its accuracy and efficiency.
- **Build Trust**: Provide confidence that the model will perform well in real-world applications.

Splitting the Data

Before evaluating a model, the dataset is typically split into training, validation, and test sets:

- **Training Set:** Used to train the model.
- **Validation Set:** Used to tune the model's hyperparameters and prevent overfitting.
- **Test Set:** Used to evaluate the final model's performance.

```javascript
const tf = require('@tensorflow/tfjs');

// Example data: features and labels
const features = tf.tensor2d([[1, 2], [2, 3], [3, 4], [4, 5], [5,
6], [6, 7]]);
const labels = tf.tensor2d([[0], [1], [0], [1], [0], [1]]);
```

```
// Split the data into training (80%) and test (20%) sets
const [trainFeatures, testFeatures] = tf.split(features, [4, 2]);
const [trainLabels, testLabels] = tf.split(labels, [4, 2]);
```

Compiling the Model

Before training, compile the model with appropriate loss functions, optimizers, and metrics. For classification tasks, common metrics include accuracy, precision, recall, and F1 score.

```
// Define a simple sequential model
const model = tf.sequential();
model.add(tf.layers.dense({units: 10, inputShape: [2],
activation: 'relu'}));
model.add(tf.layers.dense({units: 1, activation: 'sigmoid'}));

// Compile the model
model.compile({
  loss: 'binaryCrossentropy',
  optimizer: 'adam',
  metrics: ['accuracy']
});
```

Training the Model

Train the model using the training data and validate it using the validation data. The `fit` method allows you to specify a validation split or provide a separate validation dataset.

```
// Train the model with validation split
async function trainModel() {
  const history = await model.fit(trainFeatures, trainLabels, {
    epochs: 50,
    batchSize: 2,
    validationSplit: 0.2,
    callbacks: {
      onEpochEnd: (epoch, logs) => {
        console.log(`Epoch ${epoch + 1}: loss = ${logs.loss},
        accuracy = ${logs.acc}`);
      }
    }
  });
```

```
      console.log('Training complete');
      console.log(history.history);
   }

   trainModel();
```

Evaluating the Model

After training, evaluate the model's performance on the test set using the `evaluate` method. This method returns the loss and specified metrics.

```
   // Evaluate the model on the test set
   async function evaluateModel() {
      const result = await model.evaluate(testFeatures, testLabels);
      console.log(`Test loss: ${result[0].dataSync()}`);
      console.log(`Test accuracy: ${result[1].dataSync()}`);
   }

   evaluateModel();
```

Validation Techniques

Cross-Validation:

Cross-validation involves splitting the data into multiple folds and training the model multiple times, each time using a different fold as the validation set. This technique provides a more robust estimate of the model's performance.

K-Fold Cross-Validation:

In K-Fold Cross-Validation, the dataset is divided into K subsets (folds). The model is trained K times, each time using a different fold as the validation set and the remaining folds as the training set. The final performance metric is the average of the K runs.

```
   const k = 5;
   const foldSize = Math.floor(features.shape[0] / k);

   for (let i = 0; i < k; i++) {
      const validationStart = i * foldSize;
      const validationEnd = validationStart + foldSize;

      const validationFeatures = features.slice([validationStart, 0],
   [foldSize, -1]);
```

```
    const validationLabels = labels.slice([validationStart, 0],
[foldSize, -1]);

    const trainFeatures = tf.concat([
      features.slice([0, 0], [validationStart, -1]),
      features.slice([validationEnd, 0], [features.shape[0] -
      validationEnd, -1])
    ]);

    const trainLabels = tf.concat([
      labels.slice([0, 0], [validationStart, -1]),
      labels.slice([validationEnd, 0], [labels.shape[0] -
      validationEnd, -1])
    ]);

    // Train and evaluate the model for each fold
    await model.fit(trainFeatures, trainLabels, {epochs: 50,
batchSize: 2});
    const result = await model.evaluate(validationFeatures,
validationLabels);
    console.log(`Fold ${i + 1}: loss = ${result[0].dataSync()},
accuracy = ${result[1].dataSync()}`);
  }
```

Monitoring and Logging

Monitoring and logging the training process is essential for understanding how the model is learning and for diagnosing issues. TensorFlow.js provides callbacks that can be used to log metrics and visualize the training process.

```
    const tfvis = require('@tensorflow/tfjs-vis');

    async function trainModelWithVisualization() {
      const history = await model.fit(trainFeatures, trainLabels, {
        epochs: 50,
        batchSize: 2,
        validationSplit: 0.2,
        callbacks: tfvis.show.fitCallbacks(
          { name: 'Training Performance' },
          ['loss', 'val_loss', 'acc', 'val_acc'],
          { height: 200, callbacks: ['onEpochEnd'] }
```

```
    )
  });
  console.log('Training complete');
}


trainModelWithVisualization();
```

Running the Code

1. **Set Up Your Environment**:

   Ensure that Node.js is installed on your system. You can download it from the Node.js official website: https://nodejs.org/

2. **Create a Project Directory**:

   Create a new directory for your project and navigate into it using your command line interface.

   ```
   mkdir my-tfjs-project
     cd my-tfjs-project
   ```

3. **Initialize a Node.js Project**:

   Run `npm init -y` to create a `package.json` file that will manage your project's dependencies.

   ```
   npm init -y
   ```

4. **Install TensorFlow.js and TensorFlow.js-Vis**:

   Install the TensorFlow.js package for Node.js and TensorFlow.js-Vis for visualization using `npm`.

   ```
   npm install @tensorflow/tfjs @tensorflow/tfjs-vis
   ```

5. **Create a JavaScript File**:

   Create a new JavaScript file in your project directory, for example, `evaluate-model.js`, and paste the provided code into this file.

   ```
   evaluate-model.js :-
   // Import TensorFlow.js
   const tf = require('@tensorflow/tfjs');

   // Define a simple neural network model
   const model = tf.sequential();
   model.add(tf.layers.dense({ units: 1, inputShape: [1] }));
   ```

```
model.compile({ optimizer: 'sgd', loss: 'meanSquaredError' });

// Generate some synthetic data for training
const xs = tf.tensor2d([1, 2, 3, 4], [4, 1]);
const ys = tf.tensor2d([2, 3, 5, 7], [4, 1]);

// Train the model
async function train() {
  await model.fit(xs, ys, { epochs: 100 });
}

// Evaluate the model
async function evaluate() {
  const loss = model.evaluate(xs, ys);
  console.log('Loss:', await loss.data());
}

// Run the training and evaluation
async function main() {
  await train();
  await evaluate();
}

main().then(() => console.log('Done'));
```

6. **Run the Script**:

   Execute the script using Node.js by running the following command in your terminal:

   ```
   node evaluate-model.js
   ```

7. **View the Output**:

   The output will be printed to the console, showing the loss and accuracy for each epoch, as well as the final evaluation metrics on the test set.

By following these steps, you will be able to evaluate and validate machine learning models effectively in a Node.js environment using TensorFlow.js. Proper evaluation and validation are essential for ensuring that your models perform well in real-world applications, providing reliable and accurate predictions.

Fine-Tuning and Optimization

Fine-tuning and optimization are essential steps in the machine learning pipeline that help improve model performance and efficiency. These processes involve adjusting hyperparameters, leveraging pre-trained models, and applying regularization techniques to enhance the model's accuracy and generalization capabilities. In the context of Node.js and TensorFlow.js, fine-tuning and optimization can significantly impact the effectiveness of AI-driven applications.

Hyperparameter Tuning

In this section, we will go through the definition, techniques, and implementation of hyperparameter tuning.

Definition

Hyperparameters are configuration settings that are not learned from the data but are set before the training process. Examples include learning rate, batch size, and the number of layers in a neural network.

Techniques

- **Grid Search**: Exhaustively searches for the best hyperparameters by trying all possible combinations.
- **Random Search**: Randomly samples hyperparameter combinations to find the best configuration.
- **Bayesian Optimization**: Uses a probabilistic model to guide the search for the best hyperparameters.

Implementation

```
const tf = require('@tensorflow/tfjs');
const bayesopt = require('bayesopt');

const objective = (params, done) => {
  const learningRate = params.learningRate;
  const batchSize = params.batchSize;

  // Define and compile the model
  const model = tf.sequential();
  model.add(tf.layers.dense({units: 10, inputShape: [2],
activation: 'relu'}));
  model.add(tf.layers.dense({units: 1, activation: 'sigmoid'}));
  model.compile({
```

```
    loss: 'binaryCrossentropy',
    optimizer: tf.train.sgd(learningRate),
    metrics: ['accuracy']
  });

  // Train the model
  model.fit(trainFeatures, trainLabels, {
    epochs: 10,
    batchSize: batchSize,
    validationData: [valFeatures, valLabels],
    callbacks: {
      onEpochEnd: (epoch, logs) => {
        console.log(`Epoch ${epoch}: loss = ${logs.loss}`);
      }
    }
  }).then(() => {
    const valLoss = model.evaluate(valFeatures, valLabels);
    console.log(`Validation loss: ${valLoss}`);
    done(null, valLoss);
  });
};

// Define the search space for hyperparameters
const searchSpace = {
  learningRate: {min: 0.001, max: 0.1},
  batchSize: {min: 16, max: 128}
};

// Perform Bayesian optimization
bayesopt.minimize(objective, searchSpace, {iterations: 20});
```

Transfer Learning

Let us understand transfer learning, its techniques, and its implementation.

Definition

Transfer learning involves leveraging pre-trained models as a starting point for new tasks. This approach can significantly reduce training time and improve model performance.

Techniques

- **Feature Extraction**: Use the pre-trained model as a fixed feature extractor, and train only the final layers on the new dataset.
- **Fine-Tuning**: Retrain some or all of the layers of the pre-trained model on the new dataset.

Implementation

```
const baseModel = await tf.loadLayersModel('model.json');
baseModel.trainable = false; // Freeze the base model layers

const model = tf.sequential();
model.add(baseModel);
model.add(tf.layers.dense({units: 10, activation: 'relu'}));
model.add(tf.layers.dense({units: 1, activation: 'sigmoid'}));

model.compile({
  loss: 'binaryCrossentropy',
  optimizer: 'adam',
  metrics: ['accuracy']
});

await model.fit(trainFeatures, trainLabels, {
  epochs: 10,
  validationData: [valFeatures, valLabels]
});

model.json :-
{
  "modelTopology": {
    "class_name": "Functional",
    "config": {
      "layers": [
        {
          "class_name": "InputLayer",
          "config": {
            "name": "input_1",
            "dtype": "float32",
            "input_shape": [224, 224, 3]
          }
        },
        {
```

```
            "class_name": "Conv2D",
            "config": {
              "name": "conv2d",
              "filters": 32,
              "kernel_size": [3, 3],
              "activation": "relu"
            }
          },
          {
            "class_name": "MaxPooling2D",
            "config": {
              "name": "max_pooling2d",
              "pool_size": [2, 2]
            }
          },
          {
            "class_name": "Flatten",
            "config": {
              "name": "flatten"
            }
          }
        ]
      }
    },
    "weightsManifest": [
      {
        "name": "conv2d/kernel",
        "shape": [3, 3, 3, 32],
        "dtype": "float32",
        "paths": ["conv2d_weights.bin"]
      },
      {
        "name": "conv2d/bias",
        "shape": [32],
        "dtype": "float32",
        "paths": ["conv2d_bias.bin"]
      }
    ]
  }
```

Model Regularization

Let us understand model regularization with ease.

Techniques

- **L1/L2 Regularization**: Adds a penalty to the loss function to prevent overfitting.
- **Dropout**: Randomly drops units during training to prevent overfitting.
- **Early Stopping**: Stops training when the validation performance stops improving.

Implementation

```
model.add(tf.layers.dense({
  units: 10,
  inputShape: [2],
  activation: 'relu',
  kernelRegularizer: tf.regularizers.l2({l2: 0.01})
}));
model.add(tf.layers.dropout({rate: 0.5}));
```

Model Optimization

Let us understand model optimization with ease.

Techniques

- **Model Pruning**: Removes unnecessary weights to reduce model size.
- **Quantization**: Reduces the precision of the model's weights to decrease size and increase inference speed.

Implementation

```
const prunedModel = tf.sequential();
prunedModel.add(tf.layers.dense({units: 10, inputShape: [2],
activation: 'relu'}));
prunedModel.add(tf.layers.dense({units: 1, activation:
'sigmoid'}));

// Apply quantization
const quantizedModel = tf.quantization.quantize(prunedModel,
{dtype: 'int8'});
```

Deploying Models for Inference

Deploying machine learning models for inference involves making the trained models available for real-time predictions in production environments. In the context of Node.js and TensorFlow.js, this process includes loading the trained model, setting up an API for inference, and ensuring the model runs efficiently in the production environment.

Loading the Trained Model

Loading a Model

Use TensorFlow.js APIs to load a pre-trained model from a file or URL.

Implementation

```
const tf = require('@tensorflow/tfjs');

// Load the model
const model = await tf.loadLayersModel('model.json');

model.json:-
{
  "modelTopology": {
    "class_name": "Sequential",
    "config": {
      "layers": [
        {
          "class_name": "Conv2D",
          "config": {
            "name": "conv2d",
            "filters": 32,
            "kernel_size": [3, 3],
            "activation": "relu"
          }
        },
        {
          "class_name": "MaxPooling2D",
          "config": {
            "name": "max_pooling2d",
            "pool_size": [2, 2]
          }
        },
        {
```

```json
          "class_name": "Flatten",
          "config": {
            "name": "flatten"
          }
        },
        {
          "class_name": "Dense",
          "config": {
            "name": "dense",
            "units": 128,
            "activation": "relu"
          }
        },
        {
          "class_name": "Dense",
          "config": {
            "name": "dense_1",
            "units": 10,
            "activation": "softmax"
          }
        }
      ]
    }
  },
  "weightsManifest": [
    {
      "name": "conv2d/kernel",
      "shape": [3, 3, 1, 32],
      "dtype": "float32",
      "paths": ["group1-shard1of1.bin"]
    },
    {
      "name": "conv2d/bias",
      "shape": [32],
      "dtype": "float32",
      "paths": ["group2-shard1of1.bin"]
    },
    {
      "name": "dense/kernel",
      "shape": [3136, 128],
      "dtype": "float32",
      "paths": ["group3-shard1of1.bin"]
```

```
      },
      {
        "name": "dense/bias",
        "shape": [128],
        "dtype": "float32",
        "paths": ["group4-shard1of1.bin"]
      },
      {
        "name": "dense_1/kernel",
        "shape": [128, 10],
        "dtype": "float32",
        "paths": ["group5-shard1of1.bin"]
      },
      {
        "name": "dense_1/bias",
        "shape": [10],
        "dtype": "float32",
        "paths": ["group6-shard1of1.bin"]
      }
    ],
    "format": "layers-model",
    "generatedBy": "2.3.0",
    "convertedBy": "TensorFlow.js Converter v2.3.0"
  }
```

Setting Up an API for Inference

Express.js

Use Express.js to set up a RESTful API for serving model predictions.

Implementation

```
const express = require('express');
const app = express();
const port = 3000;

app.use(express.json());

app.post('/predict', async (req, res) => {
  const input = tf.tensor2d(req.body.input, [1, 2]);
  const prediction = model.predict(input);
  const output = prediction.dataSync();
  res.json({prediction: output});
```

```
});

app.listen(port, () => {
  console.log(`Server is running on http://localhost:${port}`);
});
```

Ensuring Efficient Inference

Optimizing Inference

- Use techniques such as model quantization and pruning to reduce model size and improve inference speed.

- Leverage hardware acceleration (example, GPU) for faster inference.

Implementation

```
const quantizedModel = tf.quantization.quantize(model, {dtype:
'int8'});

// Use GPU for inference
const gpuModel = tf.node.loadSavedModel('path/to/model',
['serve'], 'serve');
const input = tf.tensor2d([[1, 2]]);
const output = gpuModel.predict(input);
output.print();
```

Running the Code

Follow the succeeding steps to fine-tune, optimize, and deploy machine learning models effectively in a Node.js environment using TensorFlow.js:

1. **Set Up Your Environment**:

   Ensure that Node.js is installed on your system. You can download it from the Node.js official website: https://nodejs.org/

2. **Create a Project Directory**:

   Create a new directory for your project and navigate into it using your command line interface.

   ```
   mkdir my-tfjs-project
     cd my-tfjs-project
   ```

3. **Initialize a Node.js Project**:

   Run `npm init -y` to create a `package.json` file that will manage your project's dependencies.

   ```
   npm init -y
   ```

4. **Install TensorFlow.js and Express.js**:

   Install the TensorFlow.js package for Node.js and Express.js using `npm`.

   ```
   npm install @tensorflow/tfjs express
   ```

5. **Create JavaScript Files**:

   Create JavaScript files in your project directory for fine-tuning, optimization, and deploying models. For example, `fine-tune.js`, `optimize.js`, and `deploy.js`.

6. **Run the Scripts**:

   Execute the scripts using Node.js by running the following commands in your terminal:

   ```
   node fine-tune.js
     node optimize.js
     node deploy.js
   ```

7. **View the Output**:

   The output will be printed to the console, showing the results of fine-tuning, optimization, and model inference.

These processes are essential for ensuring that your models perform well in production, providing accurate and efficient predictions for real-world applications.

Conclusion

This chapter delved into the practical aspects of integrating artificial intelligence into web applications using the Node.js environment, powered by the TensorFlow.js library. This chapter aimed to bridge the gap between theoretical machine learning concepts and their real-world application, particularly within the server-side of the MERN stack (MongoDB, Express.js, React, Node.js). Readers learned how to leverage TensorFlow.js, a powerful and flexible library for machine learning in JavaScript, to develop, train, and deploy machine learning models directly in Node.js.

The chapter covered a comprehensive range of topics, starting with setting up TensorFlow.js in a Node.js environment. It then moved on to understanding core concepts of TensorFlow.js, such as tensors, operations, models, and layers. Readers gained insights into designing machine learning models, including selecting appropriate architectures and defining layers. The chapter also emphasized the importance of data handling and preprocessing, introducing techniques for data collection, cleaning, transformation, and augmentation to ensure high-quality training data. Training machine learning models was covered in detail, with practical examples of compiling, training, and evaluating models. Additionally, the chapter explored fine-tuning and optimization strategies, such as hyperparameter tuning, transfer learning, and regularization techniques, to enhance model performance. Finally, readers learned about deploying trained models for inference, setting up APIs for real-time predictions, and ensuring efficient model performance in production environments.

By the end of this chapter, readers should be equipped with the knowledge and skills to implement sophisticated AI features in their web applications using Node.js and TensorFlow.js. The next chapter, *Creating Intelligent User Interfaces with React*, focuses on the intersection of AI and user interface (UI) design within the MERN stack, leveraging the power of React to build dynamic and responsive web applications.

Multiple Choice Questions

1. What is the primary purpose of TensorFlow.js in a Node.js environment?

    a. To create web pages

    b. To develop, train, and deploy machine learning models

    c. To manage databases

    d. To handle HTTP requests

2. Which of the following is a key advantage of using TensorFlow.js for machine learning?

    a. It is only compatible with Python

    b. It allows for machine learning directly in the browser and Node.js

    c. It requires no setup or installation

    d. It is used for creating static websites

3. What is the first step in setting up TensorFlow.js in a Node.js environment?

    a. Writing the machine learning model

    b. Installing TensorFlow.js using npm

    c. Collecting data

    d. Deploying the model

4. Which method is used to compile a model in TensorFlow.js?

    a. `model.train()`

    b. `model.compile()`

    c. `model.fit()`

    d. `model.evaluate()`

5. What is the purpose of the `fit` method in TensorFlow.js?

   a. To compile the model

   b. To train the model on the dataset

   c. To evaluate the model's performance

   d. To deploy the model

6. Which of the following is a common technique for data preprocessing?

   a. Model quantization

   b. Data normalization

   c. Hyperparameter tuning

   d. Model pruning

7. What is the role of hyperparameter tuning in machine learning?

   a. To adjust the model's parameters to minimize the loss function

   b. To preprocess the data

   c. To deploy the model

   d. To evaluate the model's performance

8. Which technique involves using a pre-trained model as a starting point for a new task?

   a. Data augmentation

   b. Transfer learning

   c. Model pruning

   d. Cross-validation

9. What is the purpose of the `evaluate` method in TensorFlow.js?

   a. To train the model

   b. To compile the model

   c. To assess the model's performance on a test dataset

   d. To preprocess the data

10. Which of the following is a method to deploy machine learning models for inference in Node.js?

    a. Using Express.js to set up a RESTful API

    b. Using HTML to create a web page

    c. Using CSS for styling

    d. Using SQL for database management

Answers

1. b

2. b

3. b

4. b

5. b

6. b

7. a

8. b

9. c

10. a

CHAPTER 5

Creating Intelligent User Interfaces with React

Introduction

Creating Intelligent User Interfaces with React focuses on the intersection of AI and user interface (UI) design within the MERN stack, leveraging the power of React to build dynamic and responsive web applications. This chapter explores how to infuse AI-driven interactivity and personalization into React components, enhancing the user experience with smart features such as predictive text, real-time recommendations, and adaptive content layouts.

Readers will learn about the core concepts of React, including components, state, and props, and how to integrate these with AI models to create interfaces that respond intelligently to user input and behavior. The chapter will cover the use of React hooks for managing state in functional components, context for managing global data, and higher-order components for reusing logic across the application.

The tech stack highlighted in this chapter includes React as the primary library for building the UI, along with additional tools and libraries such as Axios for making HTTP requests to AI-powered backend services, and Redux for state management in more complex applications. By the end of this chapter, readers will be adept at designing and implementing UIs that are not only visually appealing but also enriched with AI capabilities, providing a seamless and intuitive user experience.

Structure

In this chapter, we will cover the following topics:

- Introduction to React and Its Ecosystem
- State Management in React

- Integrating AI into React Components
- Building Interactive UI Elements with AI
- Using Axios for API Requests
- Advanced State Management with Redux and Optimizing Its Performance

Introduction to React and its Ecosystem

React, sometimes referred to as a frontend JavaScript framework, is a powerful library created by Facebook for building user interfaces. Since its release, React has become one of the most popular tools for developing dynamic and high-performance web applications. Its component-based architecture allows developers to build encapsulated components that manage their own state, then compose them to create complex UIs. This modular approach not only promotes reusability but also makes it easier to manage and maintain large applications.

Feature	Description
JSX (JavaScript XML)	JSX is a syntax extension that allows writing HTML elements in JavaScript. It makes the code easier to understand and write. JSX is not supported by browsers directly, so it is transpiled to JavaScript using tools like Babel.
Virtual DOM	React uses a virtual DOM to optimize updates to the actual DOM. It updates the virtual DOM first, then compares it with the previous version, and only updates the parts of the actual DOM that have changed. This improves performance.
One-way Data Binding	React follows a unidirectional data flow, which means data flows in one direction from parent to child components. This makes the application more predictable and easier to debug.
Component-Based Architecture	React applications are built using components, which are reusable and self-contained pieces of UI. Each component has its own logic and controls, making it easier to manage and maintain large applications.

Figure 5.1: Features of ReactJS

Core Concepts of React

Let us understand the core concepts of React such as Components, JSX (JavaScript XML), State and Props, and Virtual DOM.

Components

Components are the building blocks of a React application. They can be thought of as custom, reusable HTML elements that can be nested, managed, and handled independently. React components come in two types: functional components and class components. Functional components are simpler and are written as JavaScript functions, while class components are more feature-rich and are written using ES6 classes.

JavaScript XML (JSX)

JSX is a syntax extension for JavaScript that looks similar to HTML. It allows developers to write HTML-like code within JavaScript, making it easier to create and visualize the structure of the UI. JSX is then transpiled to JavaScript by tools like Babel.

State and Props

State and props are two types of data that control a component. State is managed within the component (similar to variables declared within a function), while props are passed to the component from its parent (similar to function parameters). State is mutable and can change over time, while props are immutable and set by the parent component.

Virtual DOM

React uses a virtual DOM to optimize updates to the actual DOM. When the state of a component changes, React updates the virtual DOM first. It then compares the virtual DOM with a snapshot of the previous virtual DOM (a process called *reconciliation*) and updates only the parts of the actual DOM that have changed. This makes updates more efficient and improves performance.

React Ecosystem

React's ecosystem is vast and includes a variety of tools and libraries that enhance its capabilities and streamline the development process. Some of the key components of the React ecosystem include:

React Router

React Router is a standard library for routing in React applications. It enables the navigation among views of various components in a React application, allowing developers to build single-page applications with dynamic, client-side routing.

Redux

Redux is a state management library that helps manage the state of an application in a predictable way. It is particularly useful for larger applications where managing state across multiple components can become complex. Redux provides a single source of truth for the application state, making it easier to debug and test.

Next.js

Next.js is a React framework that enables server-side rendering and static site generation. It provides a robust set of features for building production-ready React applications, including automatic code splitting, optimized performance, and a simple API for routing and data fetching.

Axios

Axios is a promise-based HTTP client for making API requests. It is often used in React applications to fetch data from backend services. Axios provides a simple and intuitive API for making HTTP requests and handling responses.

Styled Components

Styled Components is a library for styling React components using tagged template literals. It allows developers to write CSS directly within their JavaScript code, enabling a more seamless and modular approach to styling components.

React DevTools

React DevTools is a browser extension that provides a set of tools for inspecting and debugging React applications. It allows developers to inspect the component hierarchy, view and edit props and state, and track component re-renders.

By understanding these core concepts and leveraging the tools within the React ecosystem, developers can build robust, scalable, and high-performance web applications. React's flexibility and extensive ecosystem make it an ideal choice for integrating AI-driven features, enabling the creation of intelligent and interactive user interfaces.

State Management in React

State management is a crucial aspect of building dynamic and interactive user interfaces with React. As applications grow in complexity, managing state efficiently becomes essential to ensure that the UI remains responsive and consistent. React provides several tools and techniques for managing state, including the use of hooks, context, and state management libraries like Redux. This section will explore these methods and how they can be used to manage state effectively in React applications.

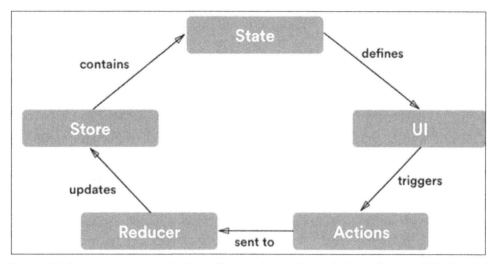

Figure 5.2: *State Management in React (Source: https://www.loginradius.com/blog/static/ 878d2cde053633bfea88a8bfcfc28e89/e5715/image1.png)*

State in React

State in React refers to a JavaScript object that holds data that may change over the lifecycle of a component. It is used to manage dynamic data and control the component's behavior and rendering.

Local State

Local state is a state that is managed within a single component. It is typically used for simple, isolated pieces of state that do not need to be shared across multiple components.

```
import React, { useState } from 'react';

function Counter() {
  const [count, setCount] = useState(0);

  return (
    <div>
      <p>You clicked {count} times</p>
      <button onClick={() => setCount(count + 1)}>Click me</
      button>
    </div>
  );
}
```

Global State

Global state is a state that needs to be shared across multiple components. Managing global state can be more complex and often requires additional tools or libraries.

React Hooks for State Management

Let's understand the different hooks like **useState** hook and **useReducer** hook in React State Management.

useState Hook

The `useState` hook is used to add state to functional components. It returns an array with two elements: the current state value and a function to update it.

```
import React, { useState } from 'react';

function Form() {
  const [firstName, setFirstName] = useState('');
  const [lastName, setLastName] = useState('');

  return (
    <div>
      <label>
        First name:
        <input value={firstName} onChange={(e) => setFirst
Name(e.target.value)} />
      </label>
      <label>
        Last name:
        <input value={lastName} onChange={(e) => setLastName
(e.target.value)} />
      </label>
      <p>Your full name is: {firstName} {lastName}</p>
    </div>
  );
}
```

useReducer Hook

The `useReducer` hook is used for managing more complex state logic. It is similar to `useState` but allows for more control over state transitions.

```
import React, { useReducer } from 'react';

const initialState = { count: 0 };

function reducer(state, action) {
  switch (action.type) {
    case 'increment':
      return { count: state.count + 1 };
    case 'decrement':
      return { count: state.count - 1 };
    default:
      throw new Error();
  }
}

function Counter() {
  const [state, dispatch] = useReducer(reducer, initialState);

  return (
    <div>
      <p>Count: {state.count}</p>
      <button onClick={() => dispatch({ type: 'increment'
})}>+</button>
      <button onClick={() => dispatch({ type: 'decrement' })}>-
</button>
    </div>
  );
}
```

Context API for Global State Management

The Context API is used to pass data through the component tree without having to pass props down manually at every level. It is useful for managing global state that needs to be accessed by many components.

```
import React, { createContext, useContext, useState } from 'react';

const ThemeContext = createContext();

function ThemeProvider({ children }) {
  const [theme, setTheme] = useState('light');

  return (
```

```
      <ThemeContext.Provider value={{ theme, setTheme }}>
        {children}
      </ThemeContext.Provider>
    );
  }

  function ThemedButton() {
    const { theme, setTheme } = useContext(ThemeContext);

    return (
      <button
        style={{ background: theme === 'light' ? '#fff' : '#333',
color: theme === 'light' ? '#000' : '#fff' }}
        onClick={() => setTheme(theme === 'light' ? 'dark' :
'light')}
      >
        Toggle Theme
      </button>
    );
  }

  function App() {
    return (
      <ThemeProvider>
        <ThemedButton />
      </ThemeProvider>
    );
  }
```

Advanced State Management with Redux

Redux is a state management library that provides a predictable state container for JavaScript applications. It is particularly useful for managing complex states in large applications.

```
import { createStore } from 'redux';

// Define initial state
const initialState = { count: 0 };

// Define reducer
function counterReducer(state = initialState, action) {
```

```
    switch (action.type) {
      case 'INCREMENT':
        return { count: state.count + 1 };
      case 'DECREMENT':
        return { count: state.count - 1 };
      default:
        return state;
    }
  }


  // Create Redux store
  const store = createStore(counterReducer);


  // Define action creators
  const increment = () => ({ type: 'INCREMENT' });
  const decrement = () => ({ type: 'DECREMENT' });


  // Dispatch actions
  store.dispatch(increment());
  store.dispatch(decrement());


  console.log(store.getState()); // { count: 0 }
```

Connecting Redux with React

To connect Redux with React, use the `react-redux` library, which provides the `Provider` component and the `connect` function.

```
import React from 'react';
import ReactDOM from 'react-dom';
import { Provider, connect } from 'react-redux';
import { createStore } from 'redux';


// Define initial state and reducer
const initialState = { count: 0 };
function counterReducer(state = initialState, action) {
  switch (action.type) {
    case 'INCREMENT':
      return { count: state.count + 1 };
    case 'DECREMENT':
```

```
      return { count: state.count - 1 };
    default:
      return state;
  }
}

// Create Redux store
const store = createStore(counterReducer);

// Define action creators
const increment = () => ({ type: 'INCREMENT' });
const decrement = () => ({ type: 'DECREMENT' });

// Define Counter component
function Counter({ count, increment, decrement }) {
  return (
    <div>
      <p>Count: {count}</p>
      <button onClick={increment}>+</button>
      <button onClick={decrement}>-</button>
    </div>
  );
}

// Map state and dispatch to props
const mapStateToProps = (state) => ({ count: state.count });
const mapDispatchToProps = { increment, decrement };

// Connect Counter component to Redux store
const ConnectedCounter = connect(mapStateToProps, mapDispatch-
ToProps)(Counter);

// Render the app
ReactDOM.render(
  <Provider store={store}>
    <ConnectedCounter />
  </Provider>,
  document.getElementById('root')
);
```

By understanding and utilizing these state management techniques, developers can build robust and scalable React applications. Effective state management ensures that the UI remains responsive and consistent, providing a seamless user experience. Whether using hooks for local state, the Context API for global state, or Redux for complex state management, React offers a variety of tools to meet the needs of any application.

Integrating AI into React Components

Integrating AI into React components involves leveraging machine learning models to create intelligent and responsive user interfaces. This integration can enhance the user experience by providing features such as predictive text, real-time recommendations, and adaptive content layouts. By combining the power of React with AI, developers can build applications that respond intelligently to user input and behavior, making the interfaces more interactive and personalized.

Figure 5.3: *Integrating AI in React Components*

Supervised Learning in React Components

Definition

Supervised learning involves training a model on a labeled dataset, where the input data is paired with the correct output. This approach is commonly used for tasks like classification and regression.

Use Cases

- **Sentiment Analysis**: Analyzing user comments to determine their sentiment (positive, negative, or neutral).
- **Product Recommendations**: Suggesting products to users based on their browsing history and preferences.

- • **Handwriting Recognition**: Converting handwritten input into digital text.

Implementation

Integrate pre-trained supervised learning models into React components using APIs or libraries like TensorFlow.js.

```
import React, { useState, useEffect } from 'react';
import * as tf from '@tensorflow/tfjs';

function SentimentAnalysis() {
  const [model, setModel] = useState(null);
  const [inputText, setInputText] = useState('');
  const [prediction, setPrediction] = useState('');

  useEffect(() => {
    async function loadModel() {
      const loadedModel = await tf.loadLayersModel('model.
json');
      setModel(loadedModel);
    }
    loadModel();
  }, []);

  const analyzeSentiment = async () => {
    if (model) {
      const inputTensor = tf.tensor([inputText]);
      const predictionTensor = model.predict(inputTensor);
      const predictionValue = predictionTensor.dataSync()[0];
      setPrediction(predictionValue > 0.5 ? 'Positive' :
'Negative');
    }
  };

  return (
    <div>
      <textarea value={inputText} onChange={(e) => setInputText(e.target.value)} />
      <button onClick={analyzeSentiment}>Analyze Sentiment</button>
      <p>Prediction: {prediction}</p>
    </div>
  );
}
```

```
    export default SentimentAnalysis;

model.json :-
[
  {
    "text": "This movie was absolutely amazing!",
    "sentiment": 1
  },
  {
    "text": "The food was terrible, wouldn't recommend it.",
    "sentiment": 0
  }
]
```

Unsupervised Learning in React Components

Definition

Unsupervised learning involves training a model on data without labeled responses. The model tries to find patterns and relationships in the data.

Use Cases

- **Clustering**: Grouping users based on their behavior patterns.
- **Dimensionality Reduction**: Simplifying data visualizations by identifying key features.

Implementation

Train unsupervised models on user data within the React application and use the insights to enhance the UI.

```
    import React, { useState, useEffect } from 'react';
    import * as tf from '@tensorflow/tfjs';

    function UserClustering() {
      const [model, setModel] = useState(null);
      const [userData, setUserData] = useState([]);
      const [clusters, setClusters] = useState([]);

      useEffect(() => {
        async function loadModel() {
          const kmeans = new tf.KMeans({ k: 3 });
          setModel(kmeans);
```

```
      }
      loadModel();
    }, []);

    const clusterUsers = async () => {
      if (model) {
        const userTensor = tf.tensor(userData);
        const clusterIndices = model.fitPredict(userTensor);
        setClusters(clusterIndices);
      }
    };

    return (
      <div>
        <button onClick={clusterUsers}>Cluster Users</button>
        <p>Clusters: {clusters.join(', ')}</p>
      </div>
    );
  }

  export default UserClustering;
```

Semi-Supervised Learning in React Components

Definition

Semi-supervised learning combines labeled and unlabeled data to improve learning accuracy. It is useful when labeled data is scarce but unlabeled data is abundant.

Use Cases

- **Content Moderation**: Using a small set of labeled comments to train a model that can then classify a larger set of unlabeled comments.
- **Spam Detection**: Identifying spam emails using a combination of labeled and unlabeled data.

Implementation

Use semi-supervised learning models to enhance the accuracy of predictions in React components.

```
    import React, { useState, useEffect } from 'react';
    import * as tf from '@tensorflow/tfjs';
```

```
    function SpamDetection() {
      const [model, setModel] = useState(null);
      const [emailText, setEmailText] = useState('');
      const [isSpam, setIsSpam] = useState(false);

      useEffect(() => {
        async function loadModel() {
          const loadedModel = await tf.loadLayersModel('semi-super-
vised-model.json');
          setModel(loadedModel);
        }
        loadModel();
      }, []);

      const detectSpam = async () => {
        if (model) {
          const inputTensor = tf.tensor([emailText]);
          const predictionTensor = model.predict(inputTensor);
          const predictionValue = predictionTensor.dataSync()[0];
          setIsSpam(predictionValue > 0.5);
        }
      };

      return (
        <div>
          <textarea value={emailText} onChange={(e) => setEmail
Text(e.target.value)} />
          <button onClick={detectSpam}>Detect Spam</button>
          <p>{isSpam ? 'Spam' : 'Not Spam'}</p>
        </div>
      );
    }

  export default SpamDetection;

semi-supervised-model.json :-

[
  {"text": "This is a great product!", "label": 1},
  {"text": "I hate this product.", "label": 0},
  {"text": "Buy now, limited time offer!", "label": 1},
  {"text": "Unsubscribe from this email.", "label": 1}
]
```

Real-Time Recommendations and Adaptive Content

Let us understand the Real-time recommendations and adaptive content briefly.

Real-Time Recommendations

Use AI models to provide real-time recommendations based on user interactions. For example, recommending products or content based on user behavior.

Adaptive Content Layouts

Adjust the layout and content of the UI dynamically based on user preferences and interactions. This can be achieved by analyzing user data and using AI models to predict the most relevant content.

Implementation

Integrate AI models that analyze user behavior and provide real-time recommendations or adapt the content layout.

```
import React, { useState, useEffect } from 'react';
 import * as tf from '@tensorflow/tfjs';

function ProductRecommendations() {
  const [model, setModel] = useState(null);
  const [userPreferences, setUserPreferences] = useState([]);
  const [recommendations, setRecommendations] = useState([]);

  useEffect(() => {
    async function loadModel() {
      const loadedModel = await tf.loadLayersModel
('recommendation-model.json');
      setModel(loadedModel);
    }
    loadModel();
  }, []);

  const getRecommendations = async () => {
    if (model) {
      const inputTensor = tf.tensor([userPreferences]);
      const predictionTensor = model.predict(inputTensor);
      const recommendedProducts = predictionTensor.dataSync();
      setRecommendations(recommendedProducts);
```

```
      }
    };

    return (
      <div>
        <button onClick={getRecommendations}>Get Recommendations</
button>
        <ul>
          {recommendations.map((product, index) => (
            <li key={index}>{product}</li>
          ))}
        </ul>
      </div>
    );
  }

  export default ProductRecommendations;
```

recommendation-model.json :-

```
[
  {
    "user_id": 1,
    "product_id": 2,
    "rating": 5,
  },
  {
    "user_id": 1,
    "product_id": 3,
    "rating": 4,
  },
  {
    "user_id": 2,
    "product_id": 1,
    "rating": 3,
  },
  {
    "user_id": 2,
    "product_id": 3,
    "rating": 5,
  }
]
```

By integrating AI into React components, developers can create intelligent and responsive user interfaces that enhance the user experience. Whether using supervised, unsupervised, or semi-supervised learning techniques, AI can provide valuable insights and capabilities that make applications more interactive and personalized. Leveraging tools like TensorFlow.js and React's powerful component-based architecture, developers can build innovative web applications that respond intelligently to user input and behavior.

Building Interactive UI Elements with AI

Building interactive UI elements with AI involves leveraging machine learning and artificial intelligence techniques to create responsive and intelligent components within a React application. These elements can significantly enhance the user experience by providing features such as predictive text input, smart recommendations, adaptive content layouts, voice and conversational interfaces, and intelligent assistance. Here are some key topics and examples of how to implement these features:

Predictive Text Input

Definition

Predictive text input uses AI models to provide users with contextual suggestions as they type, improving efficiency and reducing errors.

Implementation

Integrate language models like GPT-3 or custom-trained models into React components to provide real-time text predictions.

```
import React, { useState } from 'react';
import axios from 'axios';

function PredictiveTextInput() {
  const [inputText, setInputText] = useState('');
  const [suggestions, setSuggestions] = useState([]);

  const fetchSuggestions = async (text) => {
    const response = await axios.post('https://api.example.com/
predict', { text });
    setSuggestions(response.data.suggestions);
  };

  const handleChange = (e) => {
    const text = e.target.value;
    setInputText(text);
    fetchSuggestions(text);
```

```
    };

    return (
      <div>
        <input type="text" value={inputText} onChange=
{handleChange} />
        <ul>
          {suggestions.map((suggestion, index) => (
            <li key={index}>{suggestion}</li>
          ))}
        </ul>
      </div>
    );
  }

  export default PredictiveTextInput;
```

Smart Recommendations

Definition

Smart recommendations analyze user behavior, preferences, and contextual data to surface personalized content, products, or actions within the UI.

Implementation

Develop recommendation systems using recommender algorithms or AI-powered services like Amazon Personalize.

```
    import React, { useState, useEffect } from 'react';
    import axios from 'axios';

    function SmartRecommendations() {
      const [recommendations, setRecommendations] = useState([]);

      useEffect(() => {
        const fetchRecommendations = async () => {
          const response = await axios.get('https://api.example.
com/recommendations');
          setRecommendations(response.data);
        };
        fetchRecommendations();
      }, []);
```

```
    return (
      <div>
        <h2>Recommended for You</h2>
        <ul>
          {recommendations.map((item, index) => (
            <li key={index}>{item.name}</li>
          ))}
        </ul>
      </div>
    );
}

export default SmartRecommendations;
```

Voice and Conversational Interfaces

Definition

Integrate speech recognition and natural language processing to enable voice-driven interactions and conversational UI elements.

Implementation

Use libraries like *Web Speech* API for speech recognition and natural language processing.

```
    import React, { useState } from 'react';

    function VoiceInterface() {
      const [transcript, setTranscript] = useState('');

      const startListening = () => {
        const recognition = new window.webkitSpeechRecognition();
        recognition.onresult = (event) => {
          setTranscript(event.results[0][0].transcript);
        };
        recognition.start();
      };

      return (
        <div>
          <button onClick={startListening}>Start Listening</button>
          <p>Transcript: {transcript}</p>
        </div>
```

```
    );
}

export default VoiceInterface;
```

Using Axios for API Requests

Axios is a promise-based HTTP client for making API requests. It is often used in React applications to fetch data from backend services, including AI-powered services. Axios provides a simple and intuitive API for making HTTP requests and handling responses, making it an excellent choice for integrating AI models into React components.

Setting Up Axios

Let us understand Axios in detail, which can be used for API requests.

Installation

Install Axios using npm or yarn.

```
npm install axios
 # or
 yarn add axios
```

Basic Usage

Import Axios and use it to make GET and POST requests.

```
import axios from 'axios';

// Making a GET request
axios.get('https://api.example.com/data')
  .then(response => {
    console.log(response.data);
  })
  .catch(error => {
    console.error('Error fetching data:', error);
  });

// Making a POST request
axios.post('https://api.example.com/data', { key: 'value' })
  .then(response => {
```

```
        console.log(response.data);
      })
      .catch(error => {
        console.error('Error posting data:', error);
      });
```

Handling API Responses:

Handle API responses and errors gracefully within React components.

```
    import React, { useState } from 'react';
     import axios from 'axios';

    function ApiRequestComponent() {
      const [input, setInput] = useState('');
      const [response, setResponse] = useState('');
      const [error, setError] = useState('');

      const handleRequest = async () => {
        try {
          const result = await axios.post('https://api.example.com/
    endpoint', { input });
          setResponse(result.data);
          setError('');
        } catch (err) {
          setError('Error making request');
          setResponse('');
        }
      };

      return (
        <div>
          <input type="text" value={input} onChange={(e) => setIn-
    put(e.target.value)} />
          <button onClick={handleRequest}>Send Request</button>
          {response && <p>Response: {response}</p>}
          {error && <p>{error}</p>}
        </div>
      );
    }

    export default ApiRequestComponent;
```

Advanced State Management with Redux and Optimizing its Performance

Redux is a powerful state management library that provides a predictable state container for JavaScript applications. It is particularly useful for managing complex state in large applications, offering a centralized store and clear patterns for updating and accessing state. This section will explore advanced state management techniques with Redux and strategies for optimizing its performance in React applications.

Core Concepts of Redux

Let us analyze the core concepts of Redux, as shown in the following figure:

Concept	Description
Store	The store holds the entire state of the application. It is a single source of truth, ensuring that the state is consistent and predictable.
Actions	Actions are plain JavaScript objects that describe changes to the state. They have a `type` property and may include additional data.
Reducers	Reducers are pure functions that take the current state and an action as arguments and return a new state. They specify how the state changes in response to actions.
Dispatch	The `dispatch` function sends actions to the store, triggering the reducers to update the state.

Figure 5.4: *Core Concepts of Redux*

Connecting Redux with React

Let us observe how to connect Redux with React seamlessly.

Provider

The `Provider` component from `react-redux` makes the Redux store available to the entire application.

```
import React from 'react';
  import ReactDOM from 'react-dom';
  import { Provider } from 'react-redux';
  import store from './store';
  import App from './App';
```

```
ReactDOM.render(
  <Provider store={store}>
    <App />
  </Provider>,
  document.getElementById('root')
);

Creating the store:-
import { createStore } from 'redux';

// Reducer function
const rootReducer = (state = {}, action) => {
  switch (action.type) {
    case 'SOME_ACTION':
      return { ...state, someProperty: action.payload };
    default:
      return state;
  }
};

const store = createStore(rootReducer);

export default store;


Creating the App Component :-
import React from 'react';

function App() {
  return (
    <div>
      <h1>Hello, World!</h1>
    </div>
  );
}

export default App;
```

useSelector and useDispatch Hooks

The `useSelector` hook allows components to access the Redux state, while the `useDispatch` hook provides a way to dispatch actions.

```
import React from 'react';
  import { useSelector, useDispatch } from 'react-redux';

  function Counter() {
    const count = useSelector(state => state.count);
    const dispatch = useDispatch();

    return (
      <div>
        <p>Count: {count}</p>
        <button onClick={() => dispatch({ type: 'INCREMENT'
})}>Increment</button>
        <button onClick={() => dispatch({ type: 'DECREMENT'
})}>Decrement</button>
      </div>
    );
  }

  export default Counter;
```

Optimizing Redux Performance

Let's deep dive into how we can optimize Redux performance.

Normalization

Normalizing the state shape can improve performance by reducing the complexity of state updates and making it easier to manage relationships between entities.

```
const initialState = {
    entities: {
      users: {
        byId: {
          1: { id: 1, name: 'John' },
          2: { id: 2, name: 'Jane' }
        },
        allIds: [1, 2]
      }
    }
  };
```

Splitting Reducers

Splitting reducers into smaller, more manageable functions can improve performance and maintainability. The `combineReducers` function from Redux can be used to combine multiple reducers.

```javascript
import { combineReducers } from 'redux';

const usersReducer = (state = [], action) => {
  switch (action.type) {
    case 'ADD_USER':
      return [...state, action.payload];
    default:
      return state;
  }
};

const activitiesReducer = (state = [], action) => {
  switch (action.type) {
    case 'ADD_ACTIVITY':
      return [...state, action.payload];
    default:
      return state;
  }
};

const rootReducer = combineReducers({
  users: usersReducer,
  activities: activitiesReducer
});

const store = createStore(rootReducer);
```

Using Redux Toolkit

Redux Toolkit is the official recommended way to write Redux logic. It simplifies the Redux workflow by providing utilities like `createSlice` for defining reducers, `createAction` for creating action creators, and `createAsyncThunk` for handling asynchronous actions.

```
import { configureStore, createSlice } from '@reduxjs/toolkit';

const counterSlice = createSlice({
  name: 'counter',
  initialState: { count: 0 },
  reducers: {
    increment: state => { state.count += 1; },
    decrement: state => { state.count -= 1; }
  }
});

const store = configureStore({
  reducer: counterSlice.reducer
});

export const { increment, decrement } = counterSlice.actions;
export default store;
```

Conclusion

This chapter delved into the integration of artificial intelligence (AI) with user interface (UI) design within the MERN stack, leveraging React to build dynamic and responsive web applications. We explored how to infuse AI-driven interactivity and personalization into React components, enhancing the user experience with features such as predictive text, real-time recommendations, and adaptive content layouts. The chapter also covered the use of React hooks for managing state in functional components, context for managing global data, and higher-order components for reusing logic across the application.

The tech stack highlighted in this chapter includes React as the primary library for building the UI, along with additional tools and libraries such as Axios for making HTTP requests to AI-powered backend services, and Redux for state management in more complex applications. This chapter equips developers with the knowledge and skills to create intelligent, interactive, and personalized web applications using React and AI, ensuring that their projects are both innovative and user-centric.

The next chapter is dedicated to the pivotal role of data in powering AI functionalities within the MERN stack. It emphasizes the importance of MongoDB, a NoSQL database, in handling the diverse and voluminous datasets that AI algorithms require for training and inference.

Multiple Choice Questions

1. What is the primary purpose of React in the MERN stack?

    a. To manage databases

    b. To build dynamic and responsive user interfaces

    c. To handle server-side logic

    d. To perform data analysis

2. Which React feature allows you to write HTML-like syntax within JavaScript?

    a. Virtual DOM

    b. JSX

    c. Redux

    d. Context API

3. What is the role of the `useState` hook in React?

    a. To manage global state

    b. To handle side effects

    c. To add state to functional components

    d. To create higher-order components

4. Which library is commonly used in React applications to make HTTP requests to AI-powered backend services?

    a. Redux

    b. Axios

    c. React Router

    d. Webpack

5. What is the purpose of the `Provider` component in Redux?

    a. To create a new Redux store

    b. To connect React components to the Redux store

    c. To dispatch actions to the Redux store

    d. To define reducers for the Redux store

6. Which React hook is used to access the Redux store's state and dispatch actions?

    a. useState

    b. useEffect

    c. useContext

    d. useSelector and useDispatch

7. What is the main advantage of using the Context API in React?

    a. To manage local state within a component

    b. To handle side effects in functional components

    c. To pass data through the component tree without prop drilling

    d. To create higher-order components

8. Which of the following is a common use case for integrating AI into React components?

    a. Predictive text input

    b. Static content rendering

    c. Server-side routing

    d. Database management

9. What is the purpose of memoization in Redux?

    a. To create actions and reducers

    b. To cache the results of expensive function calls

    c. To dispatch actions to the store

    d. To connect components to the Redux store

10. Which of the following techniques can be used to optimize the performance of a Redux application?

    a. Code splitting

    b. Memoization

    c. Normalization of state

    d. All of the above

Answers

1. b

2. b

3. c

4. b

5. b

6. d

7. c

8. a

9. b

10. d

CHAPTER 6

Data Management for AI with MongoDB

Introduction

Data Management for AI with MongoDB is a chapter dedicated to the pivotal role of data in powering AI functionalities within the MERN stack. It emphasizes the importance of MongoDB, a NoSQL database, in handling the diverse and voluminous datasets that AI algorithms require for training and inference. This chapter guides readers through the best practices for schema design, data modeling, and the efficient storage and retrieval of data that AI models can utilize effectively.

The chapter introduces MongoDB's flexible document model, which is particularly well-suited for storing unstructured data, a common requirement for AI applications. Readers will learn how to use MongoDB in conjunction with Mongoose, an Object Data Modeling (ODM) library for MongoDB and Node.js, to create schemas that reflect the data needs of AI models and ensure data integrity.

Key concepts covered include indexing for performance optimization, aggregation for data analysis, and the use of MongoDB Atlas, the cloud-based database service, for scalable and secure data storage. By the end of this chapter, readers will be proficient in managing data for AI applications, understanding how to leverage MongoDB's features to support the complex data requirements of AI-driven web applications.

Structure

In this chapter, we will cover the following topics:

- Introduction to MongoDB for AI
- MongoDB Basics
- Data Modeling with MongoDB
- CRUD Operations in MongoDB
- Indexing for Performance

- Data Aggregation and Analysis
- Working with Large Datasets
- Integrating MongoDB with Node.js
- Securing AI Data

Introduction to MongoDB for AI

The chapter begins by highlighting the importance of data management in the context of AI and machine learning applications. It establishes MongoDB as a highly suitable database solution for powering AI functionalities within the MERN (MongoDB, Express, React, Node.js) stack. MongoDB's flexible document-oriented data model aligns well with the diverse and unstructured nature of data typically required by AI algorithms. Unlike traditional relational databases, MongoDB's schema-less approach allows for the storage and manipulation of complex data structures, such as nested documents and arrays, without the need for rigid data modeling upfront.

MongoDB's scalability, high availability, and built-in support for features like aggregation and indexing make it a powerful choice for managing the large and ever-growing datasets that fuel modern AI applications. The chapter also briefly mentions the benefits of using MongoDB Atlas, the cloud-hosted database service, to simplify the deployment and management of MongoDB for AI projects. MongoDB Atlas provides a fully managed, secure, and scalable environment, allowing developers to focus on building AI models and applications without worrying about the underlying infrastructure.

Figure 6.1: *Introduction to MongoDB for AI*

MongoDB Basics

This section provides a foundational overview of MongoDB's core concepts and terminology, laying the groundwork for the subsequent data management techniques covered in the chapter. It begins by explaining the basic structure of a MongoDB database, which consists of collections (similar to tables in relational databases) that store documents (akin to rows). The document data model is explored, highlighting how MongoDB stores data in flexible, JSON-like documents that can contain nested fields and arrays.

Key Concepts

Let us understand a few key concepts of MongoDB Database.

Documents: The basic unit of data in MongoDB, similar to a row in a relational database. Documents are composed of field-value pairs and are stored in BSON (Binary JSON) format.

```
{
    "_id": "unique_id",
    "name": "John Doe",
    "age": 30,
    "address": {
      "street": "123 Main St",
      "city": "Anytown",
      "state": "CA"
    },
    "hobbies": ["reading", "traveling", "swimming"]
}
```

Collections: Groups of documents, similar to tables in relational databases. Collections do not enforce a schema, allowing for flexibility in the types of documents they can store.

```
db.users.insert({
    "name": "Jane Doe",
    "age": 25,
    "email": "jane.doe@example.com"
});
```

Databases: Containers for collections. A single MongoDB instance can host multiple databases, each with its own collections and documents.

```
use myDatabase;
  db.createCollection("users");
```

CRUD Operations

Let us understand the different CRUD Operations used in the MongoDB Database.

Operation	Description	Example Command
Create	Adding new documents to a collection.	`` `db.users.insert({ "name": "Alice", "age": 28, "email": "alice@example.com" });` ``
Read	Querying documents from a collection.	`` `db.users.find({ "age": { "$gt": 25 } });` ``
Update	Modifying existing documents in a collection.	`` `db.users.update( { "name": "Alice" }, { "$set": { "email": "alice.new@example.com" } } );` ``
Delete	Removing documents from a collection.	`` `db.users.remove({ "name": "Alice" });` ``
Indexes	Indexes improve the performance of read operations by allowing the database to quickly locate documents that match a query.	`` `db.users.createIndex({ "email": 1 });` ``
Aggregation	Aggregation operations process data records and return computed results. MongoDB provides a powerful aggregation framework for data analysis.	`` `db.users.aggregate([ { "$match": { "age": { "$gt": 25 } } }, { "$group": { "_id": "$age", "count": { "$sum": 1 } } } ]);` ``

Figure 6.2: *MongoDB - CRUD Operations*

Data Modeling with MongoDB

Data modeling in MongoDB is the process of designing the structure of collections and documents to efficiently store and retrieve data. Unlike traditional relational databases, MongoDB's flexible schema allows for a more dynamic and adaptable approach to data modeling, which is particularly beneficial for AI applications that often deal with unstructured and semi-structured data. Effective data modeling ensures that the database can handle the complex data requirements of AI algorithms, providing a foundation for efficient data storage, retrieval, and analysis.

Key Concepts in MongoDB Data Modeling

Let us understand a few key concepts in MongoDB Data Modeling.

Flexible Schema:

MongoDB collections do not require documents to have the same set of fields or data types. This flexibility allows for the storage of diverse data structures within the same collection, making it easier to adapt to changing data requirements.

```
{
    "_id": "unique_id",
    "name": "John Doe",
    "age": 30,
    "address": {
      "street": "123 Main St",
      "city": "Anytown",
      "state": "CA"
    },
    "hobbies": ["reading", "traveling", "swimming"]
}
```

Embedded Data Model:

In the embedded data model, related data is stored within a single document. This approach, also known as denormalization, allows for faster read operations by reducing the need for joins.

```
{
    "_id": "unique_id",
    "name": "John Doe",
    "age": 30,
    "address": {
      "street": "123 Main St",
      "city": "Anytown",
      "state": "CA"
    },
    "hobbies": ["reading", "traveling", "swimming"]
}
```

Normalized Data Model:

In the normalized data model, related data is stored in separate documents and linked using references. This approach, also known as normalization, helps to reduce data redundancy and maintain data integrity.

```
// User document
{
```

```
  "_id": "user_id",
  "name": "John Doe"
}

// Address document
{
  "_id": "address_id",
  "user_id": "user_id",
  "street": "123 Main St",
  "city": "Anytown",
  "state": "CA"
}
```

CRUD Operations in MongoDB

CRUD operations (Create, Read, Update, Delete) are the fundamental operations for managing data in MongoDB. These operations allow users to interact with the database, perform data manipulation, and maintain data integrity. Understanding how to perform CRUD operations is essential for effectively managing data in MongoDB.

Create Operations

Insert Documents:

The `insertOne()` method is used to add a single document to a collection.

```
db.users.insertOne({
  "name": "Alice",
  "age": 28,
  "email": "alice@example.com"
});
```

The `insertMany()` method is used to add multiple documents to a collection at once.

```
db.users.insertMany([
  { "name": "Bob", "age": 32, "email": "bob@example.com" },
  { "name": "Charlie", "age": 25, "email": "charlie@example.
com" }
]);
```

Read Operations

Query Documents:

The `find()` method is used to retrieve documents from a collection based on a query.

```
db.users.find({ "age": { "$gt": 25 } });
```

The `findOne()` method is used to retrieve a single document that matches a query.

```
db.users.findOne({ "email": "alice@example.com" });
```

Update Operations

Let's understand the Update Operations of MongoDB with ease.

Modify Documents:

The `updateOne()` method is used to update a single document that matches a query.

```
db.users.updateOne(
    { "name": "Alice" },
    { "$set": { "email": "alice.new@example.com" } }
);
```

The `updateMany()` method is used to update multiple documents that match a query.

```
db.users.updateMany(
    { "age": { "$lt": 30 } },
    { "$set": { "status": "young" } }
);
```

The `replaceOne()` method is used to replace a single document that matches a query with a new document.

```
db.users.replaceOne(
    { "name": "Charlie" },
    { "name": "Charles", "age": 26, "email": "charles@example.com" }
);
```

Delete Operations

Let's understand the Delete Operations in MongoDB with ease.

Remove Documents:

The `deleteOne()` method is used to remove a single document that matches a query.

```
db.users.deleteOne({ "name": "Alice" });
```

The `deleteMany()` method is used to remove multiple documents that match a query.

```
db.users.deleteMany({ "status": "inactive" });
```

Indexing for Performance

Indexing is a critical aspect of optimizing query performance in MongoDB. Proper indexing ensures that queries are executed efficiently, reducing the time and resources required to retrieve data. This section covers best practices for creating and managing indexes in MongoDB to support high-performance AI applications.

Best Practices for Indexing

Create Indexes to Support Queries:

Indexes should be created based on the queries that are most frequently executed. This ensures that the database can quickly locate the documents that match the query criteria.

```
db.users.createIndex({ "email": 1 });
```

Compound Indexes:

Compound indexes are composed of multiple fields. They are useful for queries that filter on multiple fields. The order of fields in a compound index is important and should follow the ESR (Equality, Sort, Range) rule.

```
db.users.createIndex({ "lastName": 1, "firstName": 1 });
```

Partial Indexes:

Partial indexes only include documents that meet a specified condition. This reduces the size of the index and improves performance for queries that only need to access a subset of documents.

```
db.orders.createIndex({ "orderID": 1 }, { partialFilter
Expression: { "orderStatus": "In progress" } });
```

Multi-Key Indexes:

Multi-key indexes are used to index array fields. MongoDB creates an index key for each element in the array, allowing efficient querying of individual array elements.

```
db.users.createIndex({ "hobbies": 1 });
```

Text Search:

Text indexes are used to perform text search queries on string content. MongoDB provides a text index type that supports searching for words within a field.

```
db.articles.createIndex({ "content": "text" });
```

Data Aggregation and Analysis

Aggregation in MongoDB is a powerful tool for performing complex data analysis and transformation. The aggregation framework allows for the processing of data records and the return of computed results. This section covers the key concepts and stages of the aggregation pipeline.

Aggregation Pipeline

An aggregation pipeline consists of a series of stages that process documents. Each stage performs an operation on the input documents and passes the result to the next stage.

Stages and Operators:

Let us understand the stages and operators by understanding the following figure:

Operation	Description	Example
`$match`	Filters documents based on a specified condition	`db.orders.aggregate([{ $match: { "status": "shipped" } }])`
`$group`	Groups documents by a specified field and performs aggregation operations like sum, average, min, max, etc.	`db.orders.aggregate([{ $group: { _id: "$customerId", totalAmount: { $sum: "$amount" } } }])`
`$lookup`	Performs a left outer join with another collection	`db.orders.aggregate([{ $lookup: { from: "customers", localField: "customerId", foreignField: "_id", as: "customerDetails" } }])`
`$project`	Reshapes documents by including, excluding, or adding new fields	`db.orders.aggregate([{ $project: { orderId: 1, amount: 1, customerName: "$customerDetails.name" } }])`
`$sort`	Sorts documents based on a specified field	`db.orders.aggregate([{ $sort: { "orderDate": -1 } }])`

Figure 6.3: *Different Stages and Operators*

Working with Large Datasets

Handling large datasets in MongoDB requires careful consideration of data modeling, storage, and performance optimization techniques. This section covers strategies for managing large documents, using GridFS, sharding, batch processing, and optimizing performance for time-series data.

Handling Large Documents

Let's see how we can handle large documents in MongoDB.

Document Size Limit:

MongoDB has a maximum BSON document size of 16MB. For documents larger than this limit, MongoDB provides the GridFS API.

```
const Grid = require('gridfs-stream');
const gfs = Grid(mongoose.connection.db, mongoose.mongo);
```

GridFS:

GridFS is used to store and retrieve large files, such as images, videos, and large JSON documents, by splitting them into smaller chunks.

```
const writeStream = gfs.createWriteStream({ filename: 'largeFile' });
fs.createReadStream('largeFile').pipe(writeStream);
```

Sharding

Sharding is a method for distributing data across multiple servers. It allows MongoDB to handle large datasets by splitting collections into smaller, more manageable pieces called shards.

Implementation:

Enable sharding on a collection to distribute data across multiple shards.

```
sh.enableSharding("myDatabase");
sh.shardCollection("myDatabase.myCollection", { "shardKey": 1 });

sh - It is mainly used to set up a sharded MongoDB cluster, al-
lowing for horizontal scaling and efficient data distribution.
```

Batch Processing

Let us understand the batch processing with ease.

Batch Operations:

Batch processing involves performing operations on large datasets in smaller, manageable batches to avoid performance bottlenecks and memory issues.

```
const bulk = db.collection.initializeOrderedBulkOp();
 bulk.insert({ "name": "Alice" });
 bulk.insert({ "name": "Bob" });
 bulk.execute();
```

Time-Series Data

Let's understand the time-series data with ease.

Time-Series Collections:

MongoDB provides optimized storage and querying capabilities for time-series data, which is useful for applications that collect data at regular intervals.

```
    db.createCollection("timeSeriesData", { timeseries: { timeField:
"timestamp" } });
```

Performance Optimization:

Use indexes, sharding, and aggregation pipelines to optimize the performance of queries on large datasets.

```
    db.timeSeriesData.createIndex({ "timestamp": 1 });
```

Integrating MongoDB with Node.js

Integrating MongoDB with Node.js is a crucial step in building robust and scalable AI-driven web applications within the MERN stack. This integration allows developers to leverage MongoDB's powerful data management capabilities directly from their Node.js applications, enabling efficient data storage, retrieval, and manipulation. This section will guide you through the process of setting up and connecting MongoDB with Node.js, using the MongoDB Node.js driver and Mongoose, an Object Data Modeling (ODM) library.

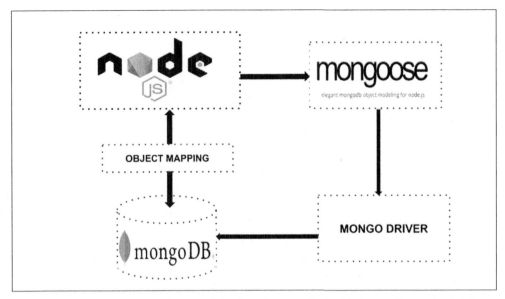

Figure 6.4: *Integrating MongoDB with Node.js (Source: https://miro.medium.com/v2/re-size:fit:880/1*6vfVDA-9P3m1y4DddcFWoA.png)*

Setting Up MongoDB and Node.js

Let us set up MongoDB and Node.js all together with ease.

Prerequisites:

- Ensure that Node.js and npm (Node Package Manager) are installed on your system. You can download them from the Node.js official website: https://nodejs.org/ .

- Install MongoDB on your local machine or use MongoDB Atlas, a cloud-based database service.

Installing MongoDB Node.js Driver:

The MongoDB Node.js driver allows you to interact with MongoDB databases from within Node.js applications. Install the driver using npm:

```
npm install mongodb
```

Installing Mongoose:

Mongoose is an ODM library for MongoDB and Node.js that provides a higher-level abstraction for working with MongoDB. Install Mongoose using npm:

```
npm install mongoose
```

Connecting to MongoDB

Let's see how we can connect to MongoDB with ease.

Using MongoDB Node.js Driver:

Create a new Node.js project and set up a connection to MongoDB using the MongoDB Node.js driver.

```
// Import MongoClient from the MongoDB package
const { MongoClient } = require('mongodb');


// Connection URI
const uri = 'mongodb://localhost:27017';


// Create a new MongoClient
const client = new MongoClient(uri, { useNewUrlParser: true,
useUnifiedTopology: true });


// Connect to the MongoDB server
async function connectToMongoDB() {
  try {
    await client.connect();
    console.log('Connected to MongoDB');
    const database = client.db('myDatabase');
    const collection = database.collection('myCollection');
    // Perform operations on the collection
  } catch (error) {
    console.error('Error connecting to MongoDB:', error);
  } finally {
    await client.close();
  }
}


connectToMongoDB();
```

Using Mongoose:

Set up a connection to MongoDB using Mongoose and define a schema and model.

```
// Import Mongoose
const mongoose = require('mongoose');
```

```
// Connection URI
const uri = 'mongodb://localhost:27017/myDatabase';


// Connect to MongoDB using Mongoose
mongoose.connect(uri, { useNewUrlParser: true, useUnifiedTopolo-
gy: true })
    .then(() => console.log('Connected to MongoDB with Mon-
goose'))
    .catch(error => console.error('Error connecting to MongoDB:',
error));


// Define a schema
const userSchema = new mongoose.Schema({
  name: String,
  age: Number,
  email: String
});


// Create a model
const User = mongoose.model('User', userSchema);


// Create and save a new user
const newUser = new User({ name: 'Alice', age: 28, email:
'alice@example.com' });
newUser.save()
  .then(() => console.log('User saved'))
  .catch(error => console.error('Error saving user:', error));
```

Performing CRUD Operations

Let us analyze the different CRUD Operations in MongoDB.

Create:

- Insert a new document into a collection using the MongoDB Node.js driver.

```
async function createDocument() {
    try {
        await client.connect();
        const database = client.db('myDatabase');
        const collection = database.collection('myCollection');
```

```
      const result = await collection.insertOne({ name: 'Bob',
  age: 32, email: 'bob@example.com' });
      console.log('Document inserted:', result.insertedId);
    } finally {
      await client.close();
    }
  }


  createDocument();
```

- Insert a new document using Mongoose.

```
  const newUser = new User({ name: 'Bob', age: 32, email: 'bob@
  example.com' });
  newUser.save()
    .then(() => console.log('User saved'))
    .catch(error => console.error('Error saving user:', error));
```

Read:

- Query documents from a collection using the MongoDB Node.js driver.

```
  async function readDocuments() {
    try {
      await client.connect();
      const database = client.db('myDatabase');
      const collection = database.collection('myCollection');
      const documents = await collection.find({ age: { $gt: 30 }
  }).toArray();
      console.log('Documents found:', documents);
    } finally {
      await client.close();
    }
  }


  readDocuments();
```

- Query documents using Mongoose.

```
  User.find({ age: { $gt: 30 } })
    .then(users => console.log('Users found:', users))
    .catch(error => console.error('Error finding users:', error));
```

Update:

- Update a document in a collection using the MongoDB Node.js driver.

```
async function updateDocument() {
  try {
    await client.connect();
    const database = client.db('myDatabase');
    const collection = database.collection('myCollection');
    const result = await collection.updateOne({ name: 'Bob' },
{ $set: { email: 'bob.new@example.com' } });
    console.log('Document updated:', result.modifiedCount);
  } finally {
    await client.close();
  }
}

updateDocument();
```

- Update a document using Mongoose.

```
User.updateOne({ name: 'Bob' }, { email: 'bob.new@example.com' })
  .then(result => console.log('User updated:', result))
  .catch(error => console.error('Error updating user:', error));
```

Delete:

- Delete a document from a collection using the MongoDB Node.js driver.

```
async function deleteDocument() {
  try {
    await client.connect();
    const database = client.db('myDatabase');
    const collection = database.collection('myCollection');
    const result = await collection.deleteOne({ name: 'Bob' });
    console.log('Document deleted:', result.deletedCount);
  } finally {
    await client.close();
  }
}

deleteDocument();
```

- Delete a document using Mongoose.

```
User.deleteOne({ name: 'Bob' })
  .then(result => console.log('User deleted:', result))
  .catch(error => console.error('Error deleting user:', error));
```

Closing the Connection

Let us understand how the MongDB Connection can be closed with ease.

- **Using MongoDB Node.js Driver:**

    Ensure that the connection to MongoDB is properly closed after operations are completed.

```
async function connectToMongoDB() {
  try {
    await client.connect();
    console.log('Connected to MongoDB');
    const database = client.db('myDatabase');
    const collection = database.collection('myCollection');
    // Perform operations on the collection
  } catch (error) {
    console.error('Error connecting to MongoDB:', error);
  } finally {
    await client.close();
  }
}

connectToMongoDB();
```

- **Using Mongoose:**

    Mongoose automatically manages the connection lifecycle, but you can manually close the connection, if needed.

```
mongoose.connection.close()
  .then(() => console.log('Mongoose connection closed'))
  .catch(error => console.error('Error closing Mongoose
connection:', error));
```

Securing AI Data

Securing AI data is paramount to ensuring the integrity, confidentiality, and availability of the data used in AI applications. MongoDB provides a robust set of security features and best practices to protect data from unauthorized access, breaches, and other security threats. This section will cover the essential security measures for securing AI data in MongoDB, including authentication, authorization, encryption, network security, and auditing.

Authentication and Authorization

Let us understand the concepts of Authentication and Authorization with ease.

Authentication:

Authentication verifies the identity of users and applications attempting to access the MongoDB database. MongoDB supports various authentication mechanisms, including SCRAM (default), x.509 certificates, LDAP, and Kerberos.

```
// Example of enabling SCRAM authentication
db.createUser({
  user: "myUser",
  pwd: "myPassword",
  roles: [{ role: "readWrite", db: "myDatabase" }]
});
```

Authorization:

Authorization determines the actions that authenticated users and applications can perform. MongoDB uses Role-Based Access Control (RBAC) to assign roles with specific permissions to users.

```
// Example of creating a user with specific roles
db.createUser({
  user: "adminUser",
  pwd: "adminPassword",
  roles: [
    { role: "dbAdmin", db: "admin" },
    { role: "readWrite", db: "myDatabase" }
  ]
});
```

Encryption

Encryption at Rest:

Encryption at rest protects data stored on disk from unauthorized access. MongoDB's WiredTiger storage engine supports native encryption at rest.

```
// Example of enabling encryption at rest
storage:
  dbPath: /var/lib/mongodb
  journal:
    enabled: true
  engine: wiredTiger
  wiredTiger:
    collectionConfig:
      blockCompressor: snappy
    engineConfig:
      cacheSizeGB: 2
    indexConfig:
      prefixCompression: true
    encryption:
      enabled: true
      keyFile: /path/to/keyfile
```

Encryption in Transit:

Encryption in transit protects data as it travels over the network between clients and MongoDB servers. MongoDB supports TLS/SSL to encrypt data in transit.

```
// Example of enabling TLS/SSL
net:
  ssl:
    mode: requireSSL
    PEMKeyFile: /etc/ssl/mongodb.pem
    CAFile: /etc/ssl/ca.pem
```

Client-Side Field Level Encryption (CSFLE):

CSFLE allows applications to encrypt specific fields before sending data to the database, providing an additional layer of security.

```
// Example of enabling CSFLE
const { ClientEncryption } = require('mongodb-client-encryption');
const client = new MongoClient(uri, {
  useNewUrlParser: true,
  useUnifiedTopology: true,
  autoEncryption: {
    keyVaultNamespace: 'encryption.__keyVault',
    kmsProviders: {
```

```
      aws: {
        accessKeyId: '<AWS_ACCESS_KEY_ID>',
        secretAccessKey: '<AWS_SECRET_ACCESS_KEY>'
      }
    }
  }
});
```

Best Practices for Securing MongoDB

Let us understand the best practices for securing MongoDB.

Role-Based Access Control (RBAC):

Implement RBAC to ensure that users have the minimum necessary permissions to perform their tasks.

```
// Example of creating a role with specific permissions
db.createRole({
    role: "readWriteRole",
    privileges: [
        { resource: { db: "myDatabase", collection: "" }, actions:
["find", "insert", "update", "remove"] }
    ],
    roles: []
});
```

Regular Updates and Patches:

Keep MongoDB and its dependencies up-to-date with the latest security patches and updates to protect against known vulnerabilities.

```
# Example of updating MongoDB
sudo apt-get update
sudo apt-get upgrade mongodb
```

Secure Configuration:

Disable unused features and configure MongoDB with secure settings to reduce the attack surface.

```
// Example of disabling server-side scripting
security:
    javascriptEnabled: false
```

Conclusion

This chapter emphasized the critical role of MongoDB in managing the diverse and voluminous datasets required for AI functionalities within the MERN stack. MongoDB's flexible document model is particularly well-suited for storing unstructured data, which is common in AI applications. The chapter guides readers through best practices for schema design, data modeling, and efficient data storage and retrieval, ensuring that AI models can utilize the data effectively.

Readers learned how to use MongoDB in conjunction with Mongoose, an Object Data Modeling (ODM) library for MongoDB and Node.js, to create schemas that reflect the data needs of AI models and ensure data integrity. Key concepts covered include indexing for performance optimization, aggregation for data analysis. By the end of this chapter, readers will be proficient in managing data for AI applications, leveraging MongoDB's features to support the complex data requirements of AI-driven web applications.

The next chapter focuses on using Express.js, a fast, unopinionated, minimalist web framework for Node.js, to create middleware that interacts with AI models, facilitating data preprocessing, decision-making, and response generation.

Multiple Choice Questions

1. What is the primary function of MongoDB in AI applications?

    a. Managing relational data

    b. Handling diverse and voluminous datasets

    c. Performing data analysis only

    d. Creating static web pages

2. Which library is commonly used with MongoDB in Node.js for schema creation?

    a. Express

    b. Mongoose

    c. React

    d. Axios

3. What type of data model does MongoDB use?

    a. Relational

    b. Document-oriented

    c.   Key-value

    d.   Graph-based

4.   What is the purpose of indexing in MongoDB?

    a.   To store data

    b.   To improve query performance

    c.   To create schemas

    d.   To delete documents

5.   Which MongoDB feature allows for the processing of data records and returning computed results?

    a.   Indexing

    b.   Aggregation

    c.   Sharding

    d.   Replication

6.   What is the maximum BSON document size in MongoDB?

    a.   8MB

    b.   16MB

    c.   32MB

    d.   64MB

7.   What is the role of MongoDB Atlas?

    a.   To provide a cloud-based database service

    b.   To create static web pages

    c.   To manage relational databases

    d.   To perform client-side rendering

8.   Which of the following is a method for distributing data across multiple servers in MongoDB?

    a.   Indexing

    b.   Aggregation

    c.   Sharding

    d.   Replication

9. What is the purpose of Mongoose in MongoDB?

    a. To perform client-side rendering

    b. To create schemas and models

    c. To manage relational data

    d. To perform data analysis only

10. What is the primary benefit of using MongoDB for AI applications?

    a. Managing relational data

    b. Handling unstructured data

    c. Creating static web pages

    d. Performing client-side rendering

Answers

1. b
2. b
3. b
4. b
5. b
6. b
7. a
8. c
9. b
10. b

CHAPTER 7

Building AI Middleware with Express.js

Introduction

Building AI Middleware with Express.js delves into the critical role of middleware in the MERN stack for integrating AI functionalities into web applications. This chapter focuses on using Express.js, a fast, unopinionated, minimalist web framework for Node.js, to create middleware that interacts with AI models, facilitating data preprocessing, decision-making, and response generation. Through Express.js, readers will learn how to efficiently bridge the gap between the frontend and AI algorithms running on the server side.

The chapter introduces the concept of middleware in web development, explaining how it operates within the request-response cycle in Express.js applications. It covers the creation of custom middleware functions that can perform tasks such as user authentication, data validation, and error handling, which are essential for AI-driven applications. Additionally, the chapter explores the integration of TensorFlow.js and other AI libraries within Express.js middleware, enabling the execution of machine learning models directly within the web server environment.

Key technologies and tools covered include Express.js for server setup and middleware configuration, TensorFlow.js for incorporating machine learning models, and Postman for testing API endpoints that utilize AI middleware. By the end of this chapter, readers will gain a comprehensive understanding of how to construct and deploy AI middleware within their Express.js applications, enhancing their web applications with intelligent features.

Structure

In this chapter, we will cover the following topics:

- Introduction to Middleware in Express.js
- Setting Up an Express.js Server
- Developing Custom AI Middleware
- Integrating TensorFlow.js with Express.js
- Data Validation and Sanitization
- Optimizing Middleware Performance

Introduction to Middleware in Express.js

Middleware is a fundamental concept in web development, particularly within the Express.js framework. Middleware functions are functions that have access to the request object (`req`), the response object (`res`), and the **next** middleware function in the application's request-response cycle. These functions can perform a variety of tasks, such as executing code, modifying the request and response objects, ending the request-response cycle, and calling the next middleware function in the stack.

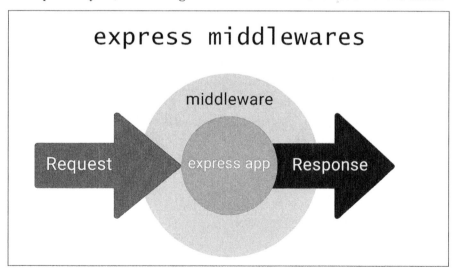

*Figure 7.1: Introduction to Middleware in Express.js (Source: https://miro.medium.com/v2/re-size:fit:1400/1*C4WbFuLBN7lFi7ETTzeSzQ.jpeg)*

Understanding Middleware

Middleware in Express.js serves as a bridge between the incoming HTTP request and the final request handler. It allows developers to intercept and manipulate requests and responses before they reach the route handlers. Middleware functions can be used to perform tasks such as logging, authentication, data validation, error handling, and more. They are invoked in the order they are added to the application, creating a stack of middleware functions that process the request sequentially.

Key Characteristics of Middleware

- **Access to Request and Response Objects**: Middleware functions can read and modify the request and response objects.

- **Next Function**: Middleware functions can call the `next()` function to pass control to the next middleware function in the stack.

- **Execution Order**: Middleware functions are executed in the order they are added to the application.

Types of Middleware

Express.js offers different types of middleware, each serving a specific purpose:

- **Application-Level Middleware:**
  - Bound to an instance of the `express` application object using `app.use()` or `app.METHOD()`.
  - Executes for every request to the application.

```
const express = require('express');
const app = express();

app.use((req, res, next) => {
  console.log('Time:', Date.now());
  next();
});

app.get('/', (req, res) => {
  res.send('Hello World');
});

app.listen(3000, () => {
  console.log('Server is running on port 3000');
});
```

- **Router-Level Middleware:**
  - Bound to an instance of `express.Router()` using `router.use()` or `router.METHOD()`.

    ○   Executes requests to routes defined within the router.

```
const express = require('express');
const router = express.Router();

router.use((req, res, next) => {
  console.log('Request URL:', req.originalUrl);
  next();
});

router.get('/user/:id', (req, res) => {
  res.send(`User ID: ${req.params.id}`);
});

const app = express();
app.use('/api', router);

app.listen(3000, () => {
  console.log('Server is running on port 3000');
});
```

- **Error-Handling Middleware:**
  - Defined with four parameters: `err`, `req`, `res`, and `next`.
  - Used to handle errors that occur during the request-response cycle.

```
const express = require('express');
const app = express();

app.use((req, res, next) => {
  const err = new Error('Something went wrong');
  err.status = 500;
  next(err);
});

app.use((err, req, res, next) => {
  res.status(err.status || 500);
  res.send({ error: err.message });
});

app.listen(3000, () => {
```

```
      console.log('Server is running on port 3000');
    });
```

- **Built-In Middleware:**
  - ○ Provided by Express.js for common tasks such as serving static files, parsing JSON, and URL-encoded data.

    ```
    const express = require('express');
    const app = express();

    app.use(express.static('public'));
    app.use(express.json());
    app.use(express.urlencoded({ extended: true }));

    app.listen(3000, () => {
      console.log('Server is running on port 3000');
    });
    ```

- **Third-Party Middleware:**
  - ○ Developed by the community and available as npm packages. Examples include `body-parser`, `morgan`, and `cors`.

    ```
    const express = require('express');
    const morgan = require('morgan');
    const cors = require('cors');
    const app = express();

    app.use(morgan('dev'));
    app.use(cors());

    app.listen(3000, () => {
      console.log('Server is running on port 3000');
    });
    ```

Middleware Chaining

Middleware functions can be chained together to create a sequence of processing steps. Each middleware function can modify the request and response objects and pass control to the next function in the stack using the `next()` function. This chaining mechanism allows for modular and reusable code.

Example of Middleware Chaining:

```javascript
const express = require('express');
const app = express();

app.use((req, res, next) => {
  console.log('First middleware');
  req.customProperty = 'Custom Value';
  next();
});

app.use((req, res, next) => {
  console.log('Second middleware');
  console.log('Custom Property:', req.customProperty);
  next();
});

app.get('/', (req, res) => {
  res.send('Hello World');
});

app.listen(3000, () => {
  console.log('Server is running on port 3000');
});
```

In this example, the first middleware function adds a custom property to the request object, and the second middleware function logs that property before passing control to the route handler.

Setting Up an Express.js Server

Setting up an Express.js server is a straightforward process that involves a few key steps. Express.js is a minimalistic and flexible web application framework for Node.js, making it easy to create robust and scalable web servers. This section will guide you through the process of setting up an Express.js server, which will serve as the foundation for building AI middleware and integrating it with your web applications.

Installing Express.js

Before you can set up an Express.js server, you need to install the Express.js package.

You can do this by creating a new directory for your project and initializing a new Node.js project with the following commands:

```
mkdir my-express-app
cd my-express-app
npm init -y
```

The `npm init -y` command creates a `package.json` file, which will manage your project's dependencies. Next, install the Express.js package by running the following command:

```
npm install express
```

Creating the Server

With Express.js installed, you can now create your server. Create a new file called `app.js` (or any name you prefer) and add the following code:

```
const express = require('express');
const app = express();
const port = 3000; // or any other port you prefer

app.get('/', (req, res) => {
  res.send('Hello, World!');
});

app.listen(port, () => {
  console.log(`Server is running on port ${port}`);
});
```

Let us break down this code:

1. `const express = require('express');`: This line imports the Express.js module.

2. `const app = express();`: This line creates an instance of the Express.js application.

3. `const port = 3000;`: This line sets the port number on which the server will listen for incoming requests.

4. `app.get('/', (req, res) => { ... });`: This line defines a route handler for the root URL (`/`). When a client sends a GET request to this URL, the server will respond with the string "*Hello, World!*".

5. `` `app.listen(port, () => { ... });` ``: This line starts the server and listens for incoming requests on the specified port. The callback function logs a message to the console, indicating that the server is running.

Running the Server

To run the Express.js server, open your terminal or command prompt, navigate to your project directory, and execute the following command:

```
node app.js
```

You should see the message "*Server is running on port 3000*" (or the port number you specified) printed in the console. Now, you can open your web browser and visit `http://localhost:3000` to see the "*Hello, World!*" message.

Adding Middleware

Express.js provides a robust middleware system that allows you to add functionality to your application. Middleware functions have access to the request object (`` `req` ``), the response object (`` `res` ``), and the `` `next` `` middleware function in the application's request-response cycle. You can add middleware functions to your Express.js application using the `` `app.use()` `` method.

Here's an example of adding a simple middleware function that logs the request method and URL:

```
const express = require('express');
const app = express();
const port = 3000;

// Middleware function to log request method and URL
app.use((req, res, next) => {
  console.log(`${req.method} ${req.url}`);
  next();
});

app.get('/', (req, res) => {
  res.send('Hello, World!');
});

app.listen(port, () => {
  console.log(`Server is running on port ${port}`);
});
```

In this example, the middleware function logs the request method and URL to the console, and then calls the `next()` function to pass control to the next middleware function in the stack.

Developing Custom AI Middleware

Developing custom AI middleware in Express.js involves creating middleware functions that interact with AI models to perform tasks such as data preprocessing, decision-making, and response generation. This section will guide you through the process of creating custom middleware functions that integrate AI capabilities into your Express.js applications, enabling intelligent features and enhancing the overall user experience.

Understanding Middleware Functions

Middleware functions in Express.js are functions that have access to the request object (`req`), the response object (`res`), and the `next` function in the application's request-response cycle. These functions can perform various tasks, such as modifying the request and response objects, executing code, and ending the request-response cycle. Middleware functions can also call the `next` function to pass control to the next middleware function in the stack.

Basic Structure of Middleware

```
function myMiddleware(req, res, next) {
    // Perform some task
    next(); // Pass control to the next middleware function
}
```

Creating Custom AI Middleware

To create custom AI middleware, you need to define middleware functions that interact with AI models. These functions can preprocess input data, run AI models, and generate responses based on the model's output.

Example: Sentiment Analysis Middleware:

This example demonstrates how to create a custom middleware function that performs sentiment analysis on user input using a pre-trained AI model.

1. **Set Up the Project**:

   Create a new directory for your project and initialize a new Node.js project.

```
mkdir ai-middleware-app
  cd ai-middleware-app
  npm init -y
```

2. **Install Dependencies**:

   Install Express.js and TensorFlow.js.

   ```
   npm install express @tensorflow/tfjs-node
   ```

3. **Create the Middleware Function**:

   Create a file named `sentimentMiddleware.js` and define the middleware function.

   ```
   const tf = require('@tensorflow/tfjs-node');


     async function loadModel() {
        const model = await tf.loadLayersModel('path/to/sentiment
   -model.json');
        return model;
      }


     const modelPromise = loadModel();


        async function sentimentMiddleware(req, res, next) {
          try {
            const model = await modelPromise;
            const inputText = req.body.text;
            const inputTensor = tf.tensor([inputText]);
            const prediction = model.predict(inputTensor);
            const sentimentScore = prediction.dataSync()[0];
            req.sentiment = sentimentScore > 0.5 ? 'Positive' :
   'Negative';
            next();
          } catch (error) {
            next(error);
          }
        }


        module.exports = sentimentMiddleware;
   ```

4. **Integrate Middleware into Express.js Application**:

Create a file named `app.js` and set up the Express.js server with the custom middleware.

```javascript
const express = require('express');
const bodyParser = require('body-parser');
const sentimentMiddleware = require('./sentimentMiddleware');

const app = express();
const port = 3000;

app.use(bodyParser.json());

app.post('/analyze', sentimentMiddleware, (req, res) => {
  res.json({ sentiment: req.sentiment });
});

app.use((err, req, res, next) => {
  console.error(err.stack);
  res.status(500).send('Something broke!');
});

app.listen(port, () => {
  console.log(`Server is running on port ${port}`);
});
```

5. **Test the Middleware**:

a. Use Postman or any other API testing tool to send a POST request to the `/analyze` endpoint with a JSON body containing the text to be analyzed.

```
{
    "text": "I love this product!"
}
```

b. The server should respond with the sentiment analysis result.

```
{
    "sentiment": "Positive"
}
```

Additional Examples of Custom AI Middleware

Let us understand it with some additional examples.

Image Classification Middleware

This example demonstrates how to create middleware that performs image classification using a pre-trained AI model.

1. **Install Additional Dependencies**:

    Install the `multer` package for handling file uploads.

    ```
    npm install multer
    ```

2. **Create the Middleware Function**:

    Create a file named `imageClassificationMiddleware.js` and define the middleware   function.

    ```
    const tf = require('@tensorflow/tfjs-node');
      const multer = require('multer');
      const upload = multer({ dest: 'uploads/' });

      async function loadModel() {
        const model = await tf.loadLayersModel('image-classifica-
    tion-model.json');
        return model;
      }

      const modelPromise = loadModel();

      async function imageClassificationMiddleware(req, res, next) {
        try {
          const model = await modelPromise;
          const imagePath = req.file.path;
          const imageBuffer = fs.readFileSync(imagePath);
          const imageTensor = tf.node.decodeImage(imageBuffer);
          const prediction = model.predict(imageTensor);
          const classIndex = prediction.argMax(-1).dataSync()[0];
          req.classification = classIndex;
          next();
        } catch (error) {
          next(error);
        }
    ```

```
        }

        module.exports = { imageClassificationMiddleware, upload };

        image-classification-model.json :-

        {
    "format": "layers-model",
    "modelTopology": {
      "class_name": "Sequential",
      "config": {
        "layers": [
          {
            "class_name": "Conv2D",
            "config": {
              "filters": 32,
              "kernel_size": [3, 3],
              "activation": "relu",
              "input_shape": [28, 28, 1]
            }
          },
          {
            "class_name": "Dense",
            "config": {
              "units": 10,
              "activation": "softmax"
            }
          }
        ]
      }
    },
    "weightsManifest": [
      {
        "paths": ["group1-shard1of2.bin"],
        "weights": [
          {
            "name": "conv2d/kernel",
            "shape": [3, 3, 1, 32],
            "dtype": "float32"
          },
        ]
      },
    ]
}
```

3. **Integrate Middleware into Express.js Application**

   Update the `app.js` file to include the image classification middleware.

   ```
   const express = require('express');
   const bodyParser = require('body-parser');
   const { imageClassificationMiddleware, upload } = require('./
   imageClassificationMiddleware');

   const app = express();
   const port = 3000;

   app.use(bodyParser.json());

   app.post('/classify', upload.single('image'), imageClassifica-
   tionMiddleware, (req, res) => {
     res.json({ classification: req.classification });
   });

   app.use((err, req, res, next) => {
     console.error(err.stack);
     res.status(500).send('Something broke!');
   });

   app.listen(port, () => {
     console.log(`Server is running on port ${port}`);
   });
   ```

4. **Test the Middleware**

   a. Use Postman or any other API testing tool to send a POST request to the `/classify` endpoint with an image file.

   b. The server should respond with the image classification result.

By following these steps, you can develop custom AI middleware in Express.js that integrates AI models into your web applications. This middleware can perform various tasks, such as data preprocessing, decision-making, and response generation, enabling intelligent features and enhancing the overall user experience.

Integrating TensorFlow.js with Express.js

Integrating TensorFlow.js with Express.js allows developers to incorporate machine learning models directly into their web server environment. This integration enables the execution of AI algorithms for tasks such as data preprocessing, decision-making, and response generation, enhancing the capabilities of web applications. This section will guide you through the process of integrating TensorFlow.js with Express.js, including setting up the environment, loading and using machine learning models, and handling requests and responses.

Setting Up the Environment

Let us set up the environment for Express.js.

Prerequisites

Ensure that Node.js and npm (Node Package Manager) are installed on your system. You can download them from the Node.js official website: https://nodejs.org/

Installing TensorFlow.js

Install TensorFlow.js for Node.js using npm.

```
npm install @tensorflow/tfjs-node
```

Installing Express.js

If you have not already, install Express.js using npm.

```
npm install express
```

Loading and Using Machine Learning Models

Let us understand it further with a detailed explanation.

Loading a Pre-Trained Model

TensorFlow.js allows you to load pre-trained models that can be used for inference. Create a file named `model.js` to load and export the model.

```
const tf = require('@tensorflow/tfjs-node');

async function loadModel() {
    const model = await tf.loadLayersModel('file://path/to/model/
model.json');
    return model;
}
```

```
        module.exports = loadModel;

model.json :-

{
  "format": "layers-model",
  "modelTopology": {
    "class_name": "Sequential",
    "config": {
      "layers": [
        {
          "class_name": "Conv2D",
          "config": {
            "filters": 32,
            "kernel_size": [3, 3],
            "activation": "relu",
            "input_shape": [28, 28, 1]
          }
        },
        {
          "class_name": "Dense",
          "config": {
            "units": 10,
            "activation": "softmax"
          }
        }
      ]
    }
  },
  "weightsManifest": [
    {
      "paths": ["group1-shard1of2.bin"],
      "weights": [
        {
          "name": "conv2d/kernel",
          "shape": [3, 3, 1, 32],
          "dtype": "float32"
        },
      ]
    }
  ]
}
```

Using the Model in Middleware

Create a middleware function that uses the loaded model to perform inference. This function will preprocess the input data, run the model, and generate a response based on the model's output.

```
const tf = require('@tensorflow/tfjs-node');
const loadModel = require('./model');


const modelPromise = loadModel();


async function aiMiddleware(req, res, next) {
  try {
    const model = await modelPromise;
    const inputData = req.body.data; // Assuming input data is
sent in the request body
    const inputTensor = tf.tensor(inputData);
    const prediction = model.predict(inputTensor);
    const outputData = prediction.dataSync();
    req.aiResult = outputData;
    next();
  } catch (error) {
    next(error);
  }
}


module.exports = aiMiddleware;
```

Integrating Middleware into Express.js Application

Let us integrate Middleware into Express.js applications with ease.

Setting Up the Server

Create a file named `app.js` to set up the Express.js server and integrate the AI middleware.

```
const express = require('express');
const bodyParser = require('body-parser');
const aiMiddleware = require('./aiMiddleware');
```

```
const app = express();
const port = 3000;

app.use(bodyParser.json());

app.post('/predict', aiMiddleware, (req, res) => {
  res.json({ result: req.aiResult });
});

app.use((err, req, res, next) => {
  console.error(err.stack);
  res.status(500).send('Something broke!');
});

app.listen(port, () => {
  console.log(`Server is running on port ${port}`);
});
```

Testing the Integration

Let us test the integration process in detail.

Using Postman

- Use Postman or any other API testing tool to send a POST request to the `/predict` endpoint with a JSON body containing the input data.

  ```
  {
    "data": [1, 2, 3, 4]
  }
  ```

- The server should respond with the prediction result from the AI model.

  ```
  {
    "result": [0.5, 0.7, 0.2, 0.9]
  }
  ```

Example: Text Classification Middleware

Let us understand the example of Text Classification Middleware with ease.

Installing Additional Dependencies

Install the `body-parser` package for parsing JSON request bodies.

```
npm install body-parser
```

Creating the Middleware Function

Create a file named `textClassificationMiddleware.js` and define the middleware function.

```
const tf = require('@tensorflow/tfjs-node');
const loadModel = require('./model');

const modelPromise = loadModel();

async function textClassificationMiddleware(req, res, next) {
  try {
    const model = await modelPromise;
    const inputText = req.body.text; // Assuming input text is
sent in the request body
    const inputTensor = tf.tensor([inputText]);
    const prediction = model.predict(inputTensor);
    const classIndex = prediction.argMax(-1).dataSync()[0];
    req.classification = classIndex;
    next();
  } catch (error) {
    next(error);
  }
}

module.exports = textClassificationMiddleware;
```

Configuring Middleware in an Express.js Environment

Update the `app.js` file to include the text classification middleware.

```
const express = require('express');
const bodyParser = require('body-parser');
const textClassificationMiddleware = require('./textClassifica-
tionMiddleware');
```

```
const app = express();
const port = 3000;

app.use(bodyParser.json());

app.post('/classify-text', textClassificationMiddleware, (req,
res) => {
    res.json({ classification: req.classification });
});

app.use((err, req, res, next) => {
    console.error(err.stack);
    res.status(500).send('Something broke!');
});

app.listen(port, () => {
    console.log(`Server is running on port ${port}`);
});
```

Testing the Middleware

- Use Postman or any other API testing tool to send a POST request to the `/classify-text` endpoint with a JSON body containing the text to be classified.

```
{
    "text": "This is a sample text for classification."
}
```

- The server should respond with the text classification result.

```
{
    "classification": 1
}
```

By following these steps, you can integrate TensorFlow.js with Express.js to create powerful AI middleware that enhances your web applications with intelligent features. This integration allows you to leverage machine learning models directly within your web server environment, enabling real-time data processing and decision-making.

Data Validation and Sanitization

Data validation and sanitization are critical steps in ensuring the integrity and security of data processed by AI middleware in Express.js applications. Proper validation and sanitization help prevent common security vulnerabilities such as SQL injection, cross-site scripting (XSS), and other forms of data corruption. This section will guide you through the best practices and techniques for validating and sanitizing data in Express.js middleware.

Importance of Data Validation and Sanitization

Let us analyze the importance of Data Validation and Sanitization with ease.

Data Validation

Data Validation ensures that the input data conforms to the expected format, type, and range. It helps in catching errors early and prevents invalid data from being processed by the AI models.

Data Sanitization

Data Sanitization removes or escapes potentially harmful characters from the input data to prevent security vulnerabilities. It ensures that the data is safe to use within the application.

Implementing Data Validation

Let us understand the implementation of Data Validation.

Using Express Validator

Express Validator is a popular library for validating and sanitizing data in Express.js applications. Install it using npm:

```
npm install express-validator
```

Setting Up Validation Middleware

Creates a middleware function that uses Express Validator to validate incoming data.

```
const { body, validationResult } = require('express-validator');

const validateInput = [
   body('email').isEmail().withMessage('Invalid email address'),
   body('age').isInt({ min: 0 }).withMessage('Age must be a
positive integer'),
   (req, res, next) => {
```

```
        const errors = validationResult(req);
        if (!errors.isEmpty()) {
          return res.status(400).json({ errors: errors.array() });
        }
        next();
    }
];

module.exports = validateInput;
```

Integrating Validation Middleware

Use the validation middleware in your Express.js routes to validate incoming data.

```
const express = require('express');
const bodyParser = require('body-parser');
const validateInput = require('./validateInput');

const app = express();
const port = 3000;

app.use(bodyParser.json());

app.post('/submit', validateInput, (req, res) => {
  res.send('Data is valid');
});

app.listen(port, () => {
  console.log(`Server is running on port ${port}`);
});
```

Implementing Data Sanitization

Let us understand the implementation of Data Sanitization with ease.

Using Express Validator for Sanitization

Express Validator also provides sanitization functions to clean the input data.

```
const { body, sanitizeBody } = require('express-validator');

const sanitizeInput = [
  body('username').trim().escape(),
```

```
    body('email').normalizeEmail(),
    (req, res, next) => {
      next();
    }
];


module.exports = sanitizeInput;
```

Integrating Sanitization Middleware

Use the sanitization middleware in your Express.js routes to sanitize incoming data.

```
const express = require('express');
const bodyParser = require('body-parser');
const sanitizeInput = require('./sanitizeInput');

const app = express();
const port = 3000;

app.use(bodyParser.json());

app.post('/register', sanitizeInput, (req, res) => {
  res.send('Data is sanitized');
});

app.listen(port, () => {
  console.log(`Server is running on port ${port}`);
});
```

By implementing data validation and sanitization, you can ensure that the data processed by your AI middleware is both valid and secure, reducing the risk of errors and vulnerabilities in your application.

Optimizing Middleware Performance

Optimizing the performance of middleware in Express.js is crucial for ensuring that your web application remains responsive and efficient, especially when integrating AI functionalities that may involve computationally intensive tasks. This section will cover best practices and techniques for optimizing middleware performance in Express.js applications.

Best Practices for Middleware Performance

Let us see the different best practices for Middleware Performance.

Minimize Synchronous Operations

Avoid blocking the event loop with synchronous operations. Use asynchronous functions and promises to handle tasks that may take time to complete.

```
const express = require('express');
const app = express();
const port = 3000;

app.use(async (req, res, next) => {
  try {
    const result = await someAsyncFunction();
    req.result = result;
    next();
  } catch (error) {
    next(error);
  }
});

app.listen(port, () => {
  console.log(`Server is running on port ${port}`);
});
```

Use Caching

Implement caching to store the results of expensive operations and reuse them for subsequent requests. This can significantly reduce the load on your server and improve response times.

```
const cache = new Map();

app.use((req, res, next) => {
  const key = req.url;
  if (cache.has(key)) {
    return res.json(cache.get(key));
  }
  res.sendResponse = res.json;
  res.json = (body) => {
    cache.set(key, body);
    res.sendResponse(body);
  };
  next();
});
```

Optimize AI Model Loading

Load AI models once during server startup and reuse the loaded models for subsequent requests. This avoids the overhead of loading models for each request.

```
const tf = require('@tensorflow/tfjs-node');
const express = require('express');
const bodyParser = require('body-parser');

const app = express();
const port = 3000;

let model;

async function loadModel() {
  model = await tf.loadLayersModel('file://path/to/model/model.
json');
}

loadModel();

app.use(bodyParser.json());

app.post('/predict', async (req, res) => {
  const inputData = req.body.data;
  const inputTensor = tf.tensor(inputData);
  const prediction = model.predict(inputTensor);
  const outputData = prediction.dataSync();
  res.json({ result: outputData });
});

app.listen(port, () => {
  console.log(`Server is running on port ${port}`);
});
```

Use Efficient Data Structures

Choose appropriate data structures for storing and processing data. For example, use arrays for sequential data and objects or maps for key-value pairs.

Limit Middleware Scope

Apply middleware only to the routes that need it. This reduces the overhead of running middleware functions for every request.

```
app.use('/api', apiMiddleware);
app.use('/admin', adminMiddleware);
```

Profile and Monitor Performance

Use profiling and monitoring tools to identify performance bottlenecks and optimize them. Tools like `pm2`, `New Relic`, *and* `AppDynamics` can help monitor the performance of your Express.js application.

Optimize Database Queries

Ensure that database queries are optimized and use indexes where appropriate. Avoid N+1 query problems by using joins or batch queries.

Implement Rate Limiting

Use rate limiting to prevent abuse and ensure fair usage of your API. This can help protect your server from being overwhelmed by too many requests.

```
const rateLimit = require('express-rate-limit');

const limiter = rateLimit({
  windowMs: 15 * 60 * 1000, // 15 minutes
  max: 100, // limit each IP to 100 requests per windowMs
});

app.use(limiter);
```

By following these best practices and techniques, you can optimize the performance of your middleware in Express.js, ensuring that your web application remains responsive and efficient even when integrating computationally intensive AI functionalities.

Conclusion

This chapter provided a comprehensive guide to integrating AI functionalities into web applications using Express.js. By leveraging the power of middleware, developers can create robust and intelligent web applications that efficiently bridge the gap between the frontend and AI algorithms running on the server side. The chapter covered essential concepts such as setting up an Express.js server, developing custom AI middleware, and integrating TensorFlow.js for executing machine learning models directly within the web server environment.

Readers learned how to create custom middleware functions for tasks such as user authentication, data validation, and error handling, which are crucial for AI-driven applications. The chapter also emphasized the importance of data validation and sanitization to ensure data integrity and security. Additionally, it provided the best practices for optimizing middleware performance, ensuring that web applications remain responsive and efficient even when handling computationally intensive AI tasks. By the end of this chapter, readers will be equipped with the knowledge and skills to construct and deploy AI middleware within their Express.js applications, enhancing their web applications with intelligent features.

The next chapter explores the fascinating world of conversational AI within the MERN ecosystem, focusing on the development of intelligent chatbots that can simulate human-like interactions.

Multiple Choice Questions

1. What is the primary role of middleware in Express.js applications?

    a. To handle database operations

    b. To manage frontend rendering

    c. To intercept and manipulate requests and responses

    d. To perform client-side validation

2. Which package is commonly used for integrating machine learning models in Express.js applications?

    a. React

    b. Mongoose

    c. TensorFlow.js

    d. Axios

3. What is the purpose of the `next` function in Express.js middleware?

    a. To terminate the request-response cycle

    b. To pass control to the next middleware function

    c. To send a response to the client

    d. To handle database queries

4. Which of the following is the best practice for optimizing middleware performance?

    a. Using synchronous operations

    b. Avoiding the use of caching

    c. Loading AI models for each request

    d. Implementing rate limiting

5. What is the primary benefit of using data validation in AI middleware?

    a. To improve frontend performance

    b. To ensure data conforms to expected formats and types

    c. To enhance database indexing

    d. To manage user sessions

6. Which middleware function is used to handle errors in Express.js applications?

    a. Application-level middleware

    b. Router-level middleware

    c. Error-handling middleware

    d. Built-in middleware

7. What is the purpose of data sanitization in AI middleware?

    a. To improve model accuracy

    b. To remove or escape potentially harmful characters

    c. To enhance user authentication

    d. To manage API requests

8. Which tool is recommended for testing API endpoints that utilize AI middleware?

    a. MongoDB Compass

    b. Postman

    c. Visual Studio Code

    d. GitHub

9. What is the benefit of loading AI models once during server startup?

    a. To reduce server memory usage

    b. To avoid the overhead of loading models for each request

    c. To improve frontend rendering speed

    d. To enhance database performance

10. Which of the following is a common use case for custom AI middleware in Express.js?

   a. Static file serving

   b. User authentication

   c. Image classification

   d. Database indexing

Answers

   1. c

   2. c

   3. b

   4. d

   5. b

   6. c

   7. b

   8. b

   9. b

   10. c

CHAPTER 8

Crafting AI-Powered Chatbots

Introduction

Crafting AI-Powered Chatbots explores the fascinating world of conversational AI within the MERN ecosystem, focusing on the development of intelligent chatbots that can simulate human-like interactions. This chapter guides readers through the entire process of building a chatbot, from understanding the basics of natural language processing (NLP) and machine learning to deploying a fully functional chatbot integrated with a MERN application.

The chapter introduces key concepts in chatbot development, including intent recognition, entity extraction, and conversation flow management. It delves into the use of Dialogflow and Microsoft Bot Framework as powerful tools for creating sophisticated chatbot experiences, highlighting their capabilities in processing and understanding user inputs. Additionally, the chapter covers the integration of these chatbots into web applications built with MongoDB, Express.js, React, and Node.js, ensuring a seamless user experience.

Readers will learn how to leverage Node.js for backend chatbot logic, React for creating interactive chat interfaces, and MongoDB for storing conversation logs and user data. By the end of this chapter, readers will be equipped with the knowledge to design, build, and deploy AI-powered chatbots that enhance user engagement and provide immediate, intelligent responses to user queries.

Structure

In this chapter, we will cover the following topics:

- Introduction to Conversational AI
- Designing a Chatbot
- Chatbot Development Platforms

- Integrating NLP with Chatbots
- Building the Chatbot Backend with Node.js
- Frontend Chat Interface with React
- Storing Conversations with MongoDB

Introduction to Conversational AI

Conversational Artificial Intelligence (AI) refers to technologies that enable computers to interact with humans using natural language. These technologies include chatbots, virtual assistants, and conversational agents, which are designed to simulate human conversation, respond to user queries, perform actions, and engage in complex dialogs.

Figure 8.1: *Introduction to Conversational AI*

Conversational AI leverages natural language processing (NLP) and machine learning (ML) to understand, process, and generate human language, making interactions with machines more intuitive and human-like.

Key Components of Conversational AI:

Let's understand the key components of Conversational AI.

Component	Description
Automatic Speech Recognition (ASR)	Converts spoken language into text, enabling voice-based interactions.
Natural Language Understanding (NLU)	Interprets and understands the meaning of the text input, identifying intents and extracting relevant entities.
Dialogue Management (DM)	Manages the flow of the conversation, keeping track of the context and determining the appropriate response.
Natural Language Generation (NLG)	Generates human-like text responses based on the processed input and the conversation context.
Text-to-Speech (TTS)	Converts text responses back into speech, enabling voice responses.

Figure 8.2: *Different key components of Conversational AI*

Conversational AI systems are commonly used in customer support, virtual assistants, and various enterprise applications to automate routine tasks, provide instant assistance, and enhance user engagement. By continuously learning from interactions, these systems improve over time, providing more accurate and relevant responses. The integration of conversational AI into web applications, particularly within the MERN (MongoDB, Express.js, React, Node.js) stack, allows for the creation of intelligent chatbots that can handle a wide range of user queries and provide a seamless user experience.

Designing a Chatbot

Designing a chatbot involves several key steps that ensure the chatbot can effectively understand and respond to user inputs, providing a seamless and engaging user experience. This section will guide you through the essential components and considerations for designing a chatbot, including defining the chatbot's purpose, understanding user needs, creating conversation flows, and selecting the appropriate technologies and tools.

Defining the Chatbot's Purpose

The first step in designing a chatbot is to define its purpose clearly. This involves understanding the specific tasks the chatbot will perform and the problems it will solve for users. Common purposes for chatbots include customer support, information retrieval, booking services, and entertainment. Defining the chatbot's purpose helps to set clear goals and objectives for its development.

Example:

- **Customer Support Chatbot**: A chatbot designed to assist customers with common queries, troubleshoot issues, and provide information about products and services.

Understanding User Needs

To design an effective chatbot, it is crucial to understand the needs and expectations of the target users. This involves researching the common questions and issues users face, as well as the language and terminology they use. User personas and journey maps can be helpful tools in this process, providing insights into user behavior and preferences.

Example:

- **User Persona**: A detailed profile of a typical user, including their demographics, goals, and pain points.
- **User Journey Map**: A visual representation of the steps a user takes to achieve a specific goal, highlighting their interactions with the chatbot.

Creating Conversation Flows

Conversation flows define the structure and logic of the interactions between the chatbot and users. These flows outline the possible paths a conversation can take, including the questions the chatbot will ask, the responses it will provide, and how it will handle different user inputs. Designing conversation flows involves creating decision trees or flowcharts that map out the dialog.

Example:

- **Greeting Flow**: The chatbot greets the user and asks how it can assist them.

    User Input: *"I need help with my order."*

    Chatbot Response: *"Sure, can you please provide your order number?"*

- **Order Status Flow**: The chatbot retrieves the order status based on the provided order number.

    User Input: "12345"

    Chatbot Response: *"Your order is currently being processed and will be shipped soon."*

Selecting Technologies and Tools

Choosing the right technologies and tools is essential for building a functional and efficient chatbot. Several platforms and frameworks are available for chatbot development, each offering different features and capabilities. Two popular options are Dialogflow and Microsoft Bot Framework.

- **Dialogflow:**

  A natural language understanding platform by Google that allows developers to design and integrate conversational user interfaces into applications. Dialogflow supports intent recognition, entity extraction, and context management.

- **Microsoft Bot Framework:**

  A comprehensive framework by Microsoft for building, testing, and deploying chatbots. It provides tools for creating conversational AI experiences, including support for multiple channels and integration with Azure Cognitive Services.

Designing the User Interface

The chatbot user interface (UI) plays a crucial role in the overall user experience. The UI should be intuitive, visually appealing, and easy to navigate. For web applications, React can be used to create interactive chat interfaces that seamlessly integrate with the backend chatbot logic.

Example:

Chat Interface with React: A React component that renders the chat window, handles user inputs, and displays chatbot responses.

```
import React, { useState } from 'react';

function ChatInterface() {
  const [messages, setMessages] = useState([]);
  const [input, setInput] = useState('');

  const sendMessage = async () => {
    const response = await fetch('/api/chat', {
      method: 'POST',
      headers: { 'Content-Type': 'application/json' },
      body: JSON.stringify({ message: input }),
    });
    const data = await response.json();
    setMessages([...messages, { user: input, bot: data.response
}]);
    setInput('');
  };

  return (
```

```
<div className="chat-interface">
  <div className="messages">
    {messages.map((msg, index) => (
      <div key={index}>
        <p><strong>You:</strong> {msg.user}</p>
        <p><strong>Bot:</strong> {msg.bot}</p>
      </div>
    ))}
  </div>
  <input
    type="text"
    value={input}
    onChange={(e) => setInput(e.target.value)}
    onKeyPress={(e) => e.key === 'Enter' && sendMessage()}
  />
  <button onClick={sendMessage}>Send</button>
</div>
);
}

export default ChatInterface;
```

Chatbot Development Platforms

When it comes to building AI-powered chatbots, selecting the right development platform is crucial. Chatbot development platforms provide the tools and frameworks necessary to create, train, and deploy chatbots that can understand and respond to user inputs effectively. This section will explore some of the most popular chatbot development platforms, including Dialogflow and Microsoft Bot Framework, highlighting their features and capabilities.

Figure 8.3: *Chatbot Development Platforms*

Dialogflow

Dialogflow, developed by Google, is a natural language understanding platform that allows developers to design and integrate conversational user interfaces into applications. It supports voice and text-based interactions and can be integrated with various messaging platforms, including Google Assistant, Facebook Messenger, and Slack.

Figure 8.4: *Dialogflow (Source: https://zweck.io/wp-content/uploads/2021/01/ivrpowers-post-04.024.jpeg)*

Key Features:

Let's understand the key features of Dialogflow.

Feature	Description
Intent Recognition	Identifies the intent behind user inputs, allowing the chatbot to understand what the user wants to achieve.
Entity Extraction	Extracts relevant entities from user inputs, such as dates, times, locations, and custom entities defined by the developer.
Context Management	Supports context management, enabling the chatbot to maintain the state of the conversation and handle multi-turn dialogues.
Pre-built Agents	Offers pre-built agents for common use cases, such as customer support and booking services, which can be customized to fit specific needs.
Integration with Google Cloud	Integrates seamlessly with Google Cloud services, providing scalability, security, and advanced analytics.

Figure 8.5: *Key features of Dialogflow*

Example Use Case:

Customer Support Chatbot: A chatbot built with Dialogflow can handle customer queries, provide information about products and services, and escalate complex issues to human agents.

Getting Started:

1. **Create a Dialogflow Agent**: Sign in to the Dialogflow console and create a new agent.

2. **Define Intents**: Create intents to represent the different actions the chatbot can perform. For example, an intent to check order status.

3. **Train the Agent**: Provide training phrases for each intent to help Dialogflow understand various ways users might express the same intent.

4. **Integrate with Your Application**: Use the Dialogflow API to integrate the chatbot with your web application or messaging platform.

Microsoft Bot Framework

The Microsoft Bot Framework is a comprehensive framework for building, testing, and deploying chatbots. It provides tools and services for creating conversational AI experiences and supports integration with multiple channels, including Microsoft Teams, Skype, and Slack.

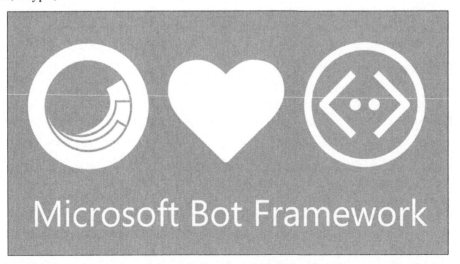

Figure 8.6: *Microsoft Bot Framework (Source: https://devsuhas.com/wp-content/uploads/2019/12/23_introtoazurebotframework.png)*

Key Features:

Let's understand the key features of Microsoft Bot Framework.

Feature	Description
Bot Builder SDK	Provides libraries and tools for building chatbots in various programming languages, including Node.js, C#, and Python.
Azure Bot Service	Offers a managed environment for deploying and scaling chatbots, with built-in support for continuous deployment and monitoring.
LUIS Integration	Integrates with Language Understanding (LUIS), a service for building natural language models that can understand user intents and extract entities.
Adaptive Cards	Supports Adaptive Cards, a framework for creating rich, interactive UI elements that can be displayed in chat interfaces.
Multi-channel Support	Allows developers to build chatbots that can be deployed across multiple channels, ensuring a consistent user experience.

Figure 8.7: Key features of Microsoft Bot Framework

Example Use Case:

Virtual Assistant: A virtual assistant built with the Microsoft Bot Framework can help users schedule appointments, set reminders, and provide personalized recommendations.

Getting Started:

1. **Create a Bot in Azure**: Sign in to the Azure portal and create a new bot using the Azure Bot Service.

2. **Develop the Bot**: Use the Bot Builder SDK to develop the bot's logic and handle user interactions.

3. **Integrate LUIS**: Create a LUIS app to define intents and entities and integrate it with your bot to enable natural language understanding.

4. **Deploy and Test**: Deploy the bot to Azure and use the Bot Framework Emulator to test its functionality.

Other Notable Chatbot Development Platforms

Let's analyze a few other notable chatbot development platforms.

Botpress

Botpress is an open-source platform for building, deploying, and managing chatbots. It offers a visual flow editor, natural language understanding, and integration with various messaging platforms.

Rasa

Rasa is an open-source framework for building conversational AI. It provides tools for training custom NLU models, managing dialog, and deploying chatbots on-premises or in the cloud.

IBM Watson Assistant

IBM Watson Assistant is a cloud-based service for building chatbots and virtual assistants. It offers advanced natural language understanding, context management, and integration with IBM Cloud services.

Amazon Lex

Amazon Lex is a service for building conversational interfaces using voice and text. It integrates with AWS services, providing scalability, security, and advanced analytics.

By selecting the right chatbot development platform, developers can leverage powerful tools and features to create sophisticated chatbots that enhance user engagement and provide intelligent responses to user queries. The next sections will delve deeper into integrating NLP with chatbots, building the chatbot backend with Node.js, creating the frontend chat interface with React, and storing conversations with MongoDB.

Integrating NLP with Chatbots

Natural Language Processing (NLP) is a critical component in the development of intelligent chatbots. NLP enables chatbots to understand, interpret, and respond to human language in a way that is both meaningful and contextually relevant. By integrating NLP with chatbots, developers can create conversational agents that can handle a wide range of user queries, provide accurate responses, and engage in natural, human-like interactions. This section will explore the key aspects of integrating NLP with chatbots, including intent recognition, entity extraction, and conversation flow management.

Figure 8.8*: Integrating NLP with Chatbots (Source: https://appinventiv.com/wp-content/up-loads/2021/08/chatbot-development-using-nlp.png)*

Key Components of NLP in Chatbots

Let's understand the key components of NLP in Chatbots.

Intent Recognition

Intent recognition is the process of identifying the user's intention behind their input. It involves classifying the input into predefined categories, such as booking a flight, checking the weather, or finding a restaurant. Intent recognition is crucial for understanding what the user wants to achieve and providing the appropriate response.

```
const intents = {
    "book_flight": ["I want to book a flight", "Can you help me
book a flight?", "Flight booking"],
    "check_weather": ["What's the weather like?", "Weather fore-
cast", "Is it going to rain today?"]
  };

  function recognizeIntent(input) {
    for (const [intent, phrases] of Object.entries(intents)) {
      if (phrases.some(phrase => input.includes(phrase))) {
        return intent;
      }
    }
    return "unknown";
  }
```

```
const userInput = "Can you help me book a flight?";
const intent = recognizeIntent(userInput);
console.log(`Recognized intent: ${intent}`);
```

Entity Extraction

Entity extraction involves identifying and extracting specific pieces of information from the user's input, such as dates, times, locations, and names. Entities provide additional context that helps the chatbot understand the details of the user's request.

```
const nlp = require('compromise');

function extractEntities(input) {
  const doc = nlp(input);
  const dates = doc.dates().out('array');
  const locations = doc.places().out('array');
  return { dates, locations };
}

const userInput = "I want to book a flight to New York on July
20th";
const entities = extractEntities(userInput);
console.log(`Extracted entities: ${JSON.stringify(entities)}`);
```

Conversation Flow Management

Conversation flow management ensures that the chatbot can handle multi-turn dialogs, maintain context, and provide coherent responses. This involves managing the state of the conversation and keeping track of previous interactions.

```
const conversationState = {};

function handleUserInput(userId, input) {
  if (!conversationState[userId]) {
    conversationState[userId] = { step: 1 };
  }

  const state = conversationState[userId];
  let response;

  switch (state.step) {
    case 1:
      response = "Where would you like to fly to?";
      state.step = 2;
      break;
    case 2:
      state.destination = input;
      response = "When would you like to fly?";
```

```
            state.step = 3;
            break;
        case 3:
            state.date = input;
            response = `Booking flight to ${state.destination} on
    ${state.date}. Is that correct?`;
            state.step = 4;
            break;
        case 4:
            if (input.toLowerCase() === "yes") {
                response = "Your flight has been booked!";
                delete conversationState[userId];
            } else {
                response = "Let's start over. Where would you like to
    fly to?";
                state.step = 2;
            }
            break;
        default:
            response = "I'm not sure how to help with that.";
    }

    return response;
}

const userId = "user123";
console.log(handleUserInput(userId, "I want to book a flight"));
console.log(handleUserInput(userId, "New York"));
console.log(handleUserInput(userId, "July 20th"));
console.log(handleUserInput(userId, "Yes"));
```

Integrating NLP Libraries and Tools

Let's integrate NLP Libraries and other tools with ease.

Using Dialogflow

Dialogflow is a powerful NLP platform by Google that provides tools for building conversational interfaces. It supports intent recognition, entity extraction, and context management. Developers can create agents, define intents, and train models using the Dialogflow console.

```
const dialogflow = require('@google-cloud/dialogflow');
const sessionClient = new dialogflow.SessionsClient();

async function detectIntent(projectId, sessionId, query,
languageCode) {
```

```
    const sessionPath = sessionClient.projectAgentSession-
Path(projectId, sessionId);
    const request = {
      session: sessionPath,
      queryInput: {
        text: {
          text: query,
          languageCode: languageCode,
        },
      },
    };

    const responses = await sessionClient.detectIntent(request);
    const result = responses[0].queryResult;
    console.log(`Detected intent: ${result.intent.displayName}`);
    console.log(`Fulfillment text: ${result.fulfillmentText}`);
  }

  detectIntent('your-project-id', '123456', 'I want to book a
flight', 'en');
```

Using Microsoft Bot Framework and LUIS

The Microsoft Bot Framework, combined with Language Understanding (LUIS), provides a comprehensive solution for building and deploying chatbots. LUIS allows developers to create custom language models that can recognize intents and extract entities.

```
  const { LuisRecognizer } = require('botbuilder-ai');

  const luisApplication = {
    applicationId: 'your-luis-app-id',
    endpointKey: 'your-luis-endpoint-key',
    endpoint: 'https://your-luis-endpoint',
  };

  const recognizer = new LuisRecognizer(luisApplication);

  async function recognizeIntent(input) {
    const recognizerResult = await recognizer.recognize({ text:
input });
    const intent = LuisRecognizer.topIntent(recognizerResult);
    console.log(`Recognized intent: ${intent}`);
  }

  recognizeIntent('I want to book a flight');
```

Benefits of Integrating NLP with Chatbots

Let's check the benefits of integrating NLP with Chatbots.

Improved User Experience

NLP enables chatbots to understand and respond to user inputs in a natural and human-like manner, providing a more engaging and satisfying user experience.

Enhanced Accuracy

By leveraging advanced NLP techniques, chatbots can accurately recognize user intents and extract relevant entities, ensuring that responses are contextually appropriate and relevant.

Scalability

NLP-powered chatbots can handle a large volume of user queries simultaneously, making them ideal for customer support and other applications where scalability is essential.

Continuous Learning

NLP models can be continuously trained and improved based on user interactions, allowing chatbots to become more accurate and effective over time.

Building the Chatbot Backend with Node.js

Node.js is an excellent choice for building the backend of an AI-powered chatbot due to its non-blocking I/O model, which allows for handling multiple concurrent requests efficiently. This section will guide you through the process of creating a robust backend for your chatbot using Node.js and Express.js.

Figure 8.9: *Building the Chatbot Backend with Node.js (Source: https://appinventiv.com/ wp-content/uploads/2021/08/chatbot-development-using-nlp.png)*

Setting Up the Project

First, let's set up a new Node.js project:

1. Create a new directory for your project:

    ```
    mkdir chatbot-backend
    cd chatbot-backend
    ```

2. Initialize a new Node.js project:

    ```
    npm init -y
    ```

3. Install necessary dependencies:

    ```
    npm install express body-parser dotenv axios
    ```

    Please note, if you are using a higher version of Node.js, that is, 20.6.0 or above, you need not to install the "dotenv" dependencies.

Creating the Server

Create a new file called `server.js` and set up a basic Express server:

```
const express = require('express');
const bodyParser = require('body-parser');
require('dotenv').config();

const app = express();
const port = process.env.PORT || 3000;
```

```
app.use(bodyParser.json());

app.listen(port, () => {
  console.log(`Server running on port ${port}`);
});
```

Integrating with a Natural Language Processing Service

For this example, we'll use Dialogflow as our NLP service. First, install the Dialogflow library:

```
npm install dialogflow
```

Now, let's create a function to process messages using Dialogflow:

```
const dialogflow = require('dialogflow');

async function processMessage(message) {
  const sessionClient = new dialogflow.SessionsClient();
  const sessionPath = sessionClient.sessionPath(process.env.DIA-
LOGFLOW_PROJECT_ID, 'unique-session-id');

  const request = {
    session: sessionPath,
    queryInput: {
      text: {
        text: message,
        languageCode: 'en-US',
      },
    },
  };

  const responses = await sessionClient.detectIntent(request);
  return responses[0].queryResult;
}
```

Creating API Endpoints

Now, let's create API endpoints for our chatbot:

```
app.post('/api/message', async (req, res) => {
  try {
    const { message } = req.body;
    const result = await processMessage(message);
    res.json({
```

```
      intent: result.intent.displayName,
      response: result.fulfillmentText,
    });
  } catch (error) {
    console.error('Error processing message:', error);
    res.status(500).json({ error: 'An error occurred while
processing the message' });
  }
});
```

Implementing Conversation Flow Management

To manage conversation flow, we can use a simple state machine. First, install the JavaScript State Machine library:

```
npm install javascript-state-machine
```

Now, let's implement a basic conversation flow:

```
const StateMachine = require('javascript-state-machine');

const conversationFlow = new StateMachine({
  init: 'greeting',
  transitions: [
    { name: 'askName', from: 'greeting', to: 'awaitingName' },
    { name: 'askQuestion', from: 'awaitingName', to: 'awaitingQ-
uestion' },
    { name: 'provideAnswer', from: 'awaitingQuestion', to:
'greeting' },
  ],
  methods: {
    onAskName: () => 'What is your name?',
    onAskQuestion: () => 'How can I help you today?',
    onProvideAnswer: (lifecycle, answer) => `Here's what I found:
${answer}`,
  },
});

app.post('/api/conversation', async (req, res) => {
  const { message, state } = req.body;

  conversationFlow.state = state;
  let response;

  switch (conversationFlow.state) {
    case 'greeting':
```

```
        conversationFlow.askName();
        response = conversationFlow.onAskName();
        break;
    case 'awaitingName':
        conversationFlow.askQuestion();
        response = conversationFlow.onAskQuestion();
        break;
    case 'awaitingQuestion':
        const answer = await processMessage(message);
        conversationFlow.provideAnswer();
        response = conversationFlow.onProvideAnswer(null, answer.
fulfillmentText);
        break;
    }

    res.json({
      response,
      newState: conversationFlow.state,
    });
});
```

Error Handling and Logging

Implement error handling and logging to ensure your chatbot backend is robust and maintainable:

```
const winston = require('winston');

const logger = winston.createLogger({
  level: 'info',
  format: winston.format.json(),
  transports: [
    new winston.transports.File({ filename: 'error.log', level:
'error' }),
    new winston.transports.File({ filename: 'combined.log' }),
  ],
});

app.use((err, req, res, next) => {
  logger.error(err.stack);
  res.status(500).send('Something broke!');
});
```

Testing the Backend

To test your chatbot backend, you can use tools like Postman or create a simple HTML page with JavaScript to send requests to your API endpoints.

Step-by-Step Procedure to Test Chatbot Backend with Postman

Let's understand the step-by-step procedure to test the chatbot backend with Postman.

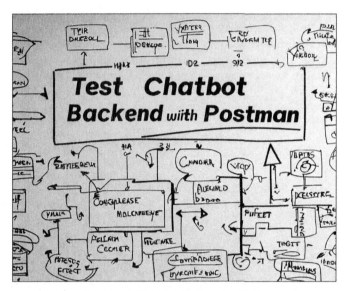

Figure 8.10: *Test Chatbot Backend with Postman*

Step 1: Install Postman

> **Download and Install**: If you haven't already, download and install Postman from the official website - https://www.postman.com/downloads/.

Step 2: Open Postman

> **Launch Postman**: Open the Postman application on your computer.

Step 3: Create a New Request

    a. **New Request**: Click the **"New"** button in the top left corner and select **"Request"**.

    b. **Name Your Request**: Give your request a name, such as **"Chatbot Message Test"**, and save it to a new or existing collection.

Step 4: Set Up the Request

    a. **HTTP Method**: Select the HTTP method as `POST` from the dropdown menu.

    b. **URL**: Enter the URL for your chatbot's API endpoint. For example, if your server is running locally on port 3000, the URL might be `http://localhost:3000/api/message`.

Step 5: Configure the Request Body

a. **Body Tab**: Click the **"Body"** tab below the URL field.

b. **Raw and JSON**: Select the **"raw"** radio button and then choose **"JSON"** from the dropdown menu on the right.

c. **JSON Payload**: Enter the JSON payload for the request body. For example:

```
{
    "userId": "user123",
    "message": "I want to book a flight"
}
```

Step 6: Send the Request

Send Button: Click the **"Send"** button to send the request to your chatbot backend.

Step 7: Review the Response

a. **Response Section**: After sending the request, review the response from the server in the lower section of Postman.

b. **Status Code**: Check the status code to ensure it is `200 OK`, indicating a successful request.

c. **Response Body**: Review the response body to see the chatbot's reply. For example:

```
{
    "intent": "book_flight",
    "response": "Sure, can you please provide your flight de-
tails?"
}
```

Step 8: Test Different Scenarios

a. **Modify Payload**: Change the message in the JSON payload to test different scenarios and intents.

b. **Send Requests**: Send multiple requests to ensure your chatbot backend handles various inputs correctly.

Step 9: Save Your Requests

Save Requests: Save your requests in a collection for future testing and reference.

Example: Testing a Conversation Flow

Let's test a conversation flow for our better understanding.

1. **Initial Request**:

    a. **Payload**:

    ```
    {
        "userId": "user123",
        "message": "I want to book a flight"
    }
    ```

    b. **Expected Response**:

    ```
    {
        "intent": "book_flight",
        "response": "Sure, can you please provide your flight
    details?"
    }
    ```

2. **Follow-up Request**:

    a. **Payload**:

    ```
    {
        "userId": "user123",
        "message": "New York on July 20th"
    }
    ```

    b. **Expected Response**:

    ```
    {
        "intent": "provide_flight_details",
        "response": "Booking flight to New York on July 20th. Is
    that correct?"
    }
    ```

3. **Confirmation Request**:

    a. **Payload**:

    ```
    {
        "userId": "user123",
        "message": "Yes"
    }
    ```

    b. **Expected Response**:

    ```
    {
        "intent": "confirm_booking",
        "response": "Your flight has been booked!"
    }
    ```

By following these steps, you can thoroughly test your chatbot backend using Postman, ensuring that it handles various user inputs and conversation flows correctly.

Frontend Chat Interface with React

Creating an interactive and user-friendly chat interface is crucial for enhancing the user experience of your AI-powered chatbot. React.js, with its component-based architecture and efficient rendering, is an excellent choice for building such interfaces. This section will guide you through the process of developing a frontend chat interface using React.js.

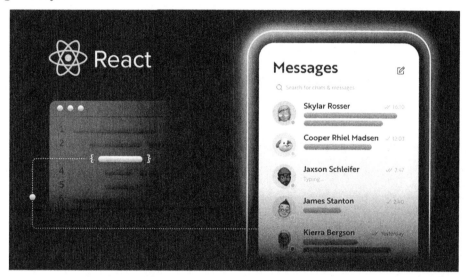

Figure 8.11: *Frontend Chat Interface with React (Source: https://media.dev.to/cdn-cgi/image/ width=1280,height=720,fit=cover,gravity=auto,format=auto/https%3A%2F%2Fdev-to-uploads. s3.amazonaws.com%2Fuploads%2Farticles%2F8ylxpg8dsaos9a1flawq.png)*

Setting Up the React Project

1. **Create a New React Application**:

   Use the **Create React App** tool to set up a new React project.

   ```
   npx create-react-app chatbot-frontend
   cd chatbot-frontend
   ```

2. **Install Necessary Dependencies**:

   Install any additional dependencies you might need, such as Axios for making HTTP requests.

   ```
   npm install axios
   ```

Building the Chat Interface

Let's build the chat interface with ease.

1. **Create the Chat Component:**

   Create a new file named `Chat.js` in the `src` directory and define the chat component.

```
import React, { useState } from 'react';
import axios from 'axios';

function Chat() {
  const [messages, setMessages] = useState([]);
  const [input, setInput] = useState('');

  const sendMessage = async () => {
    const userMessage = { text: input, sender: 'user' };
    setMessages([...messages, userMessage]);

    const response = await axios.post('/api/message', { mes-
sage: input });
    const botMessage = { text: response.data.response, sender:
'bot' };
    setMessages([...messages, userMessage, botMessage]);

    setInput('');
  };

  return (
    <div className="chat-container">
      <div className="messages">
        {messages.map((msg, index) => (
          <div key={index} className={`message ${msg.send-
er}`}>
            {msg.text}
          </div>
        ))}
      </div>
      <input
        type="text"
        value={input}
        onChange={(e) => setInput(e.target.value)}
        onKeyPress={(e) => e.key === 'Enter' && sendMessage()}
      />
      <button onClick={sendMessage}>Send</button>
    </div>
```

```
    );
  }

  export default Chat;
```

2. **Styling the Chat Interface**:

   Add some basic styles to make the chat interface look clean and user-friendly. Create a `Chat.css` file and import it into your `Chat.js` component.

```css
.chat-container {
    display: flex;
    flex-direction: column;
    height: 100vh;
    width: 400px;
    margin: auto;
    border: 1px solid #ccc;
    border-radius: 8px;
    overflow: hidden;
}

.messages {
    flex: 1;
    padding: 10px;
    overflow-y: auto;
}

.message {
    padding: 10px;
    margin: 5px 0;
    border-radius: 4px;
}

.message.user {
    background-color: #e1ffc7;
    align-self: flex-end;
}

.message.bot {
    background-color: #f1f1f1;
    align-self: flex-start;
}

input {
    padding: 10px;
    border: none;
    border-top: 1px solid #ccc;
    width: calc(100% - 20px);
```

```
    margin: 0 10px;
}

button {
    padding: 10px;
    border: none;
    background-color: #007bff;
    color: white;
    cursor: pointer;
}
```

3. **Integrate the Chat Component into the App**:

   Update the `App.js` file to include the `Chat` component.

```
import React from 'react';
import Chat from './Chat';
import './Chat.css';

function App() {
  return (
    <div className="App">
      <Chat />
    </div>
  );
}

export default App;
```

4. **Running the React Application**:

   a. Start the React development server.

```
npm start
```

   b. Open your browser and navigate to `http://localhost:3000` to see the chat interface in action.

Enhancing the Chat Interface

Let's see how we can enhance the chat interface easily.

- **Adding User Authentication**

  Implement user authentication to personalize the chat experience. You can use Firebase or any other authentication service to manage user accounts.

- **Handling Conversation Context**

  Maintain the context of the conversation to provide more relevant responses.

This can be done by storing the conversation state in the component's state or using a global state management library like Redux.

- **Implementing Real-Time Communication**

  Use WebSockets or libraries like Socket.io to enable real-time communication between the frontend and backend, providing a more responsive chat experience.

- **Adding Rich Media Support**

  Enhance the chat interface by supporting rich media, such as images, videos, and interactive elements like buttons and quick replies.

  By following these steps, you can create a robust and interactive chat interface using React.js that seamlessly integrates with your AI-powered chatbot backend.

Storing Conversations with MongoDB

Storing conversation logs and user data is essential for improving the chatbot's performance, analyzing user interactions, and maintaining context across sessions. MongoDB, with its flexible document model, is an excellent choice for storing this data. This section will guide you through the process of setting up MongoDB to store conversations and integrating it with your Node.js backend.

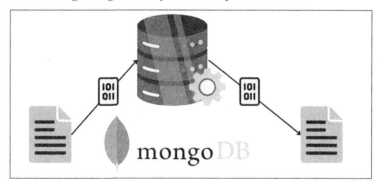

Figure 8.12: *Storing Conversations with MongoDB (Source: https://codingkakida.com/wp-content/uploads/2024/04/Storing-and-Downloading-Images-and-Videos-in-MongoDB.jpg)*

Setting Up MongoDB

Let's set up MongoDB easily.

1. **Install MongoDB**

   If you haven't already, install MongoDB on your local machine or use MongoDB Atlas for a cloud-based solution.

2. **Install Mongoose**

    Mongoose is an Object Data Modeling (ODM) library for MongoDB and Node. js. Install it using npm:

    ```
    npm install mongoose
    ```

Creating Conversation Schemas

Let's create conversation schemas easily.

Define the Conversation Schema

Create a new file named `models/Conversation.js` and define the schema for storing conversations.

```
const mongoose = require('mongoose');

const messageSchema = new mongoose.Schema({
  sender: String,
  text: String,
  timestamp: { type: Date, default: Date.now },
});

const conversationSchema = new mongoose.Schema({
  userId: String,
  messages: [messageSchema],
});

const Conversation = mongoose.model('Conversation',
conversationSchema);

module.exports = Conversation;
```

Integrating MongoDB with Node.js Backend

Let's understand it with a pictorial representation of how MongoDB can be integrated with Node.js in the backend.

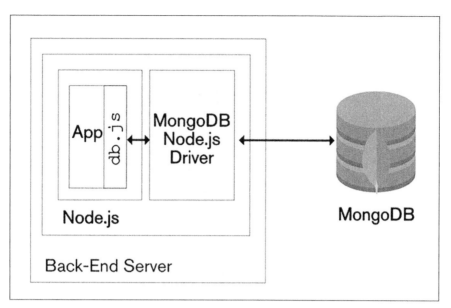

Figure 8.13: *Integrating MongoDB with Node.js Backend (Source: https://webassets.mongodb. com/_com_assets/cms/MongoDB_NodeJS_Driver-0qkvda7kk0.png)*

1. **Connect to MongoDB**:

   Update your `server.js` file to connect to MongoDB using Mongoose.

   ```
   const mongoose = require('mongoose');

   mongoose.connect(process.env.MONGODB_URI, {
     useNewUrlParser: true,
     useUnifiedTopology: true,
   }).then(() => {
     console.log('Connected to MongoDB');
   }).catch((error) => {
     console.error('Error connecting to MongoDB:', error);
   });
   ```

2. **Store Messages in MongoDB**:

   Update the API endpoint to store user and bot messages in MongoDB.

   ```
   const express = require('express');
   const bodyParser = require('body-parser');
   const mongoose = require('mongoose');
   const Conversation = require('./models/Conversation');
   const processMessage = require('./processMessage');
   // Assuming you have a function to process messages

   const app = express();
   ```

```
const port = process.env.PORT || 3000;

app.use(bodyParser.json());

app.post('/api/message', async (req, res) => {
  try {
    const { userId, message } = req.body;
    const result = await processMessage(message);

    const conversation = await Conversation.findOne({ userId })
|| new Conversation({ userId });
    conversation.messages.push({ sender: 'user', text: message
});
    conversation.messages.push({ sender: 'bot', text: result.
fulfillmentText });
    await conversation.save();

    res.json({
      intent: result.intent.displayName,
      response: result.fulfillmentText,
    });
  } catch (error) {
    console.error('Error processing message:', error);
    res.status(500).json({ error: 'An error occurred while
processing the message' });
  }
});

app.listen(port, () => {
  console.log(`Server running on port ${port}`);
});
```

Querying and Analyzing Conversations

Let's briefly understand querying and analyzing conversations.

1. **Retrieve Conversation Logs**:

   Create an API endpoint to retrieve conversation logs for analysis.

   ```
   app.get('/api/conversations/:userId', async (req, res) => {
     try {
       const { userId } = req.params;
       const conversation = await Conversation.findOne({ userId
   });
       res.json(conversation);
     } catch (error) {
   ```

```
        console.error('Error retrieving conversation:', error);
        res.status(500).json({ error: 'An error occurred while re-
trieving the conversation' });
    }
  });
```

2. **Analyze User Interactions**:

   Use the stored conversation logs to analyze user interactions, identify common queries, and improve the chatbot's responses.

Conclusion

This chapter delves into the development of intelligent chatbots within the MERN (MongoDB, Express.js, React, Node.js) ecosystem. The chapter guides readers through the entire process of building a chatbot, starting with the basics of natural language processing (NLP) and machine learning, and culminating in the deployment of a fully functional chatbot integrated with a MERN application. Key concepts covered include intent recognition, entity extraction, and conversation flow management, which are essential for creating sophisticated chatbot experiences.

The chapter explores powerful tools such as Dialogflow and Microsoft Bot Framework, highlighting their capabilities in processing and understanding user inputs. These tools enable developers to create chatbots that can simulate human-like interactions and provide intelligent responses. Additionally, the chapter covers the integration of these chatbots into web applications built with MongoDB, Express.js, React, and Node. js, ensuring a seamless user experience. Readers will learn how to leverage Node.js for backend chatbot logic, React for creating interactive chat interfaces, and MongoDB for storing conversation logs and user data.

By the end of this chapter, readers will be equipped with the knowledge and skills to design, build, and deploy AI-powered chatbots that enhance user engagement and provide immediate, intelligent responses to user queries. The chapter provides a comprehensive understanding of the technologies and methodologies involved in crafting conversational AI solutions within the MERN stack.

The next chapter delves into the advanced realms of AI by integrating image and voice recognition features into MERN stack applications.

Multiple Choice Questions

1. What is the primary focus of this chapter?

    a. Developing static web pages

    b. Building intelligent chatbots within the MERN ecosystem

    c. Managing relational databases

    d. Performing data analysis

2. Which of the following is a key concept in chatbot development covered in this chapter?

    a. Data warehousing

    b. Intent recognition

    c. Image processing

    d. Network security

3. What are Dialogflow and Microsoft Bot Framework used for in chatbot development?

    a. Creating static content

    b. Processing and understanding user inputs

    c. Managing server infrastructure

    d. Performing batch processing

4. Which technology is used for backend chatbot logic in this chapter?

    a. Angular

    b. Node.js

    c. Python

    d. Ruby on Rails

5. What is the role of React in building chatbots as discussed in this chapter?

    a. Managing database connections

    b. Creating interactive chat interfaces

    c. Handling server-side logic

    d. Performing data encryption

6. What is the purpose of MongoDB in the context of AI-powered chatbots?

   a. Storing conversation logs and user data

   b. Rendering frontend components

   c. Managing API requests

   d. Performing real-time data analysis

7. Which of the following is an example of an NLP task mentioned in the chapter?

   a. Data mining

   b. Entity extraction

   c. Image classification

   d. Network routing

8. What does conversation flow management involve in chatbot development?

   a. Managing user authentication

   b. Handling multi-turn dialogs and maintaining context

   c. Performing data validation

   d. Encrypting user data

9. Which tool is recommended for testing API endpoints that utilize AI middleware?

   a. GitHub

   b. Postman

   c. Visual Studio Code

   d. MongoDB Compass

10. What is the primary benefit of integrating AI-powered chatbots into web applications?

    a. Reducing server load

    b. Enhancing user engagement with intelligent features

    c. Improving database performance

    d. Creating static content

Answers

1. b
2. b
3. b
4. b
5. b
6. a
7. b
8. b
9. b
10. b

CHAPTER 9

Image and Voice Recognition Capabilities

Introduction

Image and Voice Recognition Capabilities delves into the advanced realms of AI by integrating image and voice recognition features into MERN stack applications. This chapter provides a comprehensive guide to implementing these cutting-edge technologies, transforming how users interact with web applications. Readers will learn about the core concepts of computer vision and speech processing and how to apply these to create more intuitive and accessible interfaces.

The chapter introduces powerful libraries such as TensorFlow.js for image recognition and Web Speech API for voice recognition, demonstrating how to leverage these tools within a Node.js environment. It covers the process of training models to recognize images and speech patterns, as well as the integration of pre-trained models for quick feature deployment.

Readers will also explore the practical aspects of incorporating these AI features into a React frontend, managing multimedia data with MongoDB, and handling audio and visual data streams with Express.js. By the end of this chapter, readers will be equipped with the skills to enhance their applications with AI-driven image and voice recognition, creating a more engaging and interactive user experience.

Structure

In this chapter, we will cover the following topics:

- Introduction to Image and Voice Recognition
- Getting Started with TensorFlow.js

- Implementing Image Recognition
- Exploring Voice Recognition Technologies
- Data Handling for Multimedia
- Creating a User Interface for Interaction
- Integrating Pre-trained Models

Introduction to Image and Voice Recognition

Image and voice recognition are two advanced capabilities of artificial intelligence (AI) transforming how users interact with web applications. These technologies enable machines to interpret and understand visual and auditory data, allowing for more intuitive and accessible interfaces. This section provides an overview of the core concepts, applications, and challenges associated with image and voice recognition.

Core Concepts

Let's understand the core concepts of Image and Voice Recognition.

Image Recognition:

Image recognition is a discipline within computer vision that involves identifying objects, patterns, and features within images. It leverages machine learning and deep learning algorithms to analyze visual data and classify images into predefined categories.

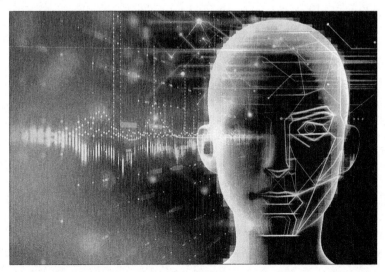

Figure 9.1: *Image Recognition (Source - https://miro.medium.com/v2/resize:fit:724 /1*doxFVXgG6Wviqjp86On9wQ.png)*

Key Techniques:

- **Object Detection**: Identifying and locating objects within an image.
- **Feature Detection and Matching**: Recognizing specific features or patterns in images, such as edges, corners, and textures.
- **Image Classification**: Categorizing images based on their content using convolutional neural networks (CNNs).

Voice Recognition:

Voice recognition, also known as speech recognition, involves converting spoken language into text. It uses acoustic and language models to interpret human speech and recognize words and phrases.

Figure 9.2: *Voice Recognition (Source - https://f5b623aa.rocketcdn.me/wp-content/up-loads/2022/10/Blog_Applications-of-Voice-Recognition-Technology.jpg)*

Key Techniques:

- **Automatic Speech Recognition (ASR)**: Converting speech waveforms into text.
- **Voice Biometrics**: Identifying individuals based on their unique vocal characteristics.
- **Natural Language Processing (NLP)**: Understanding and processing the meaning of spoken language.

Applications and Benefits

Let's understand the applications of Image and Voice Recognition.

Applications of Image Recognition:

- **Healthcare**: Diagnosing medical conditions from medical images such as X-rays and MRIs.

- **Retail**: Enhancing shopping experiences with visual search and product recommendations.
- **Security**: Implementing facial recognition for access control and surveillance.
- **Automotive**: Enabling autonomous driving through object detection and lane recognition.

Applications of Voice Recognition:

- **Virtual Assistants**: Powering assistants like Siri, Alexa, and Google Assistant to perform tasks based on voice commands.
- **Accessibility**: Providing speech-to-text services for individuals with hearing impairments.
- **Customer Service**: Automating call centers with interactive voice response (IVR) systems.
- **Smart Devices**: Controlling smart home devices through voice commands.

Benefits:

- **Enhanced User Experience**: Providing more natural and intuitive ways for users to interact with applications.
- **Increased Accessibility**: Making technology more accessible to individuals with disabilities.
- **Automation**: Streamlining processes and reducing the need for manual intervention.
- **Data Insights**: Gaining valuable insights from visual and auditory data for decision-making.

Challenges and Considerations

Let's understand the challenges and different considerations of Image and Voice Recognition.

Challenges in Image Recognition:

- **Variability in Images**: Differences in lighting, angles, and occlusions can affect the accuracy of image recognition models.
- **Data Requirements**: Training deep learning models requires large datasets and significant computational resources.
- **Privacy Concerns**: Handling and storing visual data raises privacy and security issues.

Challenges in Voice Recognition:

- **Accents and Dialects**: Variations in speech patterns can impact the accuracy of voice recognition systems.

- **Background Noise**: Ambient noise can interfere with the recognition of spoken words.
- **Out-of-Vocabulary Words**: Recognizing new or uncommon words can be challenging for speech recognition models.

Considerations:

- **Ethical Use**: Ensuring that image and voice recognition technologies are used ethically and responsibly.
- **Data Security**: Implementing robust security measures to protect sensitive visual and auditory data.
- **Model Maintenance**: Continuously updating and improving models to maintain accuracy and performance.

Getting Started with TensorFlow.js

TensorFlow.js is a powerful JavaScript library that enables developers to train and deploy machine learning models directly in the web browser or a Node.js environment. This flexibility makes it an excellent choice for integrating AI capabilities into MERN stack applications. This section will guide you through the basics of TensorFlow.js, including installation, setup, and a simple example to get you started with image and voice recognition.

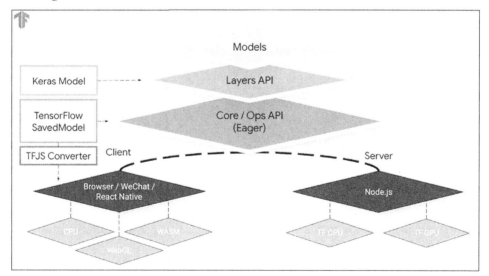

Figure 9.3: *TensorFlow.js (Source - https://res.cloudinary.com/practicaldev/image/fetch/s--oepXBlvm--/c_limit%2Cf_auto%2Cfl_progressive%2Cq_auto%2Cw_880/https://dev-to-uploads.s3.amazonaws.com/uploads/articles/m7r4grt0zkrgyx62xxx3.png)*

Understanding TensorFlow.js

TensorFlow.js is a JavaScript library developed by Google that allows you to define, train, and run machine learning models entirely in JavaScript. It supports both client-side (in the browser) and server-side (Node.js) environments, making it versatile for various applications. TensorFlow.js provides a comprehensive set of tools and APIs for building and deploying machine learning models, including support for tensors, operations, and pre-trained models.

Key Features:

Let's check the key features of TensorFlow.js with ease.

Feature	Description	Tools/Libraries
Cross-Platform	Run models in the browser or on Node.js	TensorFlow.js
GPU Acceleration	Leverage GPU acceleration for faster computations	GPU.js
Pre-trained Models	Access a wide range of pre-trained models for tasks like image classification, object detection, and speech recognition	TensorFlow.js, PyTorch, MXNet
Custom Models	Build and train custom models using JavaScript	TensorFlow.js

Figure 9.4: Key Features of TensorFlow.js

Setting Up TensorFlow.js

Let's set up the tensorflow.js easily in our system.

Installation:

There are two primary ways to install TensorFlow.js: using a CDN or via npm.

- **Using CDN:**

    Add the following script tag to your HTML file to include TensorFlow.js from a CDN:

    ```
    <script src="https://cdn.jsdelivr.net/npm/@tensorflow/
    tfjs"></script>
    ```

- **Using npm:**

  For Node.js environments, you can install TensorFlow.js using npm:

  ```
  npm install @tensorflow/tfjs
  ```

Example Setup in Node.js:

1. **Create a New Node.js Project**:

   Initialize a new Node.js project and install TensorFlow.js:

   ```
   mkdir tensorflow-js-app
     cd tensorflow-js-app
   npm init -y
   npm install @tensorflow/tfjs
   ```

2. **Create a Simple Script:**

   Create a file named `index.js` and add the following code to define and run a simple TensorFlow.js model:

   ```
   const tf = require('@tensorflow/tfjs');

   // Define a simple model
   const model = tf.sequential();
   model.add(tf.layers.dense({ units: 1, inputShape: [1] }));

   // Compile the model
   model.compile({ loss: 'meanSquaredError', optimizer: 'sgd'
   });

   // Generate some synthetic data for training
   const xs = tf.tensor2d([1, 2, 3, 4], [4, 1]);
   const ys = tf.tensor2d([1, 3, 5, 7], [4, 1]);

   // Train the model
   model.fit(xs, ys, { epochs: 10 }).then(() => {
     // Use the model to make a prediction
     model.predict(tf.tensor2d([5], [1, 1])).print();
   });
   ```

3. **Run the Script**:

   Execute the script using Node.js:

   ```
   node index.js
   ```

Implementing Image Recognition

Image recognition is a key component of computer vision that involves identifying objects, patterns, and features within images. TensorFlow.js, a powerful JavaScript library, allows developers to implement image recognition directly in the browser or a Node.js environment. This section will guide you through the process of implementing image recognition using TensorFlow.js, including setting up the environment, loading pre-trained models, and creating a simple image recognition application.

Setting Up the Environment

Let's understand the initial setup in our system.

1. **Install TensorFlow.js:**

    For Node.js environments, install TensorFlow.js using npm:

    ```
    npm install @tensorflow/tfjs @tensorflow/tfjs-node
    ```

2. **Install Additional Dependencies**:

    Install the MobileNet model for image classification:

    ```
    npm install @tensorflow-models/mobilenet
    ```

Loading and Using Pre-trained Models

TensorFlow.js provides pre-trained models like MobileNet for image classification tasks. Here's how to use MobileNet in a Node.js environment:

1. **Create an Image Recognition Script:**

    Create a file named `imageRecognition.js` and add the following code:

    ```javascript
    const tf = require('@tensorflow/tfjs-node');
    const mobilenet = require('@tensorflow-models/mobilenet');
    const fs = require('fs');
    const path = require('path');

    async function classifyImage(imagePath) {
      const imageBuffer = fs.readFileSync(imagePath);
      const imageTensor = tf.node.decodeImage(imageBuffer);

      const model = await mobilenet.load();
      const predictions = await model.classify(imageTensor);

      console.log('Predictions:', predictions);
    }

    classifyImage(path.join(__dirname, 'image.jpg'));
    ```

2. **Run the Image Recognition Script**:

Ensure you have an image named `image.jpg` in the same directory and run the script:

```
node imageRecognition.js
```

Implementing Image Recognition in a Web Application

Let's understand the implementation of Image Recognition with a suitable diagram.

Figure 9.5: *Image Recognition in a Web Application*

1. **Set Up a React Project**:

Use Create React App to set up a new React project:

```
npx create-react-app image-recognition-app
cd image-recognition-app
npm install @tensorflow/tfjs @tensorflow-models/mobilenet
```

2. **Create the Image Recognition Component**:

Create a file named `ImageRecognition.js` in the `src` directory and add the following code:

```javascript
import React, { useState } from 'react';
import * as tf from '@tensorflow/tfjs';
import * as mobilenet from '@tensorflow-models/mobilenet';

function ImageRecognition() {
  const [image, setImage] = useState(null);
  const [predictions, setPredictions] = useState([]);

  const handleImageUpload = async (event) => {
    const file = event.target.files[0];
    const imageElement = document.createElement('img');
    imageElement.src = URL.createObjectURL(file);
    imageElement.onload = async () => {
      const model = await mobilenet.load();
      const predictions = await model.classify
(imageElement);
      setPredictions(predictions);
    };
    setImage(imageElement.src);
  };

  return (
    <div>
      <h1>Image Recognition</h1>
      <input type="file" onChange={handleImageUpload} />
      {image && <img src={image} alt="Uploaded" />}
      <ul>
        {predictions.map((prediction, index) => (
          <li key={index}>
            {prediction.className}: {prediction.probability.
toFixed(2)}
          </li>
        ))}
      </ul>
    </div>
  );
}

export default ImageRecognition;
```

3. **Integrate the Component into the App**:

Update the `App.js` file to include the `ImageRecognition` component:

```
import React from 'react';
import ImageRecognition from './ImageRecognition';

function App() {
  return (
    <div className="App">
      <ImageRecognition />
    </div>
  );
}

export default App;
```

4. **Run the React Application**:

a. Start the React development server:

```
npm start
```

b. Open your browser and navigate to `http://localhost:3000` to see the image recognition interface in action.

Exploring Voice Recognition Technologies

Voice recognition, also known as speech recognition, involves converting spoken language into text. This technology enables hands-free control of devices, voice-activated assistants, and more. The Web Speech API and TensorFlow.js are powerful tools for implementing voice recognition in web applications. This section will guide you through the basics of voice recognition and how to integrate these technologies into your MERN stack applications.

Web Speech API

The Web Speech API provides two main functionalities: speech recognition (converting speech to text) and speech synthesis (converting text to speech). This API is supported in modern browsers and allows developers to create voice-enabled web applications.

1. **Setting Up Speech Recognition**:

Create an HTML file with basic elements for speech recognition:

```
<!DOCTYPE html>
  <html lang="en">
  <head>
```

```
    <meta charset="UTF-8">
    <meta name="viewport" content="width=device-width,
initial-scale=1.0">
    <title>Voice Recognition</title>
  </head>
  <body>
    <h1>Voice Recognition</h1>
    <button id="start">Start Recognition</button>
    <p id="result"></p>
    <script src="voiceRecognition.js"></script>
  </body>
  </html>
```

2. **Implementing Speech Recognition**:

   Create a file named `voiceRecognition.js` and add the following code:

```
    const startButton = document.getElementById('start');
    const resultElement = document.getElementById('result');

    const SpeechRecognition = window.SpeechRecognition || win-
dow.webkitSpeechRecognition;
    const recognition = new SpeechRecognition();

    recognition.continuous = false;
    recognition.lang = 'en-US';
    recognition.interimResults = false;
    recognition.maxAlternatives = 1;

    startButton.onclick = () => {
      recognition.start();
      console.log('Ready to receive a voice command.');
    };

    recognition.onresult = (event) => {
      const speechResult = event.results[0][0].transcript;
      resultElement.textContent = `Result: ${speechResult}`;
      console.log('Confidence: ' + event.results[0][0].confidence);
    };

    recognition.onspeechend = () => {
      recognition.stop();
    };

    recognition.onerror = (event) => {
      resultElement.textContent = `Error occurred in
recognition: ${event.error}`;
    };
```

3. **Running the Application**:

a. Open the HTML file in a browser that supports the Web Speech API (for example, Google Chrome).

b. Click the **"Start Recognition"** button and speak into your microphone. The recognized text will be displayed on the screen.

TensorFlow.js for Voice Recognition

TensorFlow.js can also be used for more advanced voice recognition tasks, such as recognizing specific commands or phrases. Here's how to implement voice command recognition using TensorFlow.js:

1. **Install Required Packages**:

```
npm install @tensorflow/tfjs @tensorflow-models/speech-commands
```

2. **Create a Voice Command Recognition Script:**

Create a file named `voiceCommandRecognition.js` and add the following code:

```
const tf = require('@tensorflow/tfjs');
const speechCommands = require('@tensorflow-models/
speech-commands');

async function recognizeCommands() {
  const recognizer = speechCommands.create('BROWSER_FFT');
  await recognizer.ensureModelLoaded();

  recognizer.listen(result => {
    const scores = result.scores;
    const words = recognizer.wordLabels();
    const highestScoreIndex = scores.indexOf(Math.max(...
scores));
    console.log(`Recognized command: ${words[highestScore
Index]}`);
  }, {
    probabilityThreshold: 0.75,
    includeSpectrogram: true,
    invokeCallbackOnNoiseAndUnknown: true,
    overlapFactor: 0.5
  });

  // Stop listening after 10 seconds
```

```
        setTimeout(() => recognizer.stopListening(), 10000);
}
```

```
recognizeCommands();
```

3. **Run the Voice Command Recognition Script**:

   Execute the script using Node.js:

   ```
   node voiceCommandRecognition.js
   ```

Data Handling for Multimedia

Handling multimedia data, such as images, audio, and video, is a crucial aspect of building AI-powered applications. In the context of the MERN stack (MongoDB, Express.js, React, Node.js), managing multimedia data efficiently involves storing, retrieving, and processing large files. This section will guide you through the best practices and techniques for handling multimedia data in MERN stack applications, including the use of GridFS for large file storage, streaming multimedia content, and integrating these capabilities into your application.

Storing Multimedia Data

Let's understand how we can store multimedia data with ease.

Using MongoDB and GridFS:

- MongoDB has a document size limit of 16MB. MongoDB provides GridFS, which is a specification for storing and retrieving large files, such as images, audio files, and videos.

- GridFS splits large files into smaller chunks and stores each chunk as a separate document. This allows for efficient storage and retrieval of large files.

Setting Up GridFS:

Let's set up the GridFS in our system.

1. **Install Mongoose and GridFS Stream:**

   ```
   npm install mongoose gridfs-stream
   ```

2. **Create a GridFS Storage Engine**:

   Create a file named `gridfs.js` to set up the GridFS storage engine.

   ```
   const mongoose = require('mongoose');
   const Grid = require('gridfs-stream');
   ```

```
mongoose.connect('mongodb://localhost:27017/mydatabase', {
  useNewUrlParser: true,
  useUnifiedTopology: true,
});


const conn = mongoose.connection;
let gfs;


conn.once('open', () => {
  gfs = Grid(conn.db, mongoose.mongo);
  gfs.collection('uploads');
});


module.exports = gfs;
```

3. **Upload Files to GridFS:**

   Create an Express route to handle file uploads using Multer and GridFS.

```
const express = require('express');
const multer = require('multer');
const { GridFsStorage } = require('multer-gridfs-storage');
const gfs = require('./gridfs');

const app = express();
const port = 3000;

const storage = new GridFsStorage({
  url: 'mongodb://localhost:27017/mydatabase',
  file: (req, file) => {
    return {
      filename: file.originalname,
      bucketName: 'uploads',
    };
  },
});

const upload = multer({ storage });

app.post('/upload', upload.single('file'), (req, res) => {
  res.json({ file: req.file });
});
```

```
app.listen(port, () => {
  console.log(`Server running on port ${port}`);
});
```

4. **Retrieve Files from GridFS**:

   Create an Express route to retrieve files from GridFS.

   ```
   app.get('/file/:filename', (req, res) => {
     gfs.files.findOne({ filename: req.params.filename }, (err, file)
   => {
       if (!file || file.length === 0) {
         return res.status(404).json({ err: 'No file exists' });
       }

       const readstream = gfs.createReadStream(file.filename);
       readstream.pipe(res);
     });
   });
   ```

Streaming Multimedia Content:

Let's understand streaming in multimedia content.

Streaming with Node.js Streams:

Node.js streams provide a way to handle large data efficiently by processing it in chunks. This is particularly useful for streaming multimedia content like audio and video.

Creating a Video Streaming Application:

1. **Set Up the Project**:

   Initialize a new Node.js project and install Express.

   ```
   mkdir video-streaming-app
     cd video-streaming-app
     npm init -y
     npm install express
   ```

2. **Create the Server**:

   Create a file named `server.js` and set up the Express server to handle video streaming.

   ```
   const express = require('express');
   const fs = require('fs');
   const path = require('path');

   const app = express();
   ```

```
      const port = 3000;

  app.get('/video', (req, res) => {
    const videoPath = path.join(__dirname, 'video.mp4');
    const stat = fs.statSync(videoPath);
    const fileSize = stat.size;
    const range = req.headers.range;

    if (range) {
      const parts = range.replace(/bytes=/, '').split('-');
      const start = parseInt(parts[0], 10);
      const end = parts[1] ? parseInt(parts[1], 10) : fileSize -
1;

      const chunksize = end - start + 1;
      const file = fs.createReadStream(videoPath, { start, end
});
      const head = {
        'Content-Range': `bytes ${start}-${end}/${fileSize}`,
        'Accept-Ranges': 'bytes',
        'Content-Length': chunksize,
        'Content-Type': 'video/mp4',
      };

      res.writeHead(206, head);
      file.pipe(res);
    } else {
      const head = {
        'Content-Length': fileSize,
        'Content-Type': 'video/mp4',
      };
      res.writeHead(200, head);
      fs.createReadStream(videoPath).pipe(res);
    }
  });

  app.listen(port, () => {
    console.log(`Server running on port ${port}`);
  });
```

3. **Create the Frontend**:

   Create an HTML file named `index.html` to display the video.

```
<!DOCTYPE html>
  <html lang="en">
  <head>
    <meta charset="UTF-8">
```

```html
    <meta name="viewport" content="width=device-width,
initial-scale=1.0">
    <title>Video Streaming</title>
  </head>
  <body>
    <h1>Video Streaming</h1>
    <video src="/video" width="600" controls></video>
  </body>
  </html>
```

4. **Serve the HTML File**:

Update the `server.js` file to serve the HTML file.

```js
app.get('/', (req, res) => {
  res.sendFile(path.join(__dirname, 'index.html'));
});
```

5. **Run the Application**:

Start the server and open your browser to `http://localhost:3000` to see the video streaming in action.

Integrating Multimedia Handling into MERN Stack

Frontend Integration with React:

Let's understand the frontend integration with React.

1. **Set Up a React Project**:

Use Create React App to set up a new React project.

```
npx create-react-app multimedia-app
  cd multimedia-app
  npm install axios
```

2. **Create a Component for Uploading Files**:

Create a file named `FileUpload.js` in the `src` directory and add the following code:

```js
import React, { useState } from 'react';
import axios from 'axios';

function FileUpload() {
  const [file, setFile] = useState(null);

  const handleFileChange = (event) => {
```

```
      setFile(event.target.files[0]);
    };

    const handleFileUpload = async () => {
      const formData = new FormData();
      formData.append('file', file);

      try {
        const response = await axios.post('/upload', formData,
{
          headers: {
            'Content-Type': 'multipart/form-data',
          },
        });
        console.log('File uploaded successfully:', response.
data);
      } catch (error) {
        console.error('Error uploading file:', error);
      }
    };

    return (
      <div>
        <h1>File Upload</h1>
        <input type="file" onChange={handleFileChange} />
        <button onClick={handleFileUpload}>Upload</button>
      </div>
    );
  }

  export default FileUpload;
```

3. **Integrate the Component into the App**:

   Update the `App.js` file to include the `FileUpload` component.

```
   import React from 'react';
   import FileUpload from './FileUpload';

   function App() {
     return (
       <div className="App">
         <FileUpload />
       </div>
     );
   }

   export default App;
```

4. **Run the React Application:**

   a. Start the React development server.

   ```
   npm start
   ```

   b. Open your browser and navigate to `http://localhost:3000` to see the file upload interface in action.

By following these steps, you can efficiently handle multimedia data in your MERN stack applications. Using GridFS for large file storage, Node.js streams for streaming content, and integrating these capabilities into your React frontend ensures a seamless and interactive user experience.

Creating a User Interface for Interaction

Creating an intuitive and interactive user interface (UI) is crucial for enhancing the user experience of AI-powered applications. This section will guide you through the process of building a user interface for image and voice recognition using React, a popular JavaScript library for building web applications. We will cover the setup, implementation, and integration of image and voice recognition features into your React application.

Setting Up the React Project

Let's understand how to set up the react project in our system.

1. **Create a New React Application:**

   Use Create React App to set up a new React project.

   ```
   npx create-react-app ai-recognition-app
     cd ai-recognition-app
   ```

2. **Install Necessary Dependencies:**

   Install TensorFlow.js for image recognition and react-speech-recognition for voice recognition.

   ```
   npm install @tensorflow/tfjs @tensorflow-models/mobilenet
   react-speech-recognition
   ```

Implementing Image and Voice Recognition

Let's implement the Image and Voice Recognition with React.js with ease.

1. **Create the Component for Image Recognition:**

   Create a file named `MyImageRecognition.js` in the `src` directory and add the following code:

```
import React, { useState } from 'react';
import * as tf from '@tensorflow/tfjs';
import * as mobilenet from '@tensorflow-models/mobilenet';

function ImageRecognition() {
  const [image, setImage] = useState(null);
  const [predictions, setPredictions] = useState([]);

  const handleImageUpload = async (event) => {
    const file = event.target.files[0];
    const imageElement = document.createElement('img');
    imageElement.src = URL.createObjectURL(file);
    imageElement.onload = async () => {
      const model = await mobilenet.load();
      const predictions = await model.classify
(imageElement);
      setPredictions(predictions);
    };
    setImage(imageElement.src);
  };

  return (
    <div>
      <h1>Image Recognition</h1>
      <input type="file" onChange={handleImageUpload} />
      {image && <img src={image} alt="Uploaded" />}
      <ul>
        {predictions.map((prediction, index) => (
          <li key={index}>
            {prediction.className}: {prediction.probability.
toFixed(2)}
          </li>
        ))}
      </ul>
    </div>
  );
}

export default ImageRecognition;
```

2. **Integrate the Component into the App**:

Update the `App.js` file to include the `MyImageRecognition` component:

```
import React from 'react';
import ImageRecognition from './MyImageRecognition';

function App() {
```

```
      return (
        <div className="App">
          <ImageRecognition />
        </div>
      );
    }

    export default App;
```

3. **Run the React Application**:

   a. Start the React development server:

   ```
   npm start
   ```

   b. Open your browser and navigate to `http://localhost:3000` to see the image recognition interface in action.

4. **Create the Voice Recognition Component**:

   Create a file named `MyVoiceRecognition.js` in the `src` directory and add the following code:

   ```
   import React, { useState } from 'react';
   import SpeechRecognition, { useSpeechRecognition } from
   'react-speech-recognition';

   function VoiceRecognition() {
      const { transcript, resetTranscript, listening,
   browserSupportsSpeechRecognition } = useSpeechRecognition();
      const [isListening, setIsListening] = useState(false);

      if (!browserSupportsSpeechRecognition) {
        return <span>Browser doesn't support speech recognition.</
   span>;
      }

      const startListening = () => {
        setIsListening(true);
        SpeechRecognition.startListening({ continuous: true });
      };

      const stopListening = () => {
        setIsListening(false);
        SpeechRecognition.stopListening();
      };

      return (
   ```

```
      <div>
        <h1>Voice Recognition</h1>
        <button onClick={startListening} disabled=
{isListening}>Start Listening</button>
        <button onClick={stopListening} disabled=
{!isListening}>Stop Listening</button>
        <button onClick={resetTranscript}>Reset</button>
        <p>{transcript}</p>
      </div>
    );
  }

  export default VoiceRecognition;
```

5. **Integrate the Voice Recognition Component into the App:**

Update the `App.js` file to include the `MyVoiceRecognition` component:

```
  import React from 'react';
  import ImageRecognition from './MyImageRecognition';
  import VoiceRecognition from './MyVoiceRecognition';

  function App() {
    return (
      <div className="App">
        <ImageRecognition />
        <VoiceRecognition />
      </div>
    );
  }

  export default App;
```

6. **Run the React Application:**

a. Start the React development server:

```
  npm start
```

b. Open your browser and navigate to `http://localhost:3000` to see the voice recognition interface in action.

7. **Styling the Components:**

Add some basic styles to make the UI look clean and user-friendly. Create a `App.css` file and import it into your `App.js` component.

```
  .App {
    text-align: center;
    padding: 20px;
```

```
    }

    h1 {
        font-size: 2em;
        margin-bottom: 20px;
    }

    input[type="file"] {
        margin-bottom: 20px;
    }

    img {
        max-width: 100%;
        height: auto;
        margin-bottom: 20px;
    }

    ul {
        list-style-type: none;
        padding: 0;
    }

    li {
        margin: 5px 0;
    }

    button {
        margin: 5px;
        padding: 10px 20px;
        font-size: 1em;
    }

    p {
        font-size: 1.2em;
        margin-top: 20px;
    }
```

8. **Integrate the Styles**:

    Update the `App.js` file to include the styles:

```
import React from 'react';
    import ImageRecognition from './MyImageRecognition';
    import VoiceRecognition from './MyVoiceRecognition';
    import './App.css';

    function App() {
        return (
```

```
      <div className=”App”>
        <ImageRecognition />
        <VoiceRecognition />
      </div>
    );
  }

  export default App;
```

9. **Start the React Server**:

   Start the React development server by using the following command:

   ```
   npm start
   ```

10. **Run the React Application:**

    Open your browser and navigate to `http://localhost:3000` to see the enhanced user interface.

By following these steps, you can create a robust and interactive user interface for image and voice recognition using React. This UI will allow users to upload images for recognition and interact with the application using voice commands, providing a more engaging and intuitive user experience.

Integrating Pre-Trained Models

Integrating pre-trained models into your MERN stack applications can significantly accelerate the development process and enhance the capabilities of your application without the need for extensive training. Pre-trained models are machine learning models that have already been trained on large datasets and can be fine-tuned or used directly for specific tasks such as image and voice recognition. This section will guide you through the process of integrating pre-trained models using TensorFlow.js and other relevant libraries.

Benefits of Using Pre-Trained Models

- **Time Efficiency**: Pre-trained models save time as they eliminate the need for training from scratch, which can be computationally expensive and time-consuming.

- **Performance**: These models are often trained on large and diverse datasets, leading to high accuracy and robustness.

- **Ease of Use**: Pre-trained models can be easily integrated into applications using high-level APIs and libraries.

Integrating Pre-Trained Models for Image Recognition

1. **Using MobileNet with TensorFlow.js:**

   MobileNet is a lightweight, efficient model designed for mobile and embedded vision applications. It is commonly used for image classification tasks.

2. **Setup:**

   Ensure TensorFlow.js and the MobileNet model are installed:

   ```
   npm install @tensorflow/tfjs @tensorflow-models/mobilenet
   ```

3. **Implementation:**

   Create a file named `imageRecognition.js` and add the following code to load and use the MobileNet model:

   ```
   const tf = require('@tensorflow/tfjs-node');
   const mobilenet = require('@tensorflow-models/mobilenet');
   const fs = require('fs');
   const path = require('path');

   async function classifyImage(imagePath) {
     const imageBuffer = fs.readFileSync(imagePath);
     const imageTensor = tf.node.decodeImage(imageBuffer);

     const model = await mobilenet.load();
     const predictions = await model.classify(imageTensor);

     console.log('Predictions:', predictions);
   }

   classifyImage(path.join(__dirname, 'image.jpg'));
   ```

4. **Run the Script:**

   Ensure you have an image named `image.jpg` in the same directory and run the script:

   ```
   node imageRecognition.js
   ```

Integrating Pre-Trained Models for Voice Recognition

1. **Using Web Speech API**:

   The Web Speech API provides speech recognition capabilities directly in the browser, allowing for easy integration of voice recognition features.

2. **Setup**:

   No additional installation is required as the Web Speech API is supported in modern browsers.

3. **Implementation**:

   Create an HTML file named `index.html` and add the following code to implement speech recognition:

```html
<!DOCTYPE html>
  <html lang="en">
  <head>
    <meta charset="UTF-8">
    <meta name="viewport" content="width=device-width,
initial-scale=1.0">
    <title>Voice Recognition</title>
  </head>
  <body>
    <h1>Voice Recognition</h1>
    <button id="start">Start Recognition</button>
    <p id="result"></p>
    <script>
      const startButton = document.getElementById('start');
      const resultElement = document.getElementById('result');

      const SpeechRecognition = window.SpeechRecognition ||
window.webkitSpeechRecognition;
      const recognition = new SpeechRecognition();

      recognition.continuous = false;
      recognition.lang = 'en-US';
      recognition.interimResults = false;
      recognition.maxAlternatives = 1;

      startButton.onclick = () => {
        recognition.start();
        console.log('Ready to receive a voice command.');
      };
```

```
          recognition.onresult = (event) => {
            const speechResult = event.results[0][0].transcript;
            resultElement.textContent = `Result: ${speechResult}`;
            console.log('Confidence: ' + event.results[0][0].
confidence);
          };

          recognition.onspeechend = () => {
            recognition.stop();
          };

          recognition.onerror = (event) => {
            resultElement.textContent = `Error occurred in
recognition: ${event.error}`;
          };
        </script>
      </body>
    </html>
```

4. **Run the Application:**

- Open the HTML file in a browser that supports the Web Speech API (for example, Google Chrome).

- Click the **"Start Recognition"** button and speak into your microphone. The recognized text will be displayed on the screen.

Conclusion

This chapter provides a comprehensive guide to integrating advanced AI features into MERN stack applications. By leveraging powerful libraries such as TensorFlow. js for image recognition and the Web Speech API for voice recognition, developers can create more intuitive and accessible interfaces. The chapter covers the core concepts of computer vision and speech processing, demonstrating how to apply these technologies within a Node.js environment.

Readers learn to train models to recognize images and speech patterns, as well as integrate pre-trained models for quick feature deployment. Practical aspects of incorporating these AI features into a React frontend, managing multimedia data with MongoDB, and handling audio and visual data streams with Express.js are also explored. By the end of this chapter, readers are equipped with the skills to enhance their applications with AI-driven image and voice recognition, creating a more engaging and interactive user experience. The next chapter delves into the creation of sophisticated recommendation engines within the MERN stack.

Multiple Choice Questions

1. What is the primary benefit of using pre-trained models in AI applications?

    a. Reducing server load

    b. Saving time and computational resources

    c. Improving database performance

    d. Creating static content

2. Which library is commonly used for image recognition in TensorFlow.js?

    a. ResNet

    b. MobileNet

    c. Inception

    d. VGGNet

3. What is the Web Speech API used for?

    a. Image classification

    b. Speech recognition and synthesis

    c. Data encryption

    d. Database management

4. How does GridFS help in managing multimedia data in MongoDB?

    a. By compressing files

    b. By splitting large files into smaller chunks

    c. By encrypting files

    d. By indexing files

5. What is the purpose of the `tf.node.decodeImage` function in TensorFlow.js?

    a. To encode images

    b. To decode image buffers into tensors

    c. To classify images

    d. To encrypt image data

6. Which method is used to start speech recognition using the Web Speech API?

   a. `recognition.stop()`

   b. `recognition.start()`

   c. `recognition.listen()`

   d. `recognition.recognize()`

7. What is the primary advantage of using pre-trained models for voice ecognition?

   a. Reduced accuracy

   b. Faster deployment

   c. Increased computational requirements

   d. Limited language support

8. Which of the following is a key feature of TensorFlow.js?

   a. Only supports server-side environments

   b. GPU acceleration for faster computations

   c. Requires Python for model training

   d. Limited to image recognition tasks

9. How can you integrate image recognition capabilities into a React frontend?

   a. By using the Web Speech API

   b. By using TensorFlow.js and pre-trained models like MobileNet

   c. By using GridFS

   d. By using Express.js

10. What is the primary focus of *Chapter 9, Image and Voice Recognition Capabilities*?

   a. Managing relational databases

   b. Integrating image and voice recognition features into MERN stack applications

   c. Performing data encryption

   d. Creating static web pages

Answers

1. b
2. b
3. b
4. b
5. b
6. b
7. b
8. b
9. b
10. b

CHAPTER 10
Personalization with Recommendation Systems

Introduction

In this chapter *Personalization with Recommendation Systems*, we delve into the creation of sophisticated recommendation engines within the MERN stack, a key feature for enhancing user engagement and satisfaction in web applications. This chapter introduces the fundamental concepts behind recommendation systems, including collaborative filtering, content-based filtering, and hybrid methods. It explains how these systems analyze user behavior and preferences to provide personalized content and product suggestions.

The chapter explores the use of machine learning libraries such as TensorFlow.js to develop the algorithms that power recommendation systems. It also discusses the role of MongoDB in storing user data and interaction logs, which are crucial for generating accurate recommendations. Readers will learn how to leverage Node.js and Express.js to build the server-side logic that processes data and serves personalized content.

Additionally, the chapter covers the integration of recommendation system functionalities into the React frontend, ensuring a seamless and dynamic user experience. By the end of this chapter, readers will have the knowledge to implement their own recommendation systems, enabling them to deliver personalized content and recommendations that resonate with their users' unique interests and behaviors.

Structure

In this chapter, we will cover the following topics:

- Introduction to Recommendation Systems
- Data Collection for Recommendations

- Building Collaborative Filtering Systems
- Content-Based Recommendation Techniques
- Hybrid Recommendation Approaches
- Machine Learning with TensorFlow.js and Integration recommendations with Node.js and Express.js
- Frontend Integration with React

Introduction to Recommendation Systems

Recommendation systems are a fundamental component of modern web applications, playing a crucial role in enhancing user engagement and satisfaction by providing personalized content and product suggestions. These systems leverage various machine learning techniques to analyze user behavior and preferences, enabling applications to deliver tailored recommendations that resonate with individual users.

Types of Recommendation Systems

There are three types of recommendation systems. Let's learn more about them.

- **Collaborative Filtering:**
  - **User-Based Collaborative Filtering**: This method recommends items based on the preferences of similar users. It identifies users with similar tastes and suggests items that those users have liked.
  - **Item-Based Collaborative Filtering**: This method recommends items based on the similarity between items. It identifies items similar to the ones the user has liked in the past and suggests those items.
- **Content-Based Filtering:**

  This method recommends items based on the characteristics of the items and the user's preferences. It uses features of the items, such as genre, keywords, or descriptions to find items similar to those the user has liked.

- **Hybrid Methods:**

  Hybrid recommendation systems combine collaborative filtering and content-based filtering to leverage the strengths of both methods. This approach can provide more accurate and diverse recommendations by considering both user behavior and item characteristics.

Core Concepts

Let's understand its core concepts with ease.

- **User Behavior Analysis**

  Recommendation systems analyze user interactions, such as clicks, views, purchases, and ratings, to understand user preferences. This data is used to build user profiles that capture individual tastes and interests.

- **Similarity Measures**

  To identify similar users or items, recommendation systems use similarity measures, such as cosine similarity, Pearson correlation, and Jaccard index. These measures quantify the similarity between users or items based on their attributes or interactions.

- **Model Training**

  Machine learning models are trained on historical user interaction data to learn patterns and relationships. These models can then predict user preferences and generate recommendations.

- **Real-Time Recommendations**

  Recommendation systems often need to provide real-time suggestions as users interact with the application. This requires efficient algorithms and data processing techniques to ensure timely and relevant recommendations.

Applications of Recommendation Systems

Let's list down a few of the applications of recommendation systems.

- **E-commerce**

  Recommendation systems are widely used in e-commerce platforms to suggest products that users are likely to purchase. By analyzing past purchases and browsing history, these systems can recommend items that match user preferences.

- **Streaming Services**

  Streaming services such as Netflix and Spotify use recommendation systems to suggest movies, TV shows, and music based on user viewing and listening habits. This helps users discover new content that aligns with their tastes.

- **Social Media**

  Social media platforms use recommendation systems to suggest friends, groups, and content that users might be interested in. By analyzing user interactions and connections, these systems enhance user engagement and retention.

- **News and Content Websites**

  News and content websites use recommendation systems to suggest articles, videos, and other content based on user reading and viewing history. This helps users find relevant and interesting content quickly.

Benefits of Recommendation Systems

Let's understand the benefits of recommendation systems with ease.

- **Enhanced User Experience**

  Personalized recommendations make it easier for users to find content and products that match their interests, leading to a more satisfying and engaging experience.

- **Increased Engagement**

  By providing relevant suggestions, recommendation systems encourage users to spend more time on the platform, exploring and interacting with recommended items.

- **Higher Conversion Rates**

  In e-commerce, personalized product recommendations can lead to higher conversion rates, as users are more likely to purchase items that align with their preferences.

- **Improved Retention**

  Recommendation systems help retain users by continuously offering fresh and relevant content, keeping users engaged and coming back to the platform.

Data Collection for Recommendations

Data collection is a critical component of building effective recommendation systems. The quality and quantity of data directly impact the accuracy and relevance of the recommendations generated. This section will cover the importance of data collection, methods for gathering user data, maintaining data quality, and ethical considerations.

Importance of Data Collection

Let's understand the importance of Data Collection with ease.

- **Foundation for Recommendations**

  Data serves as the foundation for recommendation systems. It provides the necessary information about user preferences, behaviors, and interactions, which are crucial for generating personalized recommendations.

- **Training Machine Learning Models**

  High-quality data is essential for training machine learning models that power recommendation systems. The models learn patterns and relationships from the data to predict user preferences accurately.

- **Improving User Experience**

  Collecting and analyzing user data helps in understanding user needs and preferences, enabling the delivery of personalized content and product suggestions that enhance user satisfaction and engagement.

Methods for Gathering User Data

Let's analyze the different methods for gathering user data.

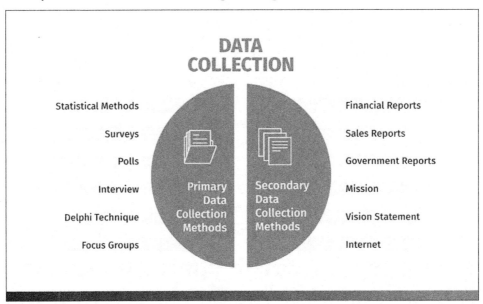

Figure 10.1: *Methods for Gathering User Data (Source -https://www.questionpro.com/blog/wp-content/uploads/2019/06/DataCollection.jpg)*

Explicit Feedback

Explicit feedback involves directly asking users for their preferences through ratings, reviews, and surveys. This method provides clear and specific insights into user preferences.

- **Ratings**: Users rate items on a scale (for example, 1 to 5 stars).
- **Reviews**: Users write detailed reviews about their experiences with items.
- **Surveys**: Users answer questions about their preferences and interests.

Implicit Feedback

Implicit feedback is collected by observing user behaviors and interactions with the application. This method is less intrusive and provides continuous data.

- **Clicks**: Tracking the items users click on.
- **Views**: Monitoring the items users view.
- **Purchases**: Recording the items users purchase.

Browsing History

Analyzing browsing history involves examining the pages users visit and the time spent on each page to understand their online behavior. This includes identifying frequently visited pages, time spent on specific websites, and the order in which pages are accessed. By analyzing browsing history, insights can be gained into user interests, preferences, and potential pain points. This information can be used to improve user experience, tailor content, and inform marketing strategies. It can also help identify trends and patterns in user behavior.

User Profiles

User profiles contain demographic information, preferences, and past interactions. This data helps in creating personalized recommendations tailored to individual users.

- **Demographics**: Age, gender, location, and so on.
- **Preferences**: Favorite genres, categories, and so on.
- **Interaction History**: Past ratings, reviews, clicks, and purchases.

Social Data

Social data includes information from social media platforms, such as likes, shares, and comments. This data provides additional context about user preferences and social influences.

- **Likes and Shares**: Items users like or share on social media.
- **Comments**: User comments and discussions on social media platforms.
- **Connections**: Information about user connections and social circles.

Maintaining Data Quality

Let's understand how we can maintain data quality with ease.

Data Cleaning

Data cleaning involves removing duplicates, correcting errors, and handling missing values to ensure the data is accurate and reliable.

- **Duplicates**: Identifying and removing duplicate entries.
- **Errors**: Correcting typographical and logical errors.
- **Missing Values**: Handling missing values through imputation or removal.

Data Normalization

Data normalization involves transforming data into a consistent format and scale, making it easier to analyze and use in machine learning models.

- **Scaling**: Adjusting numerical values to a common scale.
- **Encoding**: Converting categorical data into numerical format.

Data Enrichment

Data enrichment involves augmenting the existing data with additional information to provide more context and improve the quality of recommendations.

- **External Data Sources**: Integrating data from external sources such as third-party APIs.
- **Derived Features**: Creating new features from existing data, such as calculating average ratings or frequency of interactions.

Ethical Considerations

Let's understand ethical considerations with ease.

User Privacy

Protecting user privacy is paramount when collecting and using data for recommendations. It is essential to obtain user consent and ensure transparency about data collection practices.

- **Consent**: Obtaining explicit consent from users before collecting their data.
- **Transparency**: Communicating clearly how user data will be used and stored.

Data Security

Ensuring data security involves implementing measures to protect user data from unauthorized access, breaches, and misuse.

- **Encryption**: Encrypting data both in transit and at rest.
- **Access Control**: Restricting access to user data to authorized personnel only.

Bias and Fairness

Addressing bias and ensuring fairness in recommendation systems is crucial to providing equitable recommendations to all users.

- **Bias Detection**: Identifying and mitigating biases in the data and models.
- **Fairness**: Ensuring that recommendations are fair and do not discriminate against any user group.

Building Collaborative Filtering Systems

Collaborative filtering is a popular technique used in recommendation systems to predict a user's preferences based on the preferences of other users. It leverages the idea that users who agreed in the past will agree in the future and that users will prefer items that are similar to items they liked in the past. Collaborative filtering can be divided into two main types: user-based and item-based collaborative filtering.

User-Based Collaborative Filtering

User-based collaborative filtering recommends items to a user based on the preferences of similar users. It identifies users with similar tastes and suggests items that those users have liked.

Steps

1. **Data Collection**

   a. Gather user-item interaction data, such as ratings, clicks, or purchases.

   b. **Example**: User A likes items 1, 2, and 3; User B likes items 2, 3, and 4.

2. **Similarity Calculation**

   a. Calculate the similarity between users using similarity measures, such as cosine similarity, Pearson correlation, or Jaccard index.

   b. **Example:** Calculate the similarity between User A and User B based on their item preferences.

3. **Neighborhood Selection**

   a. Select a set of similar users (neighbors) for the target user.

   b. **Example:** Identify the top-N similar users to User A.

4. **Prediction**

   a. Predict the user's preference for an item based on the preferences of the selected neighbors.

   b. **Example:** Predict User A's rating for item 4 based on the ratings of similar users.

Implementation

Use a machine learning library like TensorFlow.js to implement user-based collaborative filtering.

```
const tf = require('@tensorflow/tfjs');
 const cosineSimilarity = (a, b) => {
   const dotProduct = tf.dot(a, b).dataSync()[0];
   const normA = tf.norm(a).dataSync()[0];
   const normB = tf.norm(b).dataSync()[0];
   return dotProduct / (normA * normB);
 };

 const userPreferences = {
   userA: [1, 1, 1, 0],
   userB: [0, 1, 1, 1],
   userC: [1, 0, 0, 1],
 };

 const targetUser = 'userA';
 const neighbors = Object.keys(userPreferences).filter(user =>
user !== targetUser);
 const similarities = neighbors.map(user => ({
   user,
   similarity: cosineSimilarity(tf.tensor(userPreferences[targe-
tUser]), tf.tensor(userPreferences[user])),
 }));

 similarities.sort((a, b) => b.similarity - a.similarity);
 console.log('Top similar users:', similarities);
```

Item-Based Collaborative Filtering

Item-based collaborative filtering recommends items to a user based on the similarity between items. It identifies items that are similar to the ones the user has liked in the past and suggests those items.

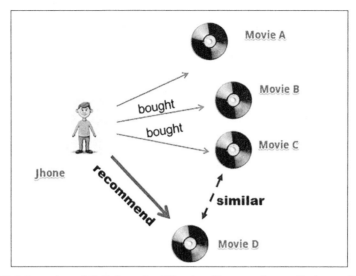

Figure 10.2: *Item-based Collaborative Filtering (Source - https://miro.medium.com /v2/resize:fit:904/1*9IYmsEsJJz-j4taOySkBYQ.png)*

Steps

1. **Data Collection**

   a. Gather user-item interaction data, such as ratings, clicks, or purchases.

   b. **Example:** Item 1 is liked by Users A and B; Item 2 is liked by Users B and C.

2. **Similarity Calculation**

   a. Calculate the similarity between items using similarity measures, such as cosine similarity, Pearson correlation, or Jaccard index.

   b. **Example:** Calculate the similarity between Item 1 and Item 2 based on user preferences.

3. **Neighborhood Selection**

   a. Select a set of similar items (neighbors) for the target item.

   b. **Example:** Identify the top-N similar items to Item 1.

4. **Prediction**

   a. Predict the user's preference for an item based on the similarity to items the user has previously liked.

   b. **Example:** Predict User A's rating for Item 2 based on the similarity to items User A has liked.

Implementation

Use a machine learning library like TensorFlow.js to implement item-based collaborative filtering.

```
const itemPreferences = {
  item1: [1, 1, 0],
  item2: [1, 0, 1],
  item3: [0, 1, 1],
};

const targetItem = 'item1';
const neighbors = Object.keys(itemPreferences).filter(item =>
item !== targetItem);
const similarities = neighbors.map(item => ({
  item,
  similarity: cosineSimilarity(tf.tensor(itemPreferences
[targetItem]), tf.tensor(itemPreferences[item])),
}));

similarities.sort((a, b) => b.similarity - a.similarity);
console.log('Top similar items:', similarities);
```

Content-Based Recommendation Techniques

Content-based recommendation techniques recommend items to users based on the characteristics of the items and the user's preferences. These techniques use the features of items, such as genre, keywords, or descriptions to find items similar to those the user has liked.

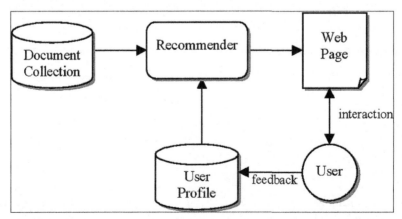

Figure 10.3: *Content-based Recommendation (Source -https://d3i71xaburhd42.cloudfront. net/4a57e0f0641b7a70fece89c14fbf5030869ededb/250px/4-Figure2-1.png)*

Key Concepts

Let's understand the key concepts of content-based recommendation techniques.

Feature Extraction

- Extract features from items to represent their characteristics. Features can include metadata, such as genre, keywords, descriptions, and other attributes.

- **Example:** Extract features from movies, such as genre (action, comedy), keywords (hero, villain), and descriptions.

User Profile

- Create a user profile that captures the user's preferences based on the features of items they have interacted with.

- **Example:** If a user likes action movies, their profile will have a high preference for the action genre.

Similarity Calculation

- Calculate the similarity between items based on their features. Common similarity measures include cosine similarity, Euclidean distance, and Jaccard index.

- **Example:** Calculate the similarity between two movies based on their genre and keywords.

Recommendation Generation

- Recommend items to the user based on the similarity between the user's profile and the features of items.

- **Example**: Recommend movies similar to the movies the user has liked.

Implementation

1. **Data Collection**

   a. Gather item metadata and user interaction data.

   b. **Example**: Collect metadata for movies and user ratings.

2. **Feature Extraction**

   a. Extract features from items to create feature vectors.

   b. **Example:** Create feature vectors for movies based on genre, keywords, and descriptions.

3. **User Profile Creation**

   a. Create user profiles based on the features of items they have interacted with.

   b. **Example**: Calculate the average feature vector for movies a user has rated highly.

4. **Similarity Calculation**

   a. Calculate the similarity between the user's profile and the features of items.

   b. **Example:** Use cosine similarity to find movies similar to the user's profile.

5. **Recommendation Generation**

   a. Recommend items to the user based on the similarity scores.

   b. **Example:** Recommend the top-N movies with the highest similarity scores to the user's profile.

Coding Implementation

Use a machine learning library like TensorFlow.js to implement content-based recommendation techniques.

```
const tf = require('@tensorflow/tfjs');

const items = {
  item1: { genre: [1, 0, 0], keywords: [1, 1, 0] },
  item2: { genre: [0, 1, 0], keywords: [0, 1, 1] },
  item3: { genre: [0, 0, 1], keywords: [1, 0, 1] },
};

const userProfile = { genre: [1, 0, 0], keywords: [1, 1, 0] };

const calculateSimilarity = (itemFeatures, userProfile) => {
  const itemTensor = tf.tensor(itemFeatures);
  const userTensor = tf.tensor(userProfile);
  return cosineSimilarity(itemTensor, userTensor);
};

const recommendations = Object.keys(items).map(item => ({
  item,
  similarity: calculateSimilarity(items[item], userProfile),
}));

recommendations.sort((a, b) => b.similarity - a.similarity);
console.log('Recommended items:', recommendations);
```

Hybrid Recommendation Approaches

Hybrid recommendation approaches combine multiple recommendation techniques to leverage the strengths of each method and mitigate their weaknesses. By integrating collaborative filtering, content-based filtering, and other methods, hybrid systems can provide more accurate, diverse, and robust recommendations.

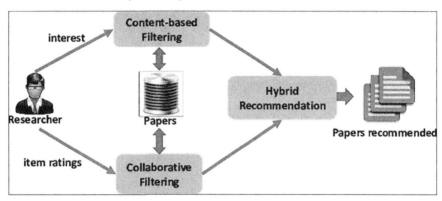

Figure 10.4: Hybrid Recommendation (Source –https://analyticsindiamag.com/ wp-content/uploads/2021/10/image-97.png)

Types of Hybrid Recommendation Approaches

Different types of recommendation approaches are:

- **Weighted Hybrid**
  - Combines the scores from different recommendation techniques by assigning weights to each method. The final recommendation score is a weighted sum of the individual scores.
  - **Example:** Combining collaborative filtering and content-based filtering with weights of 0.6 and 0.4, respectively.
- **Switching Hybrid**
  - Switches between different recommendation techniques based on specific criteria, such as user context or data availability.
  - **Example**: Using collaborative filtering for users with sufficient interaction data and content-based filtering for new users (cold start problem).
- **Mixed Hybrid**
  - Presents recommendations from multiple techniques simultaneously, allowing users to choose from diverse suggestions.
  - **Example:** Displaying recommendations from both collaborative filtering and content-based filtering on the same page.

- **Feature Augmentation**
  - Enhances one recommendation technique by incorporating features from another technique.
  - **Example:** Using content-based features (for example, item attributes) to improve collaborative filtering models.
- **Cascade Hybrid**
  - Applies multiple recommendation techniques sequentially, where the output of one technique serves as the input for the next.
  - **Example:** Using content-based filtering to narrow down the list of items and then applying collaborative filtering to rank the items.

Implementation of Hybrid Recommendation Systems

Let's implement the Hybrid Recommendation system concept with ease.

Combining Collaborative Filtering and Content-Based Filtering:

1. **Data Collection**

   a. Gather user-item interaction data and item metadata.

   b. **Example:** Collect user ratings and item attributes (for example, genre and keywords).

2. **Model Training**

   a. Train collaborative filtering and content-based filtering models separately.

   b. **Example**: Use matrix factorization for collaborative filtering and a similarity-based approach for content-based filtering.

3. **Score Combination**

   Combine the scores from both models using a weighted sum or other combination methods.

   ```
   const collaborativeScore = 0.8; // Score from collaborative
   filtering model

      const contentBasedScore = 0.7; // Score from content-based
   filtering model

      const finalScore = 0.6 * collaborativeScore + 0.4 * content-
   BasedScore;

      console.log('Final Recommendation Score:', finalScore);
   ```

4. **Recommendation Generation**:

   a. Generate the final list of recommendations based on the combined scores.

   b. **Example**: Sort items by their final scores and select the top-N items.

Machine Learning with TensorFlow.js and Integration with Node.js and Express.js

TensorFlow.js is a powerful JavaScript library that enables developers to build and run machine learning models directly in the browser or a Node.js environment.

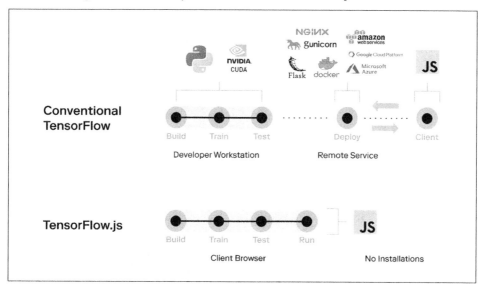

Figure 10.5: *TensorFlow.js (Source - https://cdn.analyticsvidhya.com/wp-content/up-loads/2019/05/tensorflow_diagram1.png)*

This section will guide you through the process of building and integrating machine learning algorithms for recommendation systems using TensorFlow.js, Node.js, and Express.js.

Building a Recommendation Model with TensorFlow.js

Let's understand how we can build a recommendation model with tensorflow.js.

Figure 10.6: *Building a Recommendation Model with TensorFlow.js (Source –https://*
blogger.googleusercontent.com/img/b/R29vZ2xl/AVvXsEjhmuPZTqIIWEbSo9MAQ-
jwe0PjY3-AJeM-nzZdzS8NLCSgxpXuBuLFRl4XhxqHsIS3v3ndX5oT6JBHVlSgON4oEIaG-
7WJBUEjXlsjdbFsrRp4dc2YNMr4YLH4LGHZMPnBauGNK78V50ckdLL533s7s5nD78YILLrGzLh-
tOlTFieQntHojyUgGLnJGWy/s1600/illustration.jpeg)

1. **Install TensorFlow.js**

   Install TensorFlow.js for Node.js using **npm**:

   ```
   npm install @tensorflow/tfjs @tensorflow/tfjs
   ```

2. **Create a Recommendation Model**

   Create a file named `recommendationModel.js` and add the following code
   to define and train a simple recommendation model:

   ```
   const tf = require('@tensorflow/tfjs');

       // Define the model architecture
       const model = tf.sequential();
       model.add(tf.layers.dense({ units: 10, activation: 'relu',
   inputShape: [10] }));
       model.add(tf.layers.dense({ units: 1, activation: 'sigmoid'
   }));

       // Compile the model
       model.compile({ optimizer: 'adam', loss: 'meanSquaredError'
   });
   ```

```
// Generate synthetic training data
const xs = tf.randomNormal([100, 10]);
const ys = tf.randomUniform([100, 1]);

// Train the model
model.fit(xs, ys, { epochs: 50 }).then(() => {
  console.log('Model training complete');
});

module.exports = model;
```

Integrating the Model with Node.js and Express.js

Let's understand how we can integrate the model with Node.js and Express.js with ease.

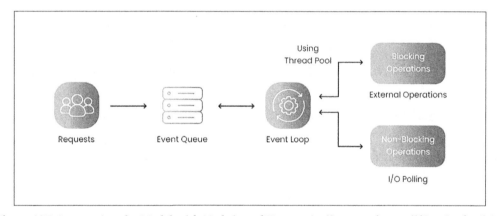

***Figure** 10.7: Integrating the Model with Node.js and Express.js (Source – https://d2ms8rpfqc4h24. cloudfront.net/introduction_to_nodejs_architecture_6bcfda5da2.jpg)*

1. **Set Up the Server:**

   Create a file named `server.js` and set up an Express server to handle recommendation requests:

```
const express = require('express');
const bodyParser = require('body-parser');
const model = require('./recommendationModel');

const app = express();
const port = 3000;

app.use(bodyParser.json());
```

```
app.post('/recommend', async (req, res) => {
  const userFeatures = tf.tensor([req.body.features]);
  const prediction = model.predict(userFeatures);
  const score = prediction.dataSync()[0];
  res.json({ score });
});

app.listen(port, () => {
  console.log(`Server running on port ${port}`);
});
```

2. **Test the Recommendation Endpoint:**

   a. Use Postman or any other API testing tool to send a POST request to `http://localhost:3000/recommend` with a JSON body containing user features:

   ```
   {
     "features": [0.1, 0.2, 0.3, 0.4, 0.5, 0.6, 0.7, 0.8, 0.9,
   1.0]
   }
   ```

   b. The server should respond with a recommendation score.

Frontend Integration with React

To provide a seamless and dynamic user experience, it's essential to integrate recommendation system functionalities into the React frontend.

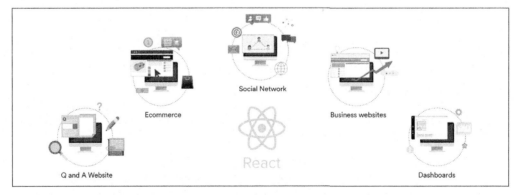

Figure 10.8: *Reactjs Applications (Source - https://www.simform.com/wp-content/up-loads/2020/02/Why-use-react-1.2-preview.png)*

This section will guide you through the process of creating a user interface for displaying recommendations and interacting with the recommendation system.

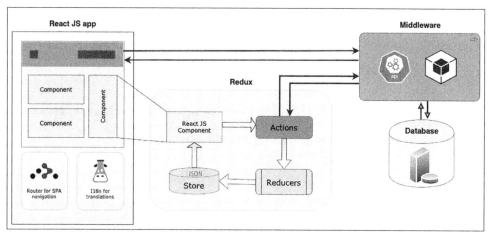

Figure 10.9: *Reactjs Architecture (Source - https://miro.medium.com/ v2/resize:fit:1400/0*wwuz-mU0KY4vsjLo)*

Setting Up the React Project

Let's set up the react project in the local system.

Figure 10.10: *Setting up the React Project (Source - https://i.ytimg.com /vi/HIdPpm-0ZNQ/maxresdefault.jpg)*

1. **Create a New React Application**

    Use Create React App to set up a new React project:

    ```
    npx create-react-app recommendation-frontend
    cd recommendation-frontend
    ```

2. **Install Axios for API Requests**

    Install Axios to handle HTTP requests to the recommendation server:

    ```
    npm install axios
    ```

Creating the Recommendation Component

1. **Create a Recommendation Component**

    Create a file named `Recommendation.js` in the `src` directory and add the following code:

    ```javascript
    import React, { useState } from 'react';
    import axios from 'axios';

    function Recommendation() {
        const [features, setFeatures] = useState(new Array(10).fill(0));
        const [score, setScore] = useState(null);

        const handleChange = (index, value) => {
          const newFeatures = [...features];
          newFeatures[index] = parseFloat(value);
          setFeatures(newFeatures);
        };

        const getRecommendation = async () => {
          const response = await axios.post
    ('http://localhost:3000/recommend', { features });
          setScore(response.data.score);
        };

        return (
          <div>
            <h1>Recommendation System</h1>
            {features.map((feature, index) => (
              <input
                key={index}
                type="number"
                value={feature}
                onChange={(e) => handleChange(index, e.target.value)}
              />
            ))}
            <button onClick={getRecommendation}>Get
    Recommendation</button>
    ```

```
                {score !== null && <p>Recommendation Score: {score}</p>}
            </div>
        );
    }
```

```
    export default Recommendation;
```

2. **Integrate the Component into the App**

   Update the `App.js` file to include the `Recommendation` component:

```
    import React from 'react';
    import Recommendation from './Recommendation';

    function App() {
      return (
        <div className="App">
          <Recommendation />
        </div>
      );
    }
```

```
    export default App;
```

3. **Run the React Application**

   a. Start the React development server:

```
      npm start
```

   b. Open your browser and navigate to `http://localhost:3000` to see the recommendation interface in action.

By following these steps, you can build and integrate hybrid recommendation systems using TensorFlow.js, Node.js, Express.js, and React. This comprehensive approach ensures that your application delivers personalized content and product suggestions, enhancing user engagement and satisfaction.

Conclusion

This chapter provides a comprehensive guide to developing sophisticated recommendation engines within the MERN stack. The chapter emphasizes the importance of understanding and implementing various recommendation techniques, including collaborative filtering, content-based filtering, and hybrid methods. By analyzing user behavior and preferences, these systems can deliver personalized content and product suggestions, significantly enhancing user engagement and satisfaction.

The chapter also explores the use of machine learning libraries such as TensorFlow. js to develop the algorithms that power recommendation systems. It discusses the critical role of MongoDB in storing user data and interaction logs, which are essential for generating accurate recommendations. Furthermore, the chapter covers the integration of recommendation system functionalities into the React frontend, ensuring a seamless and dynamic user experience. By the end of this chapter, readers will be equipped with the knowledge and skills to implement their own recommendation systems, enabling them to deliver personalized content that resonates with their users' unique interests and behaviors. The next chapter covers the entire deployment process, from preparing the application for production to selecting the right hosting platforms and ensuring scalability and reliability.

Multiple Choice Questions

1. What is the primary purpose of recommendation systems in web applications?

   a. Managing relational databases

   b. Providing personalized content and product suggestions

   c. Performing data encryption

   d. Creating static web pages

2. Which method of collaborative filtering recommends items based on the preferences of similar users?

   a. Content-based Filtering

   b. User-based Collaborative Filtering

   c. Item-based Collaborative Filtering

   d. Hybrid Methods

3. What is the key characteristic of content-based filtering?

   a. Recommending items based on the preferences of similar users

   b. Recommending items based on the characteristics of the items and the user's preferences

   c. Combining collaborative filtering and content-based filtering

   d. Using real-time data for recommendations

4. Which similarity measure is commonly used to identify similar users or items?

   a. Cosine Similarity

   b. Mean Squared Error

    c.   Gradient Descent

    d.   Cross-Entropy Loss

5.   What is the primary benefit of using hybrid recommendation methods?

    a.   Simplifying the recommendation process

    b.   Leveraging the strengths of both collaborative filtering and content-based filtering

    c.   Reducing the need for user data

    d.   Improving data encryption

6.   Which machine learning library is mentioned for developing recommendation algorithms in this chapter?

    a.   Scikit-learn

    b.   TensorFlow.js

    c.   PyTorch

    d.   Keras

7.   How do recommendation systems improve retention on social media platforms?

    a.   By providing real-time data encryption

    b.   By suggesting friends, groups, and content that users might be interested in

    c.   By reducing server load

    d.   By managing relational databases

8.   What is the role of MongoDB in recommendation systems as discussed in this chapter?

    a.   Providing real-time data encryption

    b.   Storing user data and interaction logs

    c.   Managing server infrastructure

    d.   Performing image recognition

9.   Which of the following is a key feature of TensorFlow.js?

    a.   Only supports server-side environments

    b.   GPU acceleration for faster computations

    c.   Requires Python for model training

    d.   Limited to image recognition tasks

10. How can you integrate image recognition capabilities into a React frontend?

    a.   By using the Web Speech API

    b.   By using TensorFlow.js and pre-trained models like MobileNet

    c.   By using GridFS

    d.   By using Express.js

Answers

1. b

2. b

3. b

4. a

5. b

6. b

7. b

8. b

9. b

10. b

CHAPTER 11

Deploying MERN and AI Applications

Introduction

Deploying MERN and AI Applications is a chapter that equips readers with the knowledge and tools necessary to successfully launch their AI-enhanced MERN stack applications into production. This chapter covers the entire deployment process, from preparing the application for production to selecting the right hosting platforms and ensuring scalability and reliability.

The chapter introduces key concepts such as continuous integration and continuous deployment (CI/CD), which streamline the development lifecycle, and containerization with Docker, which simplifies deployment and scaling. Readers will learn how to use platforms like Heroku for hosting and how to configure cloud services such as AWS or Google Cloud for more complex deployments that require robust infrastructure and scalability.

The chapter also discusses the importance of environment variables, security best practices, and performance monitoring using tools such as New Relic or Datadog. By the end of this chapter, readers will be well-versed in the deployment strategies and best practices that ensure their MERN and AI applications are secure, scalable, and ready for the demands of real-world usage.

Structure

In this chapter, we will cover the following topics:

- Pre-Deployment Preparation
- Understanding CI/CD Pipelines
- Containerization with Docker
- Choosing a Hosting Platform
- Cloud Services for Scalability
- Database Deployment Strategies

Pre-Deployment Preparation

Pre-deployment preparation is a crucial step in ensuring that your AI-enhanced MERN stack application is ready for production. This phase involves several key activities, including code optimization, dependency management, environment configuration, and testing. Proper preparation helps to minimize potential issues during deployment and ensures a smooth transition from development to production.

Code Optimization

- **Minification**: It involves removing unnecessary characters from the code, such as whitespace, comments, and newline characters, without affecting its functionality. This reduces the size of the files, leading to faster load times.

  Tools: *UglifyJS, Terser*

- **Bundling**: It combines multiple JavaScript files into a single file or a few files. This reduces the number of HTTP requests needed to load the application, improving performance.

  Tools: *Webpack, Rollup*

- **Tree Shaking**: It is a technique used to eliminate dead code (unused code) from the final bundle. This helps in reducing the bundle size and improving application performance.

  Tools: *Webpack, Rollup*

- **Code Splitting**: It allows you to split your code into smaller chunks that can be loaded on demand. This improves the initial load time and overall performance of the application.

  Tools: *Webpack, React.lazy, Loadable Components*

Dependency Management

- **Updating Dependencies:**

  Ensure that all dependencies are up-to-date. This helps to take advantage of the latest features, performance improvements, and security patches.

  Tools: *npm, Yarn*

- **Lockfile Management:**

  Use lockfiles (package-`lock.json` or `yarn.lock`) to ensure consistent dependency versions across different environments. This helps to avoid issues caused by version discrepancies.

- **Removing Unused Dependencies:**

  Identify and remove unused dependencies from the project. This reduces the overall size of the application and minimizes potential security vulnerabilities.

  Tools: *depcheck, npm prune*

Environment Configuration

Let us understand the environment configuration required with ease.

- **Environment Variables:**

  Use environment variables to manage configuration settings that vary between development and production environments. This includes API keys, database connection strings, and other sensitive information.

  Tools: *dotenv, process.env*

- **Configuration Files:**

  Create separate configuration files for different environments (development, staging, and production). This allows you to manage environment-specific settings easily.

  Example: *config/development.js, config/production.js*

- **Environment-Specific Builds:**

  Configure your build tools to create environment-specific builds. This ensures that the correct settings and optimizations are applied for each environment.

  Tools: *Webpack, Babel*

Testing

Let us understand the different types of testing with ease.

- **Unit Testing:**

  Write unit tests to verify the functionality of individual components and functions. This helps to catch bugs early and ensures that each part of the application works as expected.

  Tools: *Jest, Mocha, Chai*

- **Integration Testing:**

  Write integration tests to verify the interaction between different components and services. This ensures that the application works correctly as a whole.

  Tools: *Jest, Mocha, Chai, Supertest*

- **End-to-End (E2E) Testing:**

  Write end-to-end tests to simulate user interactions and verify the application's behavior from the user's perspective. This helps to ensure that the application provides a seamless user experience.

  Tools: *Cypress, Selenium, Puppeteer*

- **Performance Testing:**

  Conduct performance testing to identify and address performance bottlenecks. This ensures that the application can handle the expected load and provides a responsive user experience.

  Tools: *Lighthouse, WebPageTest, JMeter*

- **Security Testing:**

  Perform security testing to identify and address potential security vulnerabilities. This helps to protect the application and user data from malicious attacks.

  Tools: OWASP ZAP, *Burp Suite, Snyk*

Documentation

Let us understand the different documentation required for creating the applications.

- **Code Documentation:**

  Maintain comprehensive documentation for the codebase, including comments, README files, and API documentation. This helps to ensure that the code is easy to understand and maintain.

  Tools: *JSDoc, Swagger, Docusaurus*

- **Deployment Documentation:**

  Create detailed deployment documentation that outlines the steps required to deploy the application. This includes instructions for setting up the environment, running build scripts, and deploying to the hosting platform.

- **User Documentation:**

  Provide user documentation that explains how to use the application. This helps users to get started quickly and understand the features and functionality of the application.

Understanding CI/CD Pipelines

Continuous Integration (CI) and Continuous Deployment (CD) are essential practices in modern software development that streamline the development lifecycle, improve code quality, and accelerate the delivery of new features and updates. CI/CD pipelines automate the process of integrating code changes, running tests, and deploying applications, ensuring that changes are delivered quickly and reliably.

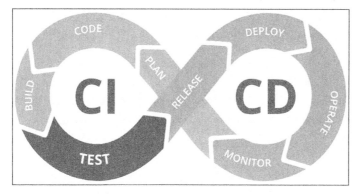

Figure 11.1: CI/CD Pipelines (Source - *https://mlops-guide.github.io/ MLOps/CICDML/ci-cd.png*)

Continuous Integration (CI)

Continuous Integration is a development practice where developers frequently integrate their code changes into a shared repository. Each integration is automatically verified by running tests to detect integration errors as early as possible.

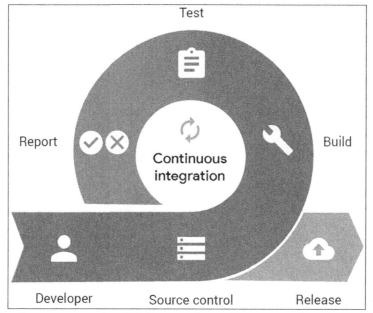

Figure 11.2: *Continuous Integration (CI) (Source - https://www.pagerduty.com/wp-content/up-loads/2020/01/continuous-integration-2.png)*

Key Components:

Let us understand a few of the key components of Continuous Integration (CI).

- **Version Control System (VCS):**

  A VCS ,such as Git, is used to manage code changes and maintain a history of modifications. Developers push their code changes to a central repository (example, GitHub, GitLab, Bitbucket).

- **Automated Build:**

  An automated build process compiles the code and packages it into deployable artifacts. This ensures that the codebase is always in a deployable state.

  Tools: *Jenkins, Travis CI, CircleCI, GitHub Actions*

- **Automated Testing:**

  Automated tests are run to verify the correctness of the code. This includes unit tests, integration tests, and end-to-end tests.

  Tools: *Jest, Mocha, Cypress, Selenium*

- **Code Quality Checks:**

  Static code analysis and linting tools are used to enforce coding standards and detect potential issues.

  Tools: *ESLint, SonarQube*

Benefits:

- **Early Detection of Errors**: By integrating code frequently and running automated tests, errors are detected early in the development process, making them easier and cheaper to fix.

- **Improved Collaboration**: CI encourages collaboration among team members by integrating changes frequently and resolving conflicts early.

- **Faster Feedback Loop**: Automated tests provide immediate feedback on the impact of code changes, allowing developers to address issues quickly.

Continuous Deployment (CD)

Continuous Deployment is the practice of automatically deploying every code change that passes the automated tests to a production environment. This ensures that new features and updates are delivered to users as soon as they are ready.

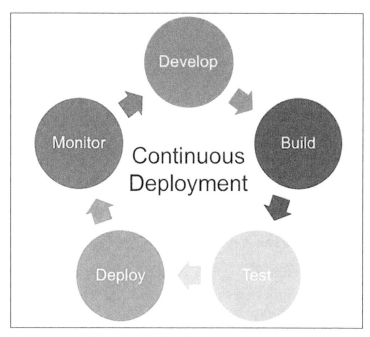

Figure 11.3: *Continuous Deployment (CD) (Source - https://miro.medium.com/v2/re-size:fit:571/1*CvCBB8-4sWnIpBSTmzcKvw@2x.jpeg)*

Key Components:

- **Automated Deployment:**

  The deployment process is automated to ensure that code changes are consistently and reliably deployed to the production environment.

  Tools: *Jenkins, GitLab CI/CD, AWS CodePipeline, Azure DevOps*

- **Environment Configuration:**

  Environment-specific configurations (example, development, staging, and production) are managed using environment variables and configuration files.

  Tools: *dotenv, Kubernetes ConfigMaps*

- **Infrastructure as Code (IaC):**

  Infrastructure is defined and managed using code, allowing for consistent and repeatable deployments.

  Tools: *Terraform, AWS CloudFormation, Ansible*

- **Monitoring and Logging:**

  Monitoring and logging tools are used to track the performance and health of the application in production. This helps in detecting and resolving issues quickly.

Tools: *New Relic, Datadog, ELK Stack (Elasticsearch, Logstash, Kibana)*

Benefits:

- **Faster Time to Market**: By automating the deployment process, new features and updates can be delivered to users quickly and frequently.

- **Reduced Risk**: Automated deployments reduce the risk of human error and ensure that deployments are consistent and reliable.

- **Improved Quality**: Continuous testing and monitoring help in maintaining the quality and stability of the application.

Implementing CI/CD Pipelines

Let us understand how we can implement CI/CD pipelines with ease.

1. **Set Up Version Control**:

   Use a version control system, such as Git, to manage your codebase. Create a repository on a platform such as GitHub, GitLab, or Bitbucket.

2. **Configure CI/CD Tools**:

   Choose a CI/CD tool that integrates with your version control system. Popular options include Jenkins, Travis CI, CircleCI, and GitHub Actions.

   Example: Setting up a CI pipeline with GitHub Actions

```
name: CI Pipeline

on: [push, pull_request]

jobs:
  build:
    runs-on: ubuntu-latest
    steps:
      - name: Checkout code
        uses: actions/checkout@v2

      - name: Set up Node.js
        uses: actions/setup-node@v2
        with:
          node-version: '14'

      - name: Install dependencies
        run: npm install

      - name: Run tests
```

```
                          run: npm test

                        - name: Build application
                          run: npm run build
```

3. **Automate Testing:**

Write and configure automated tests for your application. Ensure that tests are run as part of the CI pipeline.

Example: Using Jest for unit testing

```
// package.json
{
  "scripts": {
    "test": "jest"
  }
}
```

4. **Configure Automated Deployment:**

Set up automated deployment to a hosting platform or cloud service. This can be configured as part of the CI/CD pipeline.

Example: Deploying to Heroku using GitHub Actions

```
name: CD Pipeline

on:
  push:
    branches:
      - main

jobs:
  deploy:
    runs-on: ubuntu-latest
    steps:
      name: Checkout code
        uses: actions/checkout@v2

      name: Set up Node.js
        uses: actions/setup-node@v2
        with:
          node-version: '14'

      name: Install dependencies
        run: npm install

      name: Build application
        run: npm run build
```

```
    name: Deploy to Heroku
      env:
        HEROKU_API_KEY: ${{ secrets.HEROKU_API_KEY }}
      run: |
        git remote add heroku https://git.heroku.
com/<your-app-name>.git
        git push heroku main
```

5. **Monitor and Maintain**:

   Use monitoring and logging tools to track the performance and health of your application in production. Set up alerts to notify you of any issues.

   Example: Using Datadog for monitoring

```
    name: Monitoring

    on: [push]

    jobs:
      monitor:
        runs-on: ubuntu-latest
        steps:
          name: Checkout code
            uses: actions/checkout@v2

          name: Set up Datadog
            run: |
              DD_API_KEY=${{ secrets.DD_API_KEY }} bash -c
"$(curl -L https://s3.amazonaws.com/dd-agent/scripts/install_
script.sh)"
```

By understanding and implementing CI/CD pipelines, you can streamline the development lifecycle, improve code quality, and accelerate the delivery of new features and updates. The next sections will delve into containerization with Docker, choosing a hosting platform, and configuring cloud services for scalability to further enhance the deployment process.

Containerization with Docker

Containerization is a technology that packages an application and its dependencies into a standardized unit called a container. Containers are lightweight, portable, and consistent across different environments, making them ideal for deploying applications. Docker is the most widely used containerization platform, providing tools and features to build, ship, and run containers. This section will guide you through the process of containerizing your MERN and AI applications using Docker.

Benefits of Containerization

Let us list down the benefits of containerization with ease.

- **Portability:**

  Containers encapsulate an application and its dependencies, ensuring that it runs consistently across different environments, from development to production.

- **Isolation:**

  Containers provide isolated environments for applications, preventing conflicts between dependencies and improving security.

- **Scalability:**

  Containers can be easily scaled up or down to handle varying workloads, making them ideal for applications with fluctuating demand.

- **Efficiency:**

  Containers are lightweight and share the host system's kernel, allowing for efficient resource utilization and faster startup times compared to traditional virtual machines.

Setting Up Docker

Let us understand the steps for setting up Docker.

1. **Install Docker:**

   Download and install Docker from the official website, https://www.docker.com/get-started, for your operating system (Windows, macOS, or Linux).

2. **Verify Installation:**

   Open a terminal or command prompt and run the following command to verify that Docker is installed correctly:

   ```
   docker --version
   ```

Creating a Dockerfile

A Dockerfile is a text file that contains instructions for building a Docker image. The Docker image is a snapshot of the application and its dependencies, which can be used to create containers.

1. **Create a Dockerfile:**

   In the root directory of your MERN application, create a file named `Dockerfile` and add the following content:

   ```
   # Use an official Node.js runtime as a parent image
   FROM node:14

   # Set the working directory
   WORKDIR /app

   # Copy package.json and package-lock.json
   COPY package*.json ./

   # Install dependencies
   RUN npm install

   # Copy the rest of the application code
   COPY . .

   # Build the application (if applicable)
   RUN npm run build

   # Expose the port the app runs on
   EXPOSE 3000

   # Define the command to run the application
   CMD ["npm", "start"]
   ```

2. **Build the Docker Image:**

   Run the following command in the terminal to build the Docker image:

   ```
   docker build -t my-mern-app .
   ```

3. **Run the Docker Container:**

   a. Run the following command to start a container from the Docker image:

   ```
   docker run -p 3000:3000 my-mern-app
   ```

   b. The application should now be accessible at `http://localhost:3000`.

Docker Compose for Multi-Container Applications

Docker Compose is a tool for defining and running multi-container Docker applications. It uses a YAML file to configure the application's services, networks, and volumes.

1. **Create a Docker Compose File:**

    In the root directory of your project, create a file named `docker-compose.yml` and add the following content:

    ```
    version: '3'
      services:
        web:
          build: .
          ports:
            - "3000:3000"
          depends_on:
            - mongo
        mongo:
          image: mongo
          ports:
            - "27017:27017"
    ```

2. **Build and Run the Application**:

    a. Run the following command to build and start the application using Docker Compose:

    ```
    docker-compose up
    ```

    b. Docker Compose will start the web service (your MERN application) and the MongoDB service, linking them together.

Best Practices for Docker

Now, let us see the best practices for using Docker.

1. **Use Multi-Stage Builds**:

    Multi-stage builds allow you to create smaller, more efficient Docker images by separating the build and runtime stages.

Example:

```
# Stage 1: Build
FROM node:14 AS builder
WORKDIR /app
COPY package*.json ./
RUN npm install
COPY . .
RUN npm run build

# Stage 2: Runtime
FROM node:14
WORKDIR /app
```

```
COPY --from=builder /app .
EXPOSE 3000
CMD ["npm", "start"]
```

2. **Optimize Layer Caching**:

Docker caches each layer of the image, so order your Dockerfile instructions to maximize cache efficiency. For example, place instructions that change less frequently (example, installing dependencies) before those that change more frequently (example, copying source code).

3. **Minimize Image Size:**

Use smaller base images (example, `node:alpine` instead of `node:14`) and remove unnecessary files to reduce the size of the Docker image.

Example:

```
FROM node:14-alpine
WORKDIR /app
COPY package*.json ./
RUN npm install
COPY . .
RUN npm run build
EXPOSE 3000
CMD ["npm", "start"]
```

4. **Security Considerations:**

Use official base images and keep them up-to-date to minimize security vulnerabilities.

Avoid running containers as the root user. Use a non-root user instead.

Example:

```
FROM node:14
WORKDIR /app
COPY package*.json ./
RUN npm install
COPY . .
RUN npm run build
EXPOSE 3000
USER node
CMD ["npm", "start"]
```

By following these steps and best practices, you can effectively containerize your MERN and AI applications using Docker. Containerization simplifies deployment, improves consistency across environments, and enhances scalability. The next sections will cover choosing a hosting platform, configuring cloud services for scalability, and database deployment strategies to further streamline the deployment process.

Choosing a Hosting Platform

Choosing the right hosting platform is a critical step in deploying your AI-enhanced MERN stack application. The hosting platform you select will impact the performance, scalability, security, and cost of your application. This section will guide you through the factors to consider when choosing a hosting platform and provide an overview of popular hosting options.

Factors to Consider

Let us understand the factors for choosing a Hosting platform.

- **Scalability:**

  Ensure the hosting platform can scale your application to handle increased traffic and workload. Look for features such as auto-scaling and load balancing.

- **Performance:**

  Evaluate the performance capabilities of the hosting platform, including server response times, network latency, and data transfer speeds.

- **Cost:**

  Consider the pricing model of the hosting platform. Some platforms charge based on usage, while others offer fixed pricing plans. Make sure to account for potential hidden costs.

- **Ease of Use:**

  Choose a platform that is easy to set up and manage. Look for intuitive user interfaces, comprehensive documentation, and robust customer support.

- **Security:**

  Assess the security features offered by the hosting platform, such as SSL certificates, firewalls, DDoS protection, and compliance with industry standards.

- **Integration with CI/CD:**

  Ensure the hosting platform integrates well with your CI/CD pipeline to streamline the deployment process.

- **Support for AI and Machine Learning:**

  If your application includes AI and machine learning components, verify that the hosting platform supports the necessary libraries and frameworks.

Popular Hosting Platforms

Here, let us see and understand the different hosting platforms.

- **Heroku:**

  Heroku is a cloud platform that allows developers to build, run, and operate applications entirely in the cloud. It is known for its simplicity and ease of use.

  Features:

  o   Supports multiple programming languages, including Node.js.

  o   Easy deployment with Git.

  o   Add-ons for databases, caching, monitoring, and more.

  o   Auto-scaling and load balancing.

Use Case: Ideal for small to medium-sized applications and rapid development.

- **Amazon Web Services (AWS):**

  AWS is a comprehensive cloud computing platform that offers a wide range of services, including computing power, storage, and databases.

  Features:

  o   Elastic Beanstalk for easy application deployment.

  o   EC2 for customizable virtual servers.

  o   RDS for managed relational databases.

  o   S3 for scalable storage.

  o   Lambda for serverless computing.

Use Case: Suitable for applications requiring high scalability, flexibility, and advanced cloud services.

- **Google Cloud Platform (GCP):**

  GCP is a suite of cloud computing services offered by Google, providing infrastructure, platform, and serverless computing.

  Features:

  o   App Engine for fully managed serverless applications.

  o   Compute Engine for virtual machines.

  o   Kubernetes Engine for container orchestration.

  o   BigQuery for data analytics.

  o   AI and machine learning services.

Use Case: Ideal for data-intensive applications and those leveraging Google's AI and machine learning capabilities.

- **Microsoft Azure:**

  Azure is Microsoft's cloud computing platform, offering a wide range of services for building, deploying, and managing applications.

  Features:

  o   App Service for web apps and APIs.

  o   Virtual Machines for customizable computing.

  o   Azure SQL Database for managed relational databases.

  o   Azure Functions for serverless computing.

  o   AI and machine learning services.

Use Case: Suitable for enterprises and applications that integrate with Microsoft products and services.

- **DigitalOcean:**

  DigitalOcean is a cloud infrastructure provider focused on simplicity and developer-friendly tools.

  Features:

  o   Droplets for scalable virtual machines.

  o   Managed Databases for PostgreSQL, MySQL, and Redis.

  o   Kubernetes for container orchestration.

  o   Spaces for object storage.

  o   App Platform for easy application deployment.

Use Case: Ideal for startups and small to medium-sized applications looking for cost-effective and straightforward cloud solutions.

Deployment Examples

Let us understand and see how we can deploy on different platforms.

Deploying to Heroku:

1. **Set Up Heroku CLI:**

    a. Install the Heroku CLI from the official website: https://devcenter.heroku.com/articles/heroku-cli

    b. Log in to your Heroku account:

    ```
    heroku login
    ```

2. **Create a Heroku App**:

   Create a new Heroku app:

   ```
   heroku create my-mern-app
   ```

3. **Deploy the Application**:

   Push your code to Heroku:

   ```
   git push heroku main
   ```

4. **Set Environment Variables:**

   Set environment variables using the Heroku CLI:

   ```
   heroku config:set NODE_ENV=production
   ```

5. **Open the Application:**

   Open the deployed application in your browser:

   ```
   heroku open
   ```

Deploying to AWS Elastic Beanstalk:

1. **Set Up AWS CLI:**

   a.   Install the AWS CLI from the official website (https://aws.amazon.com/cli/).

   b.   Configure your AWS credentials:

   ```
   aws configure
   ```

2. **Initialize Elastic Beanstalk:**

   Initialize your Elastic Beanstalk application:

   ```
   eb init -p node.js my-mern-app
   ```

3. **Create an Environment:**

   Create a new environment for your application:

   ```
   eb create my-mern-app-env
   ```

4. **Deploy the Application:**

   Deploy your application to Elastic Beanstalk:

   ```
   eb deploy
   ```

5. **Open the Application:**

   Open the deployed application in your browser:

   ```
   eb open
   ```

By carefully considering the factors mentioned and exploring the features of popular hosting platforms, you can choose the best hosting solution for your AI-enhanced MERN stack application. The right hosting platform will ensure that your application is secure, scalable, and performant, meeting the demands of real-world usage. The next sections will cover configuring cloud services for scalability and database deployment strategies to further enhance the deployment process.

Cloud Services for Scalability

Cloud services provide the infrastructure and tools necessary to ensure that your MERN and AI applications can scale efficiently to handle varying levels of demand. Leveraging cloud services allows you to dynamically adjust resources, optimize performance, and maintain high availability. This section will explore key cloud services and strategies for achieving scalability.

Key Cloud Services

Let us analyze the different cloud services with ease.

- **Amazon Web Services (AWS):**
  - o **Elastic Beanstalk**: A platform-as-a-service (PaaS) that simplifies the deployment and management of applications. It automatically handles capacity provisioning, load balancing, and scaling.
  - o **Elastic Compute Cloud (EC2)**: Provides resizable compute capacity in the cloud. EC2 instances can be scaled up or down based on demand.
  - o **Auto Scaling**: Automatically adjusts the number of EC2 instances in response to changes in demand.
  - o **Relational Database Service (RDS)**: A managed relational database service that provides scalability and high availability for databases.
- **Google Cloud Platform (GCP):**

  App Engine: A fully managed serverless platform for building and deploying applications. It automatically scales applications based on traffic.

  - o **Compute Engine**: Offers scalable virtual machines for running applications. Instances can be resized and scaled based on demand.
  - o **Kubernetes Engine**: A managed Kubernetes service for deploying, managing, and scaling containerized applications.
  - o **Cloud SQL**: A fully managed relational database service that provides scalability and high availability.

- **Microsoft Azure:**
  - **App Service**: A fully managed platform for building, deploying, and scaling web apps. It supports auto-scaling and load balancing.
  - **Virtual Machines**: Provides scalable virtual machines for running applications. Instances can be resized and scaled based on demand.
  - **Azure Kubernetes Service (AKS)**: A managed Kubernetes service for deploying, managing, and scaling containerized applications.
  - **Azure SQL Database**: A fully managed relational database service that provides scalability and high availability.
- **DigitalOcean:**
  - **Droplets**: Scalable virtual machines for running applications. Droplets can be resized and scaled based on demand.
  - **Kubernetes**: A managed Kubernetes service for deploying, managing, and scaling containerized applications.
  - **Managed Databases**: Provides scalable and high-availability database services for PostgreSQL, MySQL, and Redis.

Strategies for Achieving Scalability

Let us see the different strategies for achieving scalability for cloud services.

- **Auto Scaling:**
  - Configure auto-scaling policies to automatically adjust the number of compute instances based on demand. This ensures that your application can handle traffic spikes and maintain performance.
  - **Example:** AWS Auto Scaling, GCP Autoscaler, Azure Autoscale
- **Load Balancing:**
  - Use load balancers to distribute incoming traffic across multiple instances. This improves the application's availability and reliability by preventing any single instance from becoming a bottleneck.
  - **Example:** AWS Elastic Load Balancing, GCP Load Balancing, Azure Load Balancer
- **Container Orchestration:**
  - Use container orchestration platforms such as Kubernetes to manage and scale containerized applications. Kubernetes automates the deployment, scaling, and management of containers.
  - **Example:** AWS EKS, GCP GKE, Azure AKS, DigitalOcean Kubernetes

- **Serverless Computing:**
  - ○ Leverage serverless computing services to run code without provisioning or managing servers. Serverless functions automatically scale based on demand and only charge for the compute time used.
  - ○ **Example:** AWS Lambda, GCP Cloud Functions, Azure Functions
- **Database Scaling:**
  - ○ Use managed database services that offer built-in scalability features, such as read replicas, sharding, and automatic scaling.
  - ○ **Example:** AWS RDS, GCP Cloud SQL, Azure SQL Database
- **Caching:**
  - ○ Implement caching strategies to reduce the load on your backend and improve response times. Use distributed caching services to store frequently accessed data.
  - ○ **Example**: AWS ElastiCache, GCP Memorystore, Azure Cache for Redis

Database Deployment Strategies

Deploying and managing databases in a scalable, reliable, and secure manner is crucial for the success of your MERN and AI applications. This section will cover various database deployment strategies, including managed database services, replication, sharding, and backup and recovery.

Managed Database Services

Managed database services provide a hassle-free way to deploy and manage databases. These services handle tasks such as provisioning, patching, backups, and scaling, allowing you to focus on your application.

- **Amazon Relational Database Service (RDS):**
  - ○ Supports multiple database engines, including MySQL, PostgreSQL, MariaDB, Oracle, and SQL Server.
  - ○ **Features:** Automated backups, snapshots, multi-AZ deployments for high availability, read replicas for scaling read operations.
- **Google Cloud SQL:**
  - ○ Supports MySQL, PostgreSQL, and SQL Server.
  - ○ **Features:** Automated backups, point-in-time recovery, high availability with failover, read replicas for scaling read operations.

- **Azure SQL Database:**
  - A fully managed relational database service with built-in high availability and scalability.
  - **Features**: Automated backups, geo-replication, read replicas, built-in security, and compliance.
- **DigitalOcean Managed Databases:**
  - Supports PostgreSQL, MySQL, and Redis.
  - **Features:** Automated backups, high availability with failover, read replicas, end-to-end encryption.

Replication

Replication involves creating copies of your database to improve availability, fault tolerance, and read performance. There are two main types of replication:

- **Master-Slave Replication:**
  - The master database handles write operations, while one or more slave databases handle read operations. Changes made to the master are asynchronously replicated to the slaves.
  - **Benefits:** Improved read performance, fault tolerance, and load distribution.
- **Master-Master Replication:**
  - Multiple master databases handle both read and write operations. Changes made to any master are replicated to all other masters.
  - **Benefits:** High availability, fault tolerance, and load distribution.

Sharding

Sharding involves partitioning your database into smaller, more manageable pieces called shards. Each shard contains a subset of the data, and together, they form the complete dataset. Sharding helps to distribute the load and improve performance.

- **Horizontal Sharding:**
  - Data is distributed across multiple shards based on a shard key (example, user ID). Each shard contains a subset of rows.
  - **Benefits:** Improved performance, scalability, and fault tolerance.
- **Vertical Sharding:**
  - Data is distributed across multiple shards based on columns. Each shard contains a subset of columns.
  - **Benefits:** Improved performance and scalability for specific queries.

Backup and Recovery

Implementing a robust backup and recovery strategy is essential to protect your data and ensure business continuity in case of failures or data loss.

- **Automated Backups:**
  - Schedule automated backups to create regular snapshots of your database. Ensure that backups are stored securely and are easily accessible for recovery.
  - **Example**: AWS RDS automated backups, GCP Cloud SQL automated backups, Azure SQL Database automated backups.

- **Point-in-Time Recovery:**
  - Enable point-in-time recovery to restore your database to a specific moment in time. This is useful for recovering from accidental data deletions or corruption.
  - **Example:** AWS RDS point-in-time recovery, GCP Cloud SQL point-in-time recovery.

- **Disaster Recovery:**
  - Implement disaster recovery plans to ensure that your database can be restored quickly in case of a major failure or disaster. This may involve setting up cross-region replication and maintaining offsite backups.
  - **Example:** AWS RDS cross-region read replicas, GCP Cloud SQL cross-region replicas, Azure SQL Database geo-replication.

- **Testing Backups:**

  Regularly test your backups to ensure that they can be restored successfully. This helps to identify and address any issues with the backup process.

By leveraging cloud services for scalability and implementing effective database deployment strategies, you can ensure that your MERN and AI applications are robust, scalable, and reliable.

Conclusion

This chapter provided a comprehensive guide to launching AI-enhanced MERN stack applications into production. By covering the entire deployment process, this chapter equipped readers with the essential knowledge and tools to ensure their applications are secure, scalable, and reliable. Key concepts such as continuous integration and continuous deployment (CI/CD) streamline the development lifecycle, while containerization with Docker simplifies deployment and scaling. Readers learned how to choose the right hosting platforms, configure cloud services for scalability, and implement effective database deployment strategies.

The chapter emphasized the importance of environment variables, security best practices, and performance monitoring using tools such as New Relic or Datadog. By the end of this chapter, readers should be well-prepared to deploy their applications, ensuring they meet the demands of real-world usage and provide a seamless experience for users. This knowledge empowers developers to confidently launch and manage their AI-enhanced MERN applications in production environments.

The next chapter emphasizes the importance of safeguarding applications against potential vulnerabilities and threats, particularly when dealing with sensitive AI-driven processes and data.

Multiple Choice Questions

1. What is the primary purpose of CI/CD in the deployment process?

    a.   Managing relational databases

    b.   Streamlining the development lifecycle

    c.   Performing data encryption

    d.   Creating static web pages

2. Which tool is commonly used for containerization in deployment?

    a.   GitHub

    b.   Docker

    c.   Jenkins

    d.   Terraform

3. What is a key benefit of using cloud services for scalability?

    a.   Increased server load

    b.   Dynamic adjustment of resources

    c.   Reduced security features

    d.   Fixed pricing plans

4. Which platform is known for its simplicity and ease of use for hosting applications?

    a.   AWS

    b.   Google Cloud

    c.   Heroku

    d.   Microsoft Azure

5.   What is the role of environment variables in deployment?

    a.   Managing user authentication

    b.   Storing configuration settings that vary between environments

    c.   Performing data encryption

    d.   Creating static web pages

6.   Which tool is used for performance monitoring in production environments?

    a.   ESLint

    b.   Webpack

    c.   New Relic

    d.   Babel

7.   What does containerization with Docker provide for applications?

    a.   Increased complexity

    b.   Portability and consistency across environments

    c.   Reduced scalability

    d.   Manual deployment processes

8.   Which cloud service is used for serverless computing?

    a.   AWS Lambda

    b.   Google Compute Engine

    c.   Azure Virtual Machines

    d.   DigitalOcean Droplets

9.   What is a key consideration when choosing a hosting platform?

    a.   Limited scalability

    b.   Ease of use and integration with CI/CD

    c.   Reduced performance

    d.   Fixed pricing plans

10. Which strategy is used to ensure database availability and scalability?

    a.   Manual backups

    b.   Sharding and replication

    c.   Fixed server resources

    d.   Static web pages

Answers

1.   b

2.   b

3.   b

4.   c

5.   b

6.   c

7.   b

8.   a

9.   b

10. b

CHAPTER 12

Security Practices for AI-Enabled MERN Applications

Introduction

Security Practices for AI-Enabled MERN Applications is a crucial chapter that addresses the security implications of deploying AI within the MERN stack. This chapter emphasizes the importance of safeguarding applications against potential vulnerabilities and threats, particularly when dealing with sensitive AI-driven processes and data. Readers will be introduced to a range of security concepts, including authentication, authorization, data encryption, and secure API design.

The chapter discusses the implementation of security measures such as JSON Web Tokens (JWT) for secure user authentication, OAuth for third-party authorization, and HTTPS protocols for encrypted data transmission. It also covers the use of security-focused middleware in Express.js, such as helmet and rate-limiting, to protect against common web attacks such as cross-site scripting (XSS) and denial-of-service (DoS) attacks.

Technologies and tools such as MongoDB Atlas for secure database hosting, bcrypt for hashing passwords, and environment variable management tools for protecting API keys and credentials are also explored. By the end of this chapter, readers will have a comprehensive understanding of the best practices and tools required to secure their AI-enabled MERN applications, ensuring the integrity and privacy of user data.

Structure

In this chapter, we will cover the following topics:

- Understanding Security in the MERN Stack
- Securing the Application Layer

- Authentication and Authorization
- Data Encryption and Protection
- Secure API Design
- Database Security with MongoDB
- Securing AI Models and Data

Understanding Security in the MERN Stack

Security is a critical consideration when developing AI-enabled applications using the MERN stack (MongoDB, Express.js, React, Node.js). Ensuring the security of your application involves protecting both the backend and frontend components from potential vulnerabilities and threats. This section will provide an overview of key security concepts and practices relevant to the MERN stack.

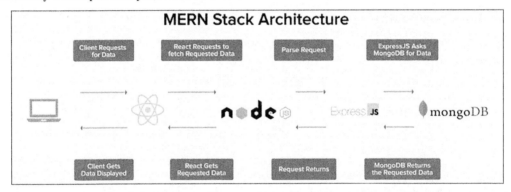

Figure 12.1: *MERN Stack Architecture (Source - https://www.tatvasoft.com/blog/wp-content/uploads/2023/05/MERN-Stack-Architecture-1.jpg)*

Key Security Concepts

Let us understand the key security concepts of MERN Stack with ease.

- **Authentication**:

  Authentication is the process of verifying the identity of a user or system. In MERN applications, this often involves using JSON Web Tokens (JWT) to securely authenticate users.

- **Authorization:**

  Authorization determines what an authenticated user is allowed to do within the application. It involves setting permissions and access controls to ensure users can only access resources they are permitted to.

- **Data Encryption:**

  Encryption is the process of converting data into a secure format that can only be read by someone with the correct decryption key. This is crucial for protecting sensitive data during transmission and storage.

- **Secure API Design:**

  Designing secure APIs involves implementing measures to protect against common web vulnerabilities, such as cross-site scripting (XSS), cross-site request forgery (CSRF), and SQL injection.

- **Database Security:**

  Securing the database involves implementing access controls, encryption, and regular audits to protect data from unauthorized access and breaches.

- **Security Best Practices:**

  Implementing best practices such as using HTTPS for encrypted data transmission, managing environment variables securely, and regularly updating dependencies to patch vulnerabilities.

Security Challenges in the MERN Stack

Let us analyze and understand the security challenges in the MERN Stack.

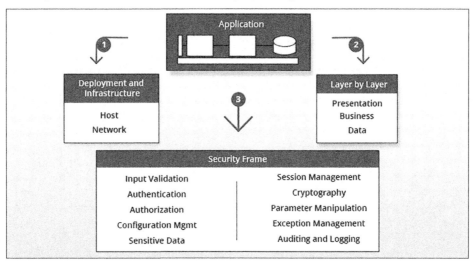

***Figure 12.2**: Security Challenges in the MERN Stack (Source - https://www.vtnetzwelt.com/ wp-content/uploads/2019/05/app-security-best-practices.jpg)*

- **Data Breaches:**

  Unauthorized access to sensitive data can lead to data breaches. Protecting user data with encryption and secure access controls is essential.

- **Injection Attacks:**

  Injection attacks, such as SQL injection and NoSQL injection, can compromise the database. Validating and sanitizing user inputs can prevent these attacks.

- **Cross-Site Scripting (XSS):**

  XSS attacks involve injecting malicious scripts into web pages viewed by other users. Using security-focused middleware and escaping user inputs can mitigate XSS risks.

- **Denial-of-Service (DoS) Attacks:**

  DoS attacks aim to make the application unavailable to users by overwhelming it with traffic. Implementing rate limiting and monitoring can help protect against DoS attacks.

- **Man-in-the-Middle (MitM) Attacks:**

  MitM attacks occur when an attacker intercepts communication between the client and server. Using HTTPS and secure communication protocols can prevent MitM attacks.

Security Tools and Technologies

Let us analyze the different security tools and technologies that can be used in the MERN Stack.

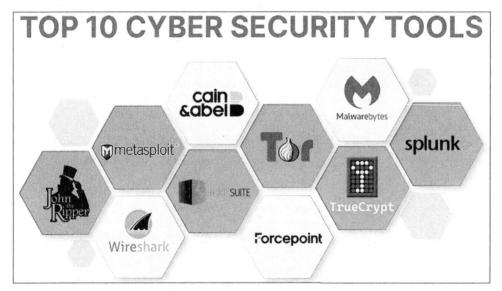

Figure 12.3: *Cyber Security Tools (Source - https://images.shiksha.com/mediadata/ugcDocuments/images/wordpressImages/2022_11_MicrosoftTeams-image-168.jpg)*

- **Helmet:**

  Helmet is an Express.js middleware that helps secure applications by setting various HTTP headers. It can protect against common vulnerabilities such as XSS and clickjacking.

- **Rate Limiting:**

  Rate limiting controls the number of requests a user can make to the server within a given timeframe, protecting against DoS attacks.

- **MongoDB Atlas:**

  MongoDB Atlas provides secure database hosting with features such as encryption at rest, network isolation, and automated backups.

- **Bcrypt:**

  Bcrypt is a library for hashing passwords securely, making it difficult for attackers to retrieve the original passwords even if they gain access to the hashed data.

- **Environment Variable Management:**

  Tools such as dotenv help manage environment variables securely, protecting sensitive information such as API keys and credentials.

By understanding these security concepts and challenges, developers can implement robust security measures to protect their AI-enabled MERN applications. The subsequent sections will delve deeper into securing the application layer, implementing authentication and authorization, and designing secure APIs.

Securing the Application Layer

Securing the application layer is essential for protecting your AI-enabled MERN applications from potential vulnerabilities and threats. This involves implementing various security measures to safeguard both the backend and frontend components of your application. Here are key strategies for securing the application layer:

Backend Security

Let us understand the backend security with ease.

- **Use HTTPS:**

  Ensure all data transmitted between the client and server is encrypted using HTTPS. This prevents man-in-the-middle attacks and protects sensitive information.

- **Security-Focused Middleware:**
  - **Helmet**: Use Helmet to set secure HTTP headers in Express.js applications. It helps protect against common vulnerabilities such as cross-site scripting (XSS) and clickjacking.

    ```
    const helmet = require('helmet');
    app.use(helmet());
    ```

  - **Rate Limiting**: Implement rate limiting to control the number of requests a user can make in a given timeframe, protecting against denial-of-service (DoS) attacks.

    ```
    const rateLimit = require('express-rate-limit');
    const limiter = rateLimit({
      windowMs: 15 * 60 * 1000, // 15 minutes
      max: 100, // limit each IP to 100 requests per windowMs
    });
    app.use(limiter);
    ```

- **Input Validation and Sanitization:**
  - Validate and sanitize all user inputs to prevent injection attacks such as SQL injection and NoSQL injection.
  - Use libraries such as express-validator for input validation.

    ```
    const { body, validationResult } = require('express-validator');
    app.post('/data', [
      body('email').isEmail(),
      body('password').isLength({ min: 5 })
    ], (req, res) => {
      const errors = validationResult(req);
      if (!errors.isEmpty()) {
        return res.status(400).json({ errors: errors.array()
    });
      }
      // Process the request
    });
    ```

- **Error Handling:**
  - Implement comprehensive error handling to prevent the exposure of sensitive information in error messages.

o   Use error-handling middleware in Express.js.

```
app.use((err, req, res, next) => {
  console.error(err.stack);
  res.status(500).send('Something went wrong!');
});
```

Frontend Security

Let us understand the front-end security with ease.

- **Content Security Policy (CSP):**
  o   Implement CSP to prevent XSS attacks by specifying which sources of content are allowed to be loaded.
  o   Configure CSP headers using Helmet.

```
app.use(helmet.contentSecurityPolicy({
  directives: {
    defaultSrc: ["'self'"],
    scriptSrc: ["'self'", 'trusted-cdn.com'],
    objectSrc: ["'none'"],
    upgradeInsecureRequests: [],
  },
}));
```

- **Cross-Origin Resource Sharing (CORS):**
  o   Configure CORS to control which domains can access your API, preventing unauthorized cross-origin requests.
  o   Use the cors middleware in Express.js.

```
const cors = require('cors');
app.use(cors({
  origin: 'https://your-frontend-domain.com'
}));
```

- **Secure Local Storage:**
  o   Avoid storing sensitive information such as tokens in local storage or session storage, as they are vulnerable to XSS attacks.
  o   Use secure cookies with the HttpOnly and Secure flags for storing session tokens.

- **Third-Party Libraries:**
  - ○ Regularly update third-party libraries and dependencies to patch known vulnerabilities.
  - ○ Use tools such as **npm** audit to identify and fix security issues.

    ```
    npm audit fix
    ```

By implementing these security measures, you can effectively secure the application layer of your AI-enabled MERN applications, protecting them from common vulnerabilities and ensuring the integrity and privacy of user data. The next sections will delve into authentication and authorization, data encryption and protection, and designing secure APIs.

Authentication and Authorization

Authentication and authorization are critical components of securing AI-enabled MERN applications. They ensure that only legitimate users can access the application and that users have the appropriate permissions to perform actions within the system.

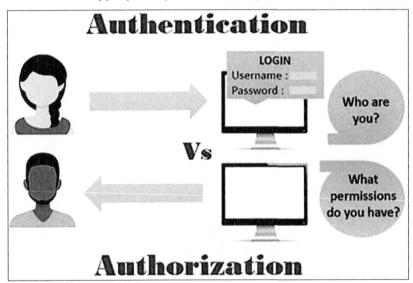

Figure 12.4: *Authentication and Authorization (Source - https://miro.medium.com/v2/re-size:fit:413/0*nrG185aDIksAga3W.jpg)*

Authentication

Authentication is the process of verifying the identity of a user or system. It ensures that the user is who they claim to be by validating credentials such as usernames, passwords, or biometric data.

Figure 12.5: *Authentication (Source - https://www.rd.com/wp-content/uploads/2022/04/RD-Two-Factor-Authentication-FT.jpg)*

Implementing Authentication with JSON Web Tokens (JWT):

- **JWT** is a compact and self-contained way to securely transmit information between parties as a JSON object. It is commonly used for authentication in MERN applications.

- **Structure**: A JWT consists of three parts: Header, Payload, and Signature.

- **Usage**: When a user logs in, the server generates a JWT and sends it to the client. The client includes this token in the Authorization header of subsequent requests.

Example:

```
const jwt = require('jsonwebtoken');

// Generate JWT
const token = jwt.sign({ userId: user._id }, process.env.JWT_
SECRET, { expiresIn: '1h' });

// Verify JWT
jwt.verify(token, process.env.JWT_SECRET, (err, decoded) => {
  if (err) {
    return res.status(401).json({ message: 'Unauthorized' });
  }
  req.user = decoded;
  next();
});
```

Authorization

Authorization determines what an authenticated user is allowed to do within the application. It involves setting permissions and access controls to ensure users can only access resources they are permitted to.

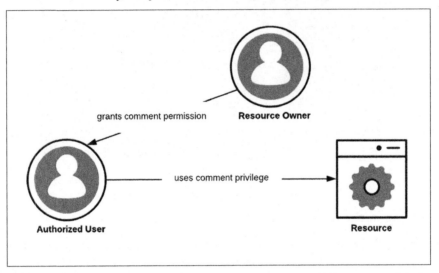

Figure 12.6: *Authentication (Source - https://images.ctfassets.net/kbkgmx9upatd/4ahsyxBLr-wLdhPuQ6dia8z/6ac8eed02315eb774b1dbd11d56e0737/authorization-process-diagram.png)*

Role-Based Access Control (RBAC):

RBAC is a common authorization strategy where users are assigned roles, and each role has specific permissions.

Implementation: Define roles and permissions in your application and check them before allowing access to resources.

Example:

```
const checkRole = (role) => (req, res, next) => {
  if (req.user.role !== role) {
    return res.status(403).json({ message: 'Forbidden' });
  }
  next();
};

// Protect a route with RBAC
app.get('/admin', checkRole('admin'), (req, res) => {
  res.send('Welcome, admin!');
});
```

Data Encryption and Protection

Data encryption and protection are essential for safeguarding sensitive information in AI-enabled MERN applications. Encryption ensures that data is secure both at rest and in transit, preventing unauthorized access.

Data Encryption

Let us see how data encryption is important and essential in AI-enabled MERN applications.

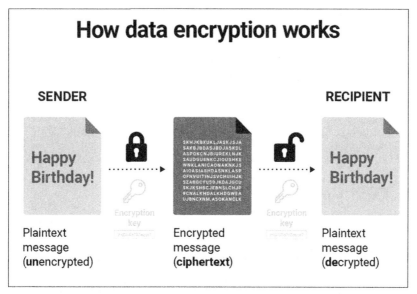

Figure 12.7: *Data Encryption (Source - https://blogapp.bitdefender.com/cyberpedia/ content/images/2022/08/How-data-encryption-works.jpg)*

Encryption at Rest:

Encrypting data stored in databases or files ensures that even if the storage medium is compromised, the data remains secure.

MongoDB Atlas: Provides encryption at rest by default, ensuring that your database data is protected.

Encryption in Transit:

Encrypting data in transit protects it from interception during transmission between the client and server.

HTTPS: Use HTTPS to encrypt data transmitted over the network.

Example:

Setting Up HTTPS:

```
const https = require('https');
const fs = require('fs');
const express = require('express');
const app = express();

const options = {
  key: fs.readFileSync('server.key'),
  cert: fs.readFileSync('server.cert'),
};

https.createServer(options, app).listen(3000, () => {
  console.log('Server is running on https://localhost:3000');
});
```

Data Protection

Let us check how data protection is essential for MERN Stack applications.

Figure 12.8: Data Protection (Source - https://media.licdn.com/dms/image/D4D12AQHsiYEp-faY45Q/article-cover_image-shrink_720_1280/0/1690758226816?e=1729123200&v=beta&t=b_YF8-i6FQ3poWRiC9s9v0pyCv3mfHzjvEfPvNb6r5Q)

Hashing Passwords:

Use a secure hashing algorithm such as **bcrypt** to hash passwords before storing them in the database. This ensures that even if the database is compromised, the original passwords cannot be retrieved.

Example:

```
const bcrypt = require('bcrypt');


// Hash a password
const saltRounds = 10;
bcrypt.hash('myPlaintextPassword', saltRounds, (err, hash) => {
   // Store hash in your password DB.
});


// Verify a password
bcrypt.compare('myPlaintextPassword', hash, (err, result) => {
   if (result) {
      // Passwords match
   } else {
      // Passwords do not match
   }
});
```

Environment Variables:

Use environment variables to store sensitive information such as API keys and database credentials. This keeps them out of your codebase and reduces the risk of exposure.

Example:

```
require('dotenv').config();
const dbConnection = process.env.DB_CONNECTION;
```

By implementing robust authentication, authorization, data encryption, and protection strategies, you can ensure that your AI-enabled MERN applications are secure and resilient against potential threats. The following sections will cover secure API design, database security with MongoDB, and securing AI models and data.

Secure API Design

Designing secure APIs is crucial for protecting your AI-enabled MERN applications from potential vulnerabilities and threats. Secure API design involves implementing measures to safeguard data, ensure proper authentication and authorization, and protect against common web attacks.

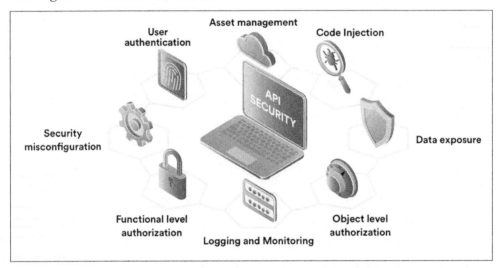

Figure 12.9: *Secure API Design (Source - https://www.simform.com/wp-content/up-loads/2020/12/API-Security-Best-Practices-for-Web-Apps-Rest-APIs-and-API-Gateways-Simform.png)*

Key Practices for Secure API Design

Let us understand the key practices for securing API Design with ease.

- **Use HTTPS:**
  - Always use HTTPS to encrypt data in transit, preventing interception by malicious actors.

- **Authentication and Authorization:**
  - Implement robust authentication mechanisms, such as OAuth or JWT, to verify the identity of users and clients.
  - Use role-based access control (RBAC) to manage permissions and ensure users can only access resources they are authorized to.

- **Input Validation and Sanitization:**
  - Validate and sanitize all inputs to prevent injection attacks, such as SQL injection and cross-site scripting (XSS).
  - Use libraries such as express-validator to enforce input validation.

- **Rate Limiting**:
  - ○ Implement rate limiting to prevent abuse and protect against denial-of-service (DoS) attacks.
  - ○ Use middleware such as express-rate-limit to control the number of requests a user can make in a given timeframe.
- **API Gateway:**
  - ○ Use an API gateway to centralize security features, such as authentication, rate limiting, and logging.
  - ○ API gateways can help manage and secure traffic to your APIs.
- **Error Handling:**
  - ○ Implement comprehensive error handling to prevent the exposure of sensitive information in error messages.
  - ○ Use error-handling middleware to handle exceptions gracefully.
- **Logging and Monitoring:**
  - ○ Enable logging and monitoring to track API usage and detect suspicious activity.
  - ○ Use tools such as New Relic or Datadog for real-time monitoring and alerts.

Database Security with MongoDB

Securing your MongoDB database is essential to protect sensitive data and ensure compliance with security standards. MongoDB provides several features and best practices to enhance database security.

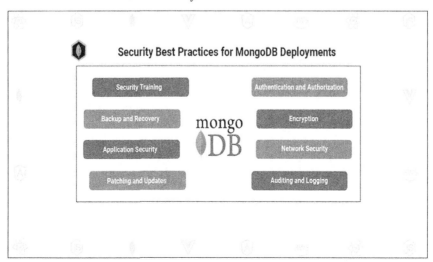

Figure 12.10: *Database Security with MongoDB (Source - https://pronteff.com/wp-content/up-loads/2023/09/Security-Best-Practices-for-MongoDB-Deployments.png)*

Key Practices for MongoDB Security

Let us emphasize the key practices for MongoDB Security in the MERN Stack applications.

- **Enable Authentication:**
  - Require users to authenticate before accessing the database. Use SCRAM-SHA-256 for secure authentication.
  - Configure authentication in the MongoDB configuration file (`mongod.conf`).
- **Role-Based Access Control (RBAC):**
  - Use RBAC to assign roles and permissions to users, ensuring they have only the necessary access to perform their tasks.
  - Define custom roles if built-in roles do not meet your needs.
- **Network Security:**
  - Limit network exposure by binding MongoDB to specific IP addresses and using firewalls to restrict access.
  - Enable TLS/SSL encryption for secure communication between clients and the server.
- **Encryption:**
  - Use encryption at rest to protect data stored in the database. MongoDB Atlas provides this feature by default.
  - Enable client-side field-level encryption for additional security.
- **Auditing:**

  Enable auditing to record user activity and database operations. This helps monitor for suspicious activities and ensures compliance with regulations.
- **Regular Updates and Patches:**

  Keep MongoDB up to date with the latest security patches to protect against known vulnerabilities.

Securing AI Models and Data

Securing AI models and data is crucial to protect against adversarial attacks and ensure the integrity and privacy of your AI systems.

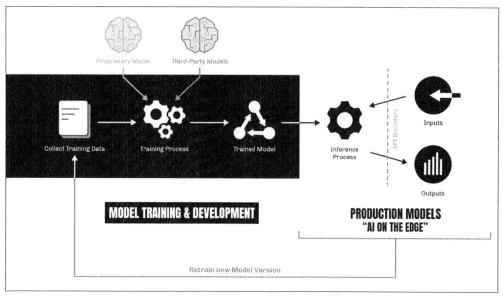

Figure 12.11: *Securing AI Models and Data (Source - https://hiddenlayer.com /wp-content/uploads/image.jpeg)*

Key Practices for AI Model Security

Let us highlight the key practices for AI Model Security with ease.

- **Data Protection:**
  - Encrypt sensitive data used for training and inference to prevent unauthorized access.
  - Use anonymization techniques to protect personally identifiable information (PII).

- **Adversarial Attack Mitigation:**
  - Implement defenses against adversarial attacks, such as input validation and anomaly detection.
  - Regularly test models for vulnerabilities and update them to address potential threats.

- **Model Integrity:**

  Use checksums or digital signatures to verify the integrity of AI models and ensure they have not been tampered with.

- **Access Control:**

  Restrict access to AI models and data to authorized personnel only. Use RBAC to manage permissions.

- **Monitoring and Logging:**
  - ○ Monitor AI model usage and performance to detect anomalies and potential security incidents.
  - ○ Implement logging to track access and modifications to AI models and data.

- **Compliance and Privacy:**

  Ensure compliance with privacy regulations, such as GDPR, by implementing data protection measures and maintaining transparency about data usage.

  By following these best practices, you can design secure APIs, protect your MongoDB databases, and safeguard your AI models and data, ensuring the integrity and privacy of your AI-enabled MERN applications.

Conclusion

This chapter provided a comprehensive guide to safeguarding applications within the MERN stack. The chapter emphasized the importance of implementing robust security measures to protect against potential vulnerabilities and threats, especially when dealing with sensitive AI-driven processes and data. Readers were introduced to essential security concepts, including authentication, authorization, data encryption, and secure API design.

The chapter covered the implementation of security measures such as JSON Web Tokens (JWT) for secure user authentication, OAuth for third-party authorization, and HTTPS protocols for encrypted data transmission. It also explored the use of security-focused middleware in Express.js, such as helmet and rate-limiting, to protect against common web attacks such as cross-site scripting (XSS) and denial-of-service (DoS) attacks. By the end of this chapter, readers should have a comprehensive understanding of the best practices and tools required to secure their AI-enabled MERN applications, ensuring the integrity and privacy of user data. The next chapter is a pivotal chapter that addresses the challenges and strategies involved in scaling AI functionalities within MERN applications

Multiple Choice Questions

1. What is the primary purpose of using JSON Web Tokens (JWT) in MERN applications?

   a. Data encryption

   b. User authentication

   c. Database management

   d. API design

2. Which protocol is essential for encrypting data in transit between the client and server?

    a. HTTP

    b. FTP

    c. HTTPS

    d. SMTP

3. What is the role of OAuth in application security?

    a. Encrypting user data

    b. Third-party authorization

    c. Database indexing

    d. Frontend development

4. Which middleware is used in Express.js to set secure HTTP headers?

    a. Morgan

    b. Helmet

    c. Body-parser

    d. Cors

5. What is the purpose of rate limiting in web applications?

    a. Enhancing user interface

    b. Controlling the number of requests to prevent DoS attacks

    c. Managing database connections

    d. Encrypting data at rest

6. Which tool is recommended for hashing passwords securely?

    a. JWT

    b. OAuth

    c. Bcrypt

    d. Helmet

7. What is a common security threat that HTTPS helps mitigate?

    a. SQL injection

    b. Man-in-the-middle attacks

    c. Cross-site scripting

    d. Buffer overflow

8. What is the main advantage of using MongoDB Atlas for database hosting?

    a. Simplified frontend development

    b. Secure database hosting with encryption at rest

    c. Faster data retrieval

    d. Enhanced image processing

9. Why is input validation important in secure API design?

    a. To improve application performance

    b. To prevent injection attacks

    c. To enhance user experience

    d. To manage server resources

10. Which practice ensures that AI models and data are protected from unauthorized access?

    a. Open access to all users

    b. Role-based access control

    c. Disabling encryption

    d. Using only local storage

Answers

1. b

2. c

3. b

4. b

5. b

6. c

7. b

8. b

9. b

10. b

CHAPTER 13

Scaling AI Features in Production

Introduction

Scaling AI Features in Production is a pivotal chapter that addresses the challenges and strategies involved in scaling AI functionalities within MERN applications as they grow and attract more users. This chapter emphasizes the importance of designing AI features with scalability in mind, ensuring that applications remain performant and responsive under varying loads. Readers will explore the use of microservices architecture to modularize AI features, facilitating easier scaling and maintenance.

The chapter introduces Kubernetes and Docker as essential tools for containerization and orchestration, allowing for the deployment of scalable applications across multiple servers. It also discusses the use of cloud services such as AWS Elastic Beanstalk and Google Cloud Platform's App Engine, which provide managed environments that automatically scale applications based on demand.

Techniques for optimizing Node.js and MongoDB performance for high-traffic scenarios are covered, including database sharding, caching strategies with Redis, and load balancing. Additionally, the chapter delves into the management of machine learning model performance, ensuring that AI features do not become bottlenecks as user demand increases.

By the end of this chapter, readers will be equipped with the knowledge to effectively scale their AI-enabled MERN applications, ensuring they can handle growth and provide a seamless user experience.

Structure

In this chapter, we will cover the following topics:

- Introduction to Scaling Challenges
- Microservices Architecture for AI

- Containerization with Docker
- Orchestration with Kubernetes
- Leveraging Cloud Platforms for Scalability
- Optimizing Node.js for High Performance

Introduction to Scaling Challenges

Scaling AI features in production is a critical aspect of developing robust MERN applications. As applications grow and attract more users, they must handle increased loads while maintaining performance and responsiveness. This section explores the common challenges associated with scaling AI functionalities and provides an overview of strategies to address them.

Common Scaling Challenges

Let us understand the common scaling challenges with ease.

- **Increased Load:**

  As user numbers grow, the demand for AI features increases. This can lead to slower response times and degraded performance if the application is not designed to scale efficiently.

- **Resource Management:**

  AI features often require significant computational resources. Efficiently managing these resources is crucial to avoid bottlenecks and ensure smooth operation.

- **Data Volume:**

  With more users, the volume of data processed by AI models increases. This requires scalable data storage solutions and efficient data processing pipelines.

- **Model Performance:**

  AI models must maintain accuracy and performance under varying loads. Ensuring that models do not become bottlenecks is essential for a seamless user experience.

- **Infrastructure Complexity:**

  Scaling AI features often involves complex infrastructure, including distributed systems and cloud services. Managing this complexity requires careful planning and robust architecture.

Strategies for Addressing Scaling Challenges

Let us analyze the strategies for addressing scaling challenges.

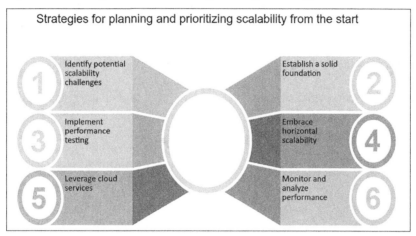

Figure 13.1: *Strategies for addressing Scaling Challenges (Source - https://fastercapital.co/i/ MVP-Scaling--Scaling-Your-Minimum-Viable-Product--Challenges-and-Solutions--Strategies- for-planning-and-prioritizing-scalability-from-the-start.webp)*

- **Microservices Architecture:**

  Modularize AI features into microservices to facilitate independent scaling and maintenance. This approach allows each service to be deployed and scaled separately based on demand.

- **Containerization:**

  Use Docker to containerize applications, ensuring consistency across environments and simplifying deployment. Containers can be easily scaled and managed using orchestration tools such as Kubernetes.

- **Cloud Platforms:**

  Leverage cloud services such as AWS Elastic Beanstalk and Google Cloud Platform's App Engine, which provide managed environments that automatically scale applications based on demand.

- **Performance Optimization:**

  Optimize Node.js and MongoDB performance for high-traffic scenarios. Implement database sharding, caching strategies with Redis, and load balancing to handle increased loads efficiently.

- **Model Management:**

  Continuously monitor and optimize machine learning model performance. Use techniques such as model retraining, versioning, and A/B testing to ensure models remain effective as user demand grows.

By understanding and addressing these scaling challenges, developers can ensure that their AI-enabled MERN applications are prepared to handle growth and provide a seamless user experience. The subsequent sections will delve deeper into microservices architecture, containerization, orchestration, and leveraging cloud platforms for scalability.

Microservices Architecture for AI

Microservices architecture is a design pattern that structures an application as a collection of loosely coupled services. Each service is independent, responsible for a specific functionality, and can be developed, deployed, and scaled independently. This approach is particularly beneficial for AI-enabled MERN applications, as it allows for modularization of AI features, facilitating easier scaling and maintenance.

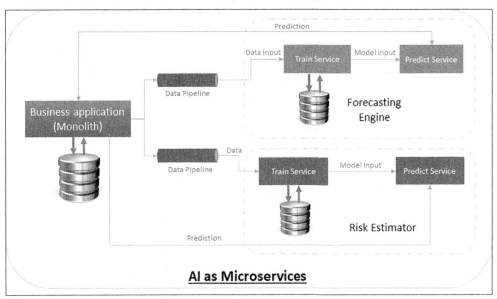

Figure 13.2: *Microservices Architecture for AI (Source –https://miro.medium.com/v2/re-size:fit:1400/1*VR1QI_2TOy0mtPD1ak7LrQ.png)*

Benefits of Microservices for AI

Let us understand the benefits of Microservices for AI with ease.

- **Scalability:**

   Microservices enable independent scaling of different components based on demand. AI services can be scaled separately from other parts of the application, optimizing resource usage.

- **Flexibility:**

  Each microservice can be developed using the most suitable technology stack, allowing for flexibility in choosing tools and frameworks for AI functionalities.

- **Resilience:**

  The failure of one microservice does not impact the entire application. This isolation enhances the resilience and reliability of the system.

- **Continuous Deployment:**

  Microservices facilitate continuous integration and deployment, allowing for rapid updates and improvements to AI features without affecting the entire application.

Implementing Microservices for AI

Let us implement the Microservices for AI with ease.

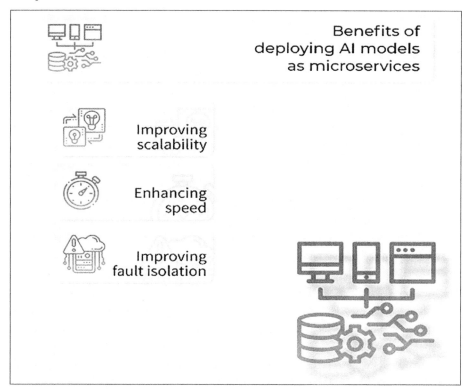

Figure 13.3: *Implementing microservices for AI (Source –https://lh6.googleusercontent.com/ proxy/SW9CLFXFjpRby2SA6SXCit6Zu7Nfv0sk_EeQna9qeoSDcqZnZiKeBmBkrSvmEwm-1fzowe5m5GxcgGvwpbmqZBKXOBM56_WuUjFhrGEv0kx8_ts5REORMnRVf6cLEv T0QR9RmGy4DIcczwgT2OE58LjJRLw7EHBmmOnzzGdw4Rmvl)*

- **Service Decomposition:**

  Identify and separate AI functionalities into distinct microservices. For example, separate services for recommendation engines, image processing, and natural language processing.

- **Communication:**

  Use lightweight protocols such as HTTP/REST or messaging systems such as RabbitMQ for communication between microservices.

- **Data Management:**

  Each microservice can have its own database, allowing for tailored data management strategies. Use database replication and sharding to handle large datasets.

- **API Gateway:**

  Implement an API gateway to manage and route requests to the appropriate microservices, providing a unified entry point for clients.

Containerization with Docker

Containerization is the process of packaging an application and its dependencies into a container, ensuring consistency across environments. Docker is a popular containerization platform that simplifies deployment and scaling of applications, making it ideal for AI-enabled MERN applications.

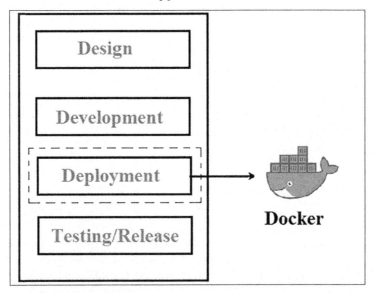

Figure 13.4: *Containerization with Docker (Source - https://media.geeksforgeeks.org/wp-content/uploads/20190915141015/dockercycle1.png)*

Key Concepts of Docker

Let us understand the key concepts of Docker.

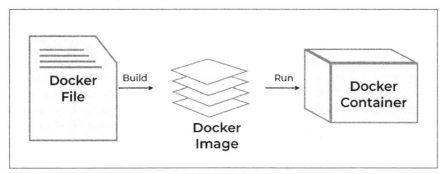

Figure 13.5: *Key concepts of Docker (Source –https://media.geeksforgeeks.org /wp-content/uploads/20230406105935/dockerfile-2.png)*

- **Containers:**

  Containers are lightweight, portable units that encapsulate an application and its dependencies. They run consistently across various environments, from development to production.

- **Docker Images:**

  A Docker image is a read-only template that contains the application code, runtime, libraries, and environment variables. Images are used to create containers.

- **Dockerfile:**

  A Dockerfile is a script containing instructions for building a Docker image. It specifies the base image, application dependencies, and commands to run the application.

- **Docker Compose:**

  Docker Compose is a tool for defining and running multi-container Docker applications. It uses a YAML file to configure application services, networks, and volumes.

Benefits of Docker for AI

Let us understand the benefits of Docker for AI.

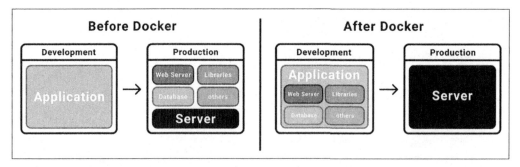

Figure 13.6: *Benefits of Docker (Source - https://media.licdn.com/dms/image/D4D12AQEu-0oURD8q93Q/article-cover_image-shrink_720_1280/0/1684544298697?e=21474 83647&v=beta&t=lvzKyMBPcYZzB8pMtiPWcLz8r02PyX1my315abKB-_8)*

- **Portability:**

  Docker containers can run consistently across different environments, from development to production, ensuring that AI models and dependencies work as expected.

- **Isolation:**

  Containers provide isolated environments, preventing conflicts between dependencies and enhancing security.

- **Scalability:**

  Containers can be easily scaled up or down to handle varying workloads, making them suitable for AI applications with fluctuating demand.

- **Efficiency:**

  Containers are lightweight and share the host system's kernel, allowing for efficient resource utilization and faster startup times compared to virtual machines.

Implementing Docker for AI

Let us implement Docker for AI with ease.

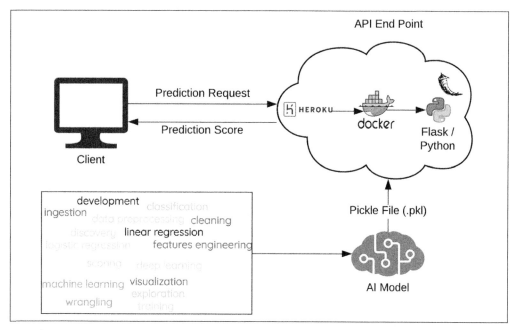

Figure 13.7: *Implementing Docker for AI (Source - https://atrium.ai/wp-content/up-loads/2021/06/DockerHerokuPython.png)*

1. **Create a Dockerfile**:

   Define the environment for your AI application in a Dockerfile, specifying the base image, dependencies, and commands to run the application.

   ```
   FROM node:14
   WORKDIR /app
   COPY package*.json ./
   RUN npm install
   COPY . .
   CMD ["node", "app.js"]
   ```

2. **Build the Docker Image**:

   Use the Dockerfile to build a Docker image for your AI application.

   ```
   docker build -t my-ai-app .
   ```

3. **Run the Docker Container**:

   Start a container from the Docker image, mapping necessary ports.

   ```
   docker run -p 3000:3000 my-ai-app
   ```

4. **Use Docker Compose**:

For applications with multiple services, use Docker Compose to define and run multi-container applications.

```
version: '3'
services:
  web:
    build: .
    ports:
      - "3000:3000"
  db:
    image: mongo
    ports:
      - "27017:27017"
```

5. **Integrate with Kubernetes**:

Use Kubernetes for orchestration and management of Docker containers, enabling automated deployment, scaling, and management of containerized applications.

By leveraging microservices architecture and Docker, developers can effectively scale AI features in MERN applications, ensuring they are modular, portable, and efficient. These strategies enable applications to handle growth and provide a seamless user experience.

Orchestration with Kubernetes

Kubernetes is a powerful open-source platform for automating the deployment, scaling, and management of containerized applications. It provides a robust framework for orchestrating Docker containers, making it an essential tool for scaling AI features in production environments.

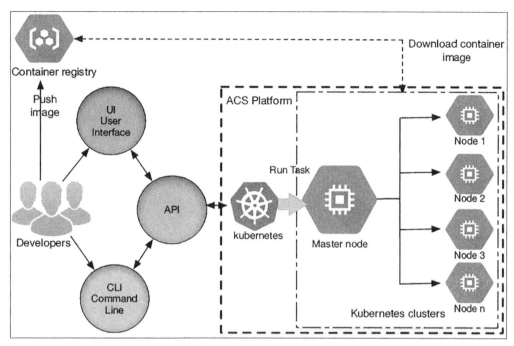

Figure 13.8: *Orchestration with Kubernetes (Source - https://www.researchgate.net/profile/ Uchechukwu-Awada/publication/325737011/figure/fig1/AS:637005562142722 @1528885369411/Kubernetes-orchestration-overview.png)*

Key Features of Kubernetes

Let us understand the key features of Kubernetes with ease.

- **Automated Deployment and Scaling:**

  Kubernetes automates the deployment of applications and scales them based on demand. It manages the desired state of applications, ensuring they run consistently across clusters.

- **Load Balancing:**

  Kubernetes provides built-in load balancing to distribute network traffic across multiple containers, ensuring high availability and reliability.

- **Self-Healing:**

  Kubernetes automatically replaces failed containers, restarts containers that fail health checks, and reschedules containers when nodes die.

- **Secret and Configuration Management:**

  Kubernetes manages sensitive information, such as passwords and API keys, securely using secrets. It also manages application configurations separately from the container images.

Implementing Kubernetes for AI

Let us implement Kubernetes for AI with ease.

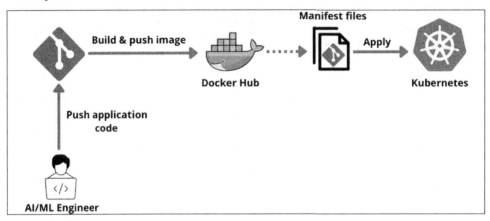

Figure 13.9: *Implementing Kubernetes for AI* (*Source –https://media.dev.to/cdn-cgi/image/ width=1000,height=420,fit=cover,gravity=auto,format=auto/https%3A%2F%2Fdev-to-uploads. s3.amazonaws.com%2Fuploads%2Farticles%2F9ycmjlrp06czknan74iv.png*)

1. **Set Up a Kubernetes Cluster**:

   Use cloud providers such as Google Kubernetes Engine (GKE), Amazon Elastic Kubernetes Service (EKS), or Azure Kubernetes Service (AKS) to set up a managed Kubernetes cluster.

2. **Define Kubernetes Manifests**:

   Create YAML files to define the desired state of your applications, including deployments, services, and configurations.

   ```
   apiVersion: apps/v1
     kind: Deployment
     metadata:
       name: ai-service
     spec:
       replicas: 3
       selector:
         matchLabels:
           app: ai-service
       template:
         metadata:
           labels:
             app: ai-service
           spec:
   ```

```
containers:
- name: ai-container
  image: my-ai-app:latest
  ports:
  - containerPort: 3000
```

3. **Deploy and Manage Applications**:

   Use `kubectl` to deploy and manage applications on the Kubernetes cluster.

   ```
   kubectl apply -f deployment.yaml
   ```

4. **Monitor and Optimize**:

   Use Kubernetes dashboards and monitoring tools, such as Prometheus and Grafana, to monitor application performance and optimize resource usage.

Leveraging Cloud Platforms for Scalability

Cloud platforms provide the infrastructure and services needed to scale AI-enabled MERN applications efficiently. They offer managed environments that automatically adjust resources based on demand, ensuring applications remain performant and responsive.

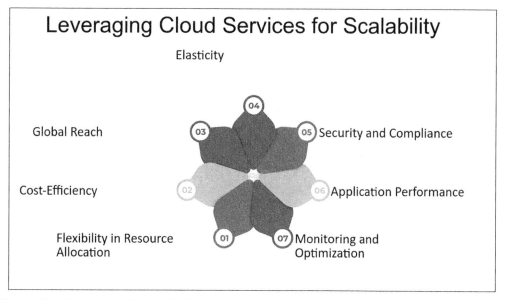

Figure 13.10: *Leveraging Cloud Platforms for Scalability (Source –https://fastercapital.co/i/Unlocking-Scalable-Solutions-with-SAP-Cloud-Platform--Leveraging-Cloud-Services-for-Scalability.webp)*

Key Cloud Platforms

Let us understand and see the key cloud platforms with ease.

- **Amazon Web Services (AWS):**
  - o **Elastic Beanstalk**: A PaaS that simplifies application deployment and scaling. It automatically handles capacity provisioning, load balancing, and scaling.
  - o **EC2**: Provides resizable compute capacity for hosting applications. Instances can be scaled based on demand.
  - o **AWS Lambda**: Offers serverless computing, automatically scaling applications based on requests.
- **Google Cloud Platform (GCP):**
  - o **App Engine**: A fully managed serverless platform that scales applications automatically based on traffic.
  - o **Compute Engine**: Offers scalable virtual machines for running applications.
  - o **Kubernetes Engine**: A managed Kubernetes service for orchestrating containerized applications.
- **Microsoft Azure:**
  - o **App Service**: A fully managed platform for building and scaling web apps. It supports auto-scaling and load balancing.
  - o **Virtual Machines**: Provides scalable virtual machines for hosting applications.
  - o **Azure Functions**: Offers serverless computing with automatic scaling.

Strategies for Leveraging Cloud Platforms

Let us see the strategies for leveraging Cloud Platforms with ease.

- **Auto Scaling:**

  Configure auto-scaling policies to automatically adjust resources based on demand, ensuring optimal performance and cost-efficiency.

- **Load Balancing:**

  Use cloud-based load balancers to distribute traffic evenly across multiple instances, enhancing application reliability and availability.

- **Serverless Architecture:**

  Leverage serverless computing to run functions in response to events, automatically scaling based on demand and reducing infrastructure management overhead.

- **Managed Databases:**

  Use managed database services to ensure high availability, scalability, and security for your application's data.

Optimizing Node.js for High Performance

Optimizing Node.js applications is crucial for handling high-traffic scenarios and ensuring that AI features remain responsive and efficient. This involves implementing best practices and techniques to improve performance and resource utilization.

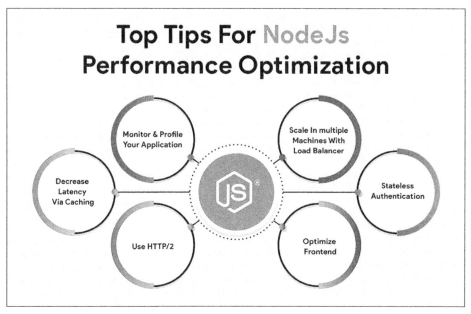

Figure 13.11: Optimizing Node.js for High Performance (Source - https://www.bacancytechnology.com/blog/wp-content/uploads/2022/05/Top-Tips-For-Node-Js-Performance-Optimization-min.jpg)

Key Optimization Techniques

Let us understand the key optimization techniques with ease.

- **Asynchronous Programming:**

  Use asynchronous programming patterns, such as callbacks, promises, and async/await, to handle concurrent operations efficiently without blocking the event loop.

- **Cluster Module:**

  Use the Node.js cluster module to take advantage of multi-core systems by spawning multiple worker processes. This improves the application's ability to handle concurrent requests.

```
const cluster = require('cluster');
const http = require('http');
const numCPUs = require('os').cpus().length;

if (cluster.isMaster) {
  for (let i = 0; i < numCPUs; i++) {
    cluster.fork();
  }
} else {
  http.createServer((req, res) => {
    res.writeHead(200);
    res.end('Hello world\n');
  }).listen(8000);
}
```

- **Caching:**

  Implement caching strategies using Redis or in-memory caches to reduce database load and improve response times for frequently accessed data.

- **Load Testing and Monitoring:**

  Conduct load testing to identify bottlenecks and optimize performance. Use monitoring tools such as New Relic or Datadog to track application metrics and performance.

- **Efficient Use of Libraries:**

  Choose lightweight and efficient libraries for your application. Regularly review and update dependencies to ensure optimal performance and security.

- **Memory Management:**

  Monitor and manage memory usage to prevent leaks and ensure efficient resource utilization. Use tools such as Node.js built-in `--inspect` flag and Chrome DevTools for profiling.

- **Compression:**

  Enable Gzip or Brotli compression to reduce the size of the response body, improving load times and reducing bandwidth usage.

- **Connection Pooling:**

  Use connection pooling for database connections to reduce the overhead of establishing new connections and improve query performance.

- **Optimize Query Performance:**

  Use indexes and optimize database queries to reduce response times and improve data retrieval efficiency.

- **Monitoring and Logging:**

  Implement monitoring and logging to track application performance and detect issues in real-time. Use tools such as New Relic, Datadog, or ELK Stack (Elasticsearch, Logstash, Kibana) for comprehensive monitoring.

By employing these strategies, developers can effectively scale AI features in MERN applications, ensuring they remain performant and responsive under varying loads. This enables applications to handle growth and provide a seamless user experience.

Conclusion

This chapter provided a comprehensive guide to addressing the challenges and strategies involved in scaling AI functionalities within MERN applications. As applications grow and attract more users, it is crucial to design AI features with scalability in mind to ensure performance and responsiveness. The chapter explored the use of microservices architecture to modularize AI features, facilitating easier scaling and maintenance.

Key tools such as Kubernetes and Docker were introduced for containerization and orchestration, enabling the deployment of scalable applications across multiple servers. The chapter also discussed leveraging cloud services such as AWS Elastic Beanstalk and Google Cloud Platform's App Engine, which provide managed environments that automatically scale applications based on demand. Techniques for optimizing Node.js and MongoDB performance, including database sharding, caching strategies with Redis, and load balancing, were covered.

By the end of this chapter, readers should be equipped with the knowledge to effectively scale their AI-enabled MERN applications, ensuring they can handle growth and provide a seamless user experience.

The next chapter provides readers with insights into the latest trends, tools, and methodologies that are driving innovation in web development and AI. It highlights the convergence of AI with technologies such as blockchain for enhanced security and data integrity, the Internet of Things (IoT) for smarter, interconnected systems, and quantum computing for solving complex computational problems at unprecedented speeds.

Multiple Choice Questions

1. What is the primary benefit of using microservices architecture for AI features?

    a. Simplified database management

    b. Independent scaling and maintenance

    c. Reduced server costs

    d. Enhanced frontend design

2. Which tool is essential for containerizing applications in a scalable way?

    a. GitHub

    b. Docker

    c. Jenkins

    d. Terraform

3. What is the role of Kubernetes in application deployment?

    a. Managing relational databases

    b. Orchestrating containerized applications

    c. Designing user interfaces

    d. Encrypting data

4. Which cloud service provides a managed environment that automatically scales applications based on demand?

    a. AWS Elastic Beanstalk

    b. GitHub Actions

    c. MongoDB Atlas

    d. Visual Studio Code

5. What is a key strategy for optimizing Node.js performance in high-traffic scenarios?

    a. Using synchronous programming

    b. Implementing caching with Redis

    c. Reducing server instances

    d. Disabling load balancing

6. How does Docker contribute to application scalability?

   a. By increasing server costs

   b. By providing lightweight, portable containers

   c. By managing frontend components

   d. By encrypting user data

7. What is the purpose of database sharding in MongoDB?

   a. To reduce data redundancy

   b. To distribute data across multiple servers

   c. To enhance user authentication

   d. To simplify API design

8. Which tool is used for load balancing in scalable applications?

   a. ESLint

   b. NGINX

   c. Babel

   d. Webpack

9. What is a benefit of using cloud platforms for AI applications?

   a. Fixed pricing plans

   b. Manual scaling

   c. Automatic resource adjustment

   d. Increased development time

10. Why is monitoring machine learning model performance important in production?

    a. To reduce server load

    b. To ensure models do not become bottlenecks

    c. To enhance frontend design

    d. To simplify database management

Answers

1. b
2. b
3. b
4. a
5. b
6. b
7. b
8. b
9. c
10. b

CHAPTER 14

Emerging Trends in AI and MERN Development

Introduction

Emerging Trends in AI and MERN Development is a forward-looking chapter that explores the cutting-edge advancements and emerging technologies shaping the future of AI within the MERN ecosystem. This chapter provides readers with insights into the latest trends, tools, and methodologies that are driving innovation in web development and AI. It highlights the convergence of AI with technologies such as blockchain for enhanced security and data integrity, the Internet of Things (IoT) for smarter, interconnected systems, and quantum computing for solving complex computational problems at unprecedented speeds.

The chapter delves into the evolution of machine learning libraries beyond TensorFlow. js, introducing readers to newer, more specialized libraries that offer advanced capabilities for specific AI tasks. It also discusses the growing importance of ethical AI and responsible development practices, emphasizing the need for transparency, fairness, and privacy in AI applications.

We will learn about the latest developments in the MERN stack, including new features in MongoDB, Express.js, React, and Node.js that facilitate the integration of AI features. The chapter also covers the role of serverless architectures in deploying scalable, cost-effective AI applications and the use of edge computing to reduce latency in AI processing.

By the end of this chapter, readers will be well-informed about the future directions of AI and MERN development, equipped with the knowledge to leverage emerging technologies and stay ahead in the rapidly evolving landscape of web development.

Structure

In this chapter, we will cover the following topics:

- Advancements in AI Technologies
- Specialized AI Libraries and Tools
- AI and Blockchain Integration
- AI in the Internet of Things (IoT)
- Quantum Computing's Impact on AI

Advancements in AI Technologies

The field of artificial intelligence (AI) is rapidly evolving, with new technologies and methodologies emerging to enhance its capabilities and applications. This section explores the latest advancements in AI technologies that are shaping the future of AI within the MERN ecosystem.

Figure 14.1: Advancements in AI Technologies (Source - https://media.licdn.com/dms/image/ D4E12AQGOV8n2ZwCdyA/article-cover_image-shrink_720_1280/0/1690289092413?e =2147483647&v=beta&t=CAHOo-KPg9cuHh6lIxA9A5af4jbN_Oso-B9o8zCgGJ0)

Key Advancements in AI

Let us understand the key advancements in AI with ease.

- **Deep Learning**:

  Deep learning, a subset of machine learning, uses neural networks with multiple layers to model complex patterns in data. Recent advancements include more efficient architectures such as Transformers, which have revolutionized natural language processing (NLP) and computer vision tasks.

- **Transfer Learning:**

  Transfer learning allows models trained on large datasets to be fine-tuned for specific tasks with smaller datasets. This technique reduces training time and resources while improving model performance.

- **Reinforcement Learning:**

  Reinforcement learning focuses on training agents to make decisions by rewarding desired behaviors. It has seen significant advancements in fields such as robotics, gaming, and autonomous systems.

- **Explainable AI (XAI):**

  As AI systems become more complex, the need for transparency and interpretability grows. Explainable AI aims to make AI decisions understandable to humans, enhancing trust and accountability.

- **Federated Learning:**

  Federated learning enables training models across decentralized devices while keeping data local. This approach enhances privacy and reduces data transfer costs, making it suitable for applications such as mobile devices and IoT.

- **AI Ethics and Fairness:**

  The focus on ethical AI development is increasing, with efforts to ensure fairness, transparency, and privacy in AI systems. Frameworks and guidelines are being developed to address biases and ethical concerns.

Impact on MERN Development

Let us understand the impact on MERN Development with ease.

- **Integration with MERN Stack:**

  The MERN stack (MongoDB, Express.js, React, and Node.js) is evolving to support advanced AI features. New tools and libraries are being developed to facilitate the integration of AI into web applications.

- **Real-Time AI Processing:**

  Advancements in AI technologies enable real-time data processing, allowing MERN applications to deliver instant insights and personalized experiences.

- **Scalability and Performance:**

  Improved AI algorithms and models enhance the scalability and performance of MERN applications, enabling them to handle larger datasets and more complex tasks efficiently.

- **Enhanced User Experience:**

  AI-driven features such as chatbots, recommendation systems, and personalized content enhance user engagement and satisfaction in MERN applications.

  By understanding these advancements in AI technologies, developers can leverage cutting-edge tools and methodologies to enhance their MERN applications, ensuring they remain competitive and innovative in a rapidly evolving digital landscape.

Specialized AI Libraries and Tools

As AI technology continues to evolve, specialized libraries and tools are emerging to address specific tasks and challenges in AI development. These libraries offer advanced capabilities, optimized performance, and ease of integration, making them invaluable for developers working within the MERN stack.

Key Specialized AI Libraries

Let us check and see the key specialized AI libraries.

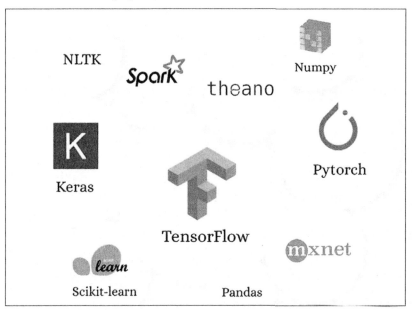

Figure 14.2: *Key specialized AI Libraries (Source -https://media.licdn.com/dms/image/D5612AQGPnXf5_T2Ulg/article-cover_image-shrink_720_1280/0/1688363717353?e =2147483647&v=beta&t=k5rLYHGX6LEt9HXS-4v2DA11AWpMCOR4IiWiJiA3tIY)*

- **PyTorch:**

  PyTorch is a popular open-source machine learning library known for its dynamic computation graph and ease of use. It is widely used for research and production in deep learning applications.

- **Scikit-learn:**

  Scikit-learn is a robust library for classical machine learning tasks such as classification, regression, and clustering. It provides simple and efficient tools for data analysis and modeling.

- **Hugging Face Transformers:**

  This library offers state-of-the-art natural language processing (NLP) models, including BERT, GPT, and T5. It simplifies the integration of advanced language models into applications.

- **OpenCV:**

  OpenCV is a comprehensive library for computer vision tasks, providing tools for image processing, video analysis, and machine learning. It is widely used for real-time applications.

- **Keras:**

  Keras is a high-level neural network API that runs on top of TensorFlow. It is designed for fast experimentation and is user-friendly, making it accessible for beginners and experts alike.

Tools for AI Development

Now, let's understand the essential tools for AI Development.

- **Jupyter Notebooks:**

  Jupyter Notebooks provide an interactive environment for data analysis and visualization, allowing developers to write and execute code in a notebook format.

- **TensorBoard:**

  TensorBoard is a visualization tool for TensorFlow that helps monitor training progress, visualize model graphs, and analyze performance metrics.

- **MLflow:**

  MLflow is an open-source platform for managing the machine learning lifecycle, including experimentation, reproducibility, and deployment.

- **Docker:**

  Docker is essential for containerizing AI applications, ensuring consistency across environments, and simplifying deployment.

- **Kubernetes:**

  Kubernetes orchestrates containerized applications, enabling automated deployment, scaling, and management of AI workloads.

Integration with the MERN Stack

Finally, let us integrate with the MERN Stack.

- **Node.js Bindings:**

  Many AI libraries offer Node.js bindings, allowing seamless integration with MERN applications. This enables developers to leverage AI capabilities directly within their web applications.

- **RESTful APIs:**

  AI models can be exposed as RESTful APIs, enabling easy integration with the MERN stack. This approach allows for scalable and modular AI services.

- **GraphQL:**

  GraphQL can be used to query AI models and services, providing a flexible and efficient way to fetch data and integrate AI features into MERN applications.

  By exploring these specialized AI libraries and tools, developers can enhance their MERN applications with advanced AI capabilities, ensuring they remain at the forefront of innovation in web development.

AI and Blockchain Integration

The integration of AI and blockchain technologies is an emerging trend that offers enhanced security, transparency, and efficiency in various applications. By combining the strengths of both technologies, developers can create innovative solutions that address complex challenges in data management, security, and automation.

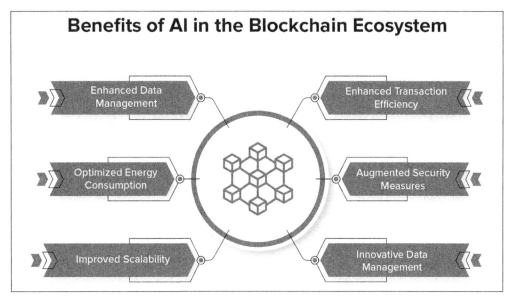

Figure 14.3: *Benefits of AI in the Blockchain Ecosystem* (*Source -https://appinventiv.com/ wp-content/uploads/2019/03/Integration-of-Blockchain-and-AI- All-You-Need-to-Know_Info-1.webp*)

Key Benefits of AI and Blockchain Integration

Let us understand the key benefits of AI and Blockchain integration.

- **Enhanced Data Security:**

  Blockchain provides a decentralized and immutable ledger, ensuring that data is securely stored and tamper-proof. This enhances the security of AI models and the data they rely on.

- **Transparency and Trust:**

  Blockchain's transparent nature allows all participants to verify data integrity, fostering trust in AI-driven processes and decisions. This is particularly valuable in industries such as finance and healthcare.

- **Decentralized AI Models:**

  AI models can be deployed across a decentralized network, reducing the risk of single points of failure and enhancing resilience. This decentralization also enables collaborative AI development and sharing.

- **Data Provenance:**

  Blockchain can track the origin and history of data used in AI models, ensuring data quality and compliance with regulatory requirements. This is crucial for maintaining ethical AI practices.

- **Smart Contracts:**

  Smart contracts on blockchain can automate AI-driven processes, executing predefined actions when certain conditions are met. This automation reduces the need for intermediaries and enhances efficiency.

Use Cases of AI and Blockchain Integration

Let us analyze the use cases of AI and Blockchain integration.

- **Supply Chain Management:**

  AI algorithms can optimize logistics and inventory management, while blockchain ensures transparency and traceability of goods throughout the supply chain.

- **Healthcare:**

  AI can analyze patient data for diagnostics, while blockchain secures medical records and ensures data privacy and integrity.

- **Financial Services:**

  AI models can assess risks and detect fraud, while blockchain enables secure and transparent transactions and record-keeping.

- **Decentralized Autonomous Organizations (DAOs):**

  AI can automate decision-making processes within DAOs, while blockchain provides a secure and transparent framework for governance and operations.

Challenges and Considerations

Let us understand the different challenges and considerations that we might have to consider for integrating AI and Blockchain.

- **Scalability:**

  Both AI and blockchain face scalability challenges. Combining the two requires careful consideration of network performance and resource management.

- **Interoperability:**

  Ensuring seamless integration between AI systems and blockchain platforms is crucial for effective implementation. Standardized protocols and interfaces can help achieve this.

- **Data Privacy:**

  While blockchain enhances data security, maintaining privacy in a transparent ledger can be challenging. Techniques such as zero-knowledge proofs can help protect sensitive information.

- **Regulatory Compliance:**

  Compliance with data protection regulations, such as GDPR, is essential when integrating AI and blockchain. Developers must ensure that data usage and storage adhere to legal requirements.

  By exploring the integration of AI and blockchain, developers can harness the combined potential of these technologies to create secure, transparent, and efficient solutions across various industries. This convergence represents a significant step forward in the evolution of digital innovation.

AI in the Internet of Things (IoT)

The integration of AI with the Internet of Things (IoT) is transforming the way devices interact and make decisions autonomously. By combining AI's data processing capabilities with IoT's connectivity, smarter and more efficient systems can be developed.

Figure 14.4: *AI in the Internet of Things (IoT)* (*Source -https://media.licdn.com/dms/image/ D5612AQFflnG8_QajhQ/article-cover_image-shrink_720_1280/0/1706444262681?e=214748364 7&v=beta&t=bBWDPy9f2lblUDTCuzmKIL6UkZxcRj-NGi-yDZKEWW8)*

Key Benefits of AI in IoT

Let us understand the key benefits of AI in IoT.

- **Enhanced Data Analysis:**

  AI algorithms can process and analyze vast amounts of data generated by IoT devices, extracting valuable insights and enabling real-time decision-making.

- **Predictive Maintenance:**

  AI-driven predictive analytics can forecast equipment failures and maintenance needs, reducing downtime and extending the lifespan of devices.

- **Automation and Control:**

  AI enables IoT systems to automate processes and control devices autonomously, improving efficiency and reducing the need for human intervention.

- **Personalization:**

  AI can tailor IoT device interactions based on user preferences and behavior, enhancing user experience and satisfaction.

Applications of AI in IoT

Let us understand and study the different applications of AI in IoT.

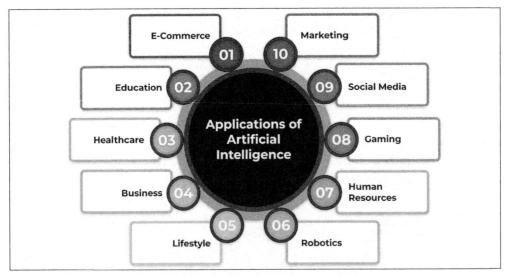

Figure 14.5: Applications of AI in IoT (Source –*https://www.solulab.com/wp-content/up-loads/2024/01/Applications-of-AI.jpg*)

- **Smart Homes:**

  AI-powered IoT devices in smart homes can learn user habits and preferences to automate lighting, heating, and security systems.

- **Industrial IoT:**

  In manufacturing, AI can optimize production processes, monitor equipment health, and improve supply chain efficiency.

- **Healthcare:**

  AI and IoT devices can monitor patient health in real-time, providing alerts and insights to healthcare providers for better patient care.

- **Smart Cities:**

  AI can analyze data from IoT sensors in smart cities to optimize traffic flow, reduce energy consumption, and enhance public safety.

Challenges and Considerations

Let us understand the challenges and considerations for using AI and IoT.

- **Data Security and Privacy:**

  The integration of AI and IoT raises concerns about data security and privacy. Ensuring secure data transmission and storage is crucial.

- **Interoperability:**

  Achieving seamless communication between diverse IoT devices and platforms is essential for effective AI integration.

- **Scalability:**

  As the number of IoT devices grows, scalable AI solutions are needed to handle the increased data volume and processing demands.

- **Latency:**

  Reducing latency in AI processing is critical for real-time applications. Edge computing can help by processing data closer to the source.

  By leveraging AI in IoT, developers can create intelligent systems that enhance efficiency, automate processes, and provide personalized experiences, driving innovation across various industries.

Impact of Quantum Computing on AI

Quantum computing is poised to revolutionize the field of artificial intelligence by providing unprecedented computational power. This section explores how quantum computing can impact AI development, particularly within the MERN ecosystem.

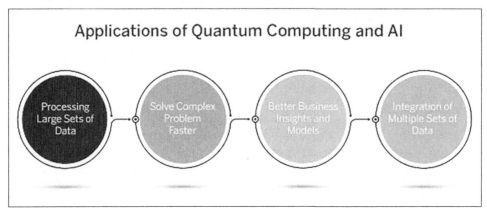

Figure 14.6: *Applications of Quantum Computing and AI (Source –https://www.bbvaopenmind. com/wp-content/uploads/2021/03/BBVA-OpenMind-Banafa-Quantum-Computing-and-IA.jpg)*

Key Impacts of Quantum Computing on AI

Let us study the key impacts of Quantum Computing on AI.

- **Enhanced Computational Power:**

  Quantum computers can process complex calculations much faster than classical computers, enabling the training of AI models on larger datasets and solving problems previously considered intractable.

- **Improved Optimization:**

  Quantum algorithms can enhance optimization processes in AI, leading to more efficient neural networks and better-performing models.

- **Accelerated Machine Learning:**

  Quantum computing can speed up machine learning tasks such as data classification, clustering, and regression, improving the efficiency of AI applications.

- **Advanced Data Analysis:**

  The ability to analyze vast amounts of data quickly allows for more sophisticated AI models and insights, enhancing decision-making and predictive analytics.

Potential Applications

Let us check the different potential applications.

- **Drug Discovery:**

  Quantum computing can accelerate the simulation of molecular interactions, aiding in the discovery of new drugs and therapies.

- **Financial Modeling:**

  Quantum algorithms can optimize complex financial models, improving risk assessment and investment strategies.

- **Cryptography:**

  Quantum computing can both challenge and enhance cryptographic techniques, impacting data security and encryption methods.

- **Supply Chain Optimization:**

  Quantum computing can optimize logistics and supply chain operations, reducing costs and improving efficiency.

Challenges and Considerations

Let us understand the different challenges and considerations.

- **Technical Complexity:**

  Developing quantum algorithms and integrating them with existing AI systems requires specialized knowledge and expertise.

- **Scalability:**

  While quantum computing offers immense potential, scaling quantum systems for widespread use remains a challenge.

- **Cost and Accessibility:**

  Quantum computing technology is currently expensive and not widely accessible, limiting its immediate impact on AI development.

- **Ethical Implications:**

  The power of quantum computing necessitates careful consideration of ethical implications, particularly in areas such as data privacy and security.

  By understanding the potential impact of quantum computing on AI, developers can prepare to leverage this emerging technology to enhance their AI-enabled MERN applications, driving innovation and efficiency in web development.

Conclusion

This chapter provided a comprehensive overview of the latest advancements and technologies shaping the future of AI within the MERN ecosystem. By exploring cutting-edge trends, such as the convergence of AI with blockchain, IoT, and quantum computing, readers gain insights into how these technologies enhance security, efficiency, and computational power. The chapter also highlighted the evolution of machine learning libraries beyond TensorFlow.js, introducing specialized tools that offer advanced capabilities for specific AI tasks.

Emphasizing the importance of ethical AI and responsible development practices, the chapter underscores the need for transparency, fairness, and privacy in AI applications. Additionally, it covered the latest developments in the MERN stack and the role of serverless architectures and edge computing in deploying scalable, cost-effective AI applications. We also learned to leverage emerging technologies, ensuring that we remain competitive and innovative in the rapidly evolving landscape of web development. The next chapter is dedicated to showcasing the practical application and impact of integrating AI within the MERN ecosystem through two compelling case studies.

Multiple Choice Questions

1. What is a key benefit of integrating AI with blockchain technology?

    a. Increased data redundancy

    b. Enhanced security and data integrity

    c. Simplified user interfaces

    d. Reduced computational power

2. How does AI enhance IoT systems?

    a. By reducing device connectivity

    b. By enabling real-time data analysis and automation

    c. By increasing data storage requirements

    d. By limiting device interactions

3. What is the role of quantum computing in AI development?

    a. Simplifying frontend design

    b. Providing enhanced computational power for complex problems

    c. Reducing server costs

    d. Managing relational databases

4. Which library is known for its dynamic computation graph and ease of use in deep learning?

    a. TensorFlow.js

    b. PyTorch

    c. OpenCV

    d. Scikit-learn

5. What is the primary focus of ethical AI development?

    a. Enhancing data storage

    b. Ensuring transparency, fairness, and privacy

    c. Increasing computational speed

    d. Simplifying user interfaces

6. How does edge computing benefit AI applications?

    a. By increasing latency

    b. By reducing latency and processing data closer to the source

    c. By simplifying data encryption

    d. By increasing server costs

7. What is a significant advantage of serverless architectures in AI applications?

    a. Fixed resource allocation

    b. Scalable, cost-effective deployment

    c. Increased manual intervention

    d. Reduced security features

8. Which technology is used to automate AI-driven processes with predefined conditions?

    a. RESTful APIs

    b. Smart contracts on blockchain

    c. GraphQL

    d. Docker containers

9. What is the primary benefit of using specialized AI libraries?

    a. Simplified database management

    b. Advanced capabilities for specific AI tasks

    c. Reduced computational requirements

    d. Enhanced frontend design

10. How does the MERN stack support AI integration?

    a. By limiting server-side capabilities

    b. By providing tools and libraries for seamless AI feature integration

    c. By focusing solely on frontend development

    d. By reducing data processing capabilities

Answers

1. b
2. b
3. b
4. b
5. b
6. b
7. b
8. b
9. b
10. b

CHAPTER 15

Case Studies and Real-World Success Stories

Introduction

Case Studies and Real-World Success Stories is a chapter dedicated to showcasing the practical application and impact of integrating AI within the MERN ecosystem through two compelling case studies. This chapter aims to inspire and educate readers by demonstrating how the concepts, technologies, and methodologies discussed throughout the book have been successfully implemented in real-world projects. Each case study will delve into the challenges faced, the solutions implemented, and the outcomes achieved, providing valuable insights and lessons.

The first case study will explore a dynamic e-commerce platform that leverages AI for personalized product recommendations, using technologies such as MongoDB for data storage, Express.js for server-side logic, React for building a responsive UI, and Node.js for backend development. It will highlight the use of TensorFlow.js for developing the machine learning models that drive the recommendation engine.

The second case study will focus on a customer service chatbot designed to enhance user engagement and automate responses. This project will showcase the integration of natural language processing (NLP) techniques, utilizing libraries, such as Dialogflow, for understanding user queries and generating appropriate responses within a MERN-based application.

By the end of this chapter, readers will have a clear understanding of how AI and MERN technologies can be combined to solve real-world problems, driving innovation and improving user experiences. These case studies will serve as a source of inspiration and a practical guide for readers looking to embark on their own AI-driven projects within the MERN ecosystem.

Structure

In this chapter, we will cover the following topics:

- Introduction to Real-World AI Applications
- Case Study 1: AI-Driven E-Commerce Platform
- Case Study 2: Customer Service Chatbot

Introduction to Real-World AI Applications

The integration of artificial intelligence (AI) within the MERN stack has opened up new possibilities for creating innovative and impactful web applications. This section introduces the practical applications of AI in real-world scenarios, highlighting how AI technologies can enhance user experiences, drive business growth, and solve complex challenges. **Artificial Intelligence (AI)** has rapidly evolved from a theoretical concept to a practical reality, permeating various aspects of our daily lives. AI applications, driven by machine learning and deep learning algorithms, are revolutionizing industries and transforming the way we interact with technology.

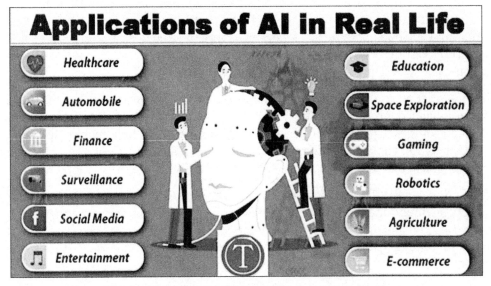

Figure 15.1: *Real World AI Applications (Source -https://i.ytimg.com /vi/fcOcrd9C7VA/sddefault.jpg)*

Key AI Concepts

Before delving into real-world applications, let us briefly discuss some fundamental AI concepts:

- **Machine Learning:** Machine learning (ML) is a subset of artificial intelligence (AI) that provides computers with the ability to learn from data without being explicitly programmed. This means that ML algorithms can automatically improve their performance on a task by learning from experience, rather than relying on manual instructions or predefined rules.

- **Deep Learning:** Deep learning is a subset of machine learning that utilizes artificial neural networks to model complex patterns in data. These neural networks are composed of multiple layers of interconnected nodes (neurons) that process and transform the input data through a series of nonlinear transformations. This allows deep learning models to automatically learn and represent complex features from raw data, enabling them to perform tasks such as image recognition, speech recognition, and natural language processing.

- **Natural Language Processing (NLP):** Natural Language Processing (NLP) is a subset of artificial intelligence that focuses on enabling computers to understand, interpret, and generate human language. It involves the use of computational linguistics, machine learning, and deep learning to analyze and process text or voice data, allowing computers to grasp the full meaning, including the speaker's or writer's intentions and emotions.

- **Computer Vision:** Computer vision is a field of artificial intelligence (AI) that focuses on enabling computers to interpret and understand visual information from the real world. It involves the use of AI algorithms to process digital images and videos, allowing computers to automatically identify, classify, and analyze objects and their surroundings. This technology is used in various applications, including object detection, facial recognition, and autonomous vehicles.

Real-World AI Applications

AI is being leveraged across a wide spectrum of industries, from healthcare to finance and entertainment. Here are some prominent examples:

- **Healthcare:**
  - **Diagnosis:** AI-powered systems can analyze medical images (X-rays, MRIs) to detect diseases such as cancer more accurately and efficiently.
  - **Drug Discovery:** AI can accelerate the process of discovering new drugs by simulating molecular interactions and predicting their effectiveness.

- o **Personalized Medicine:** AI algorithms can tailor treatment plans to individual patients based on their genetic makeup and medical history.

- **Finance:**
  - o **Fraud Detection:** AI models can identify fraudulent transactions by analyzing patterns in financial data.
  - o **Algorithmic Trading:** AI-driven systems can execute trades at high speed and frequency based on market data analysis.
  - o **Credit Scoring:** AI can assess creditworthiness more accurately by considering a broader range of factors beyond traditional credit history.

- **Customer Service:**
  - o **Chatbots:** AI-powered chatbots can provide instant customer support and answer queries efficiently.
  - o **Sentiment Analysis:** AI can analyze customer feedback to understand their emotions and improve product or service offerings.

- **Manufacturing:**
  - o **Predictive Maintenance:** AI can predict equipment failures before they occur, reducing downtime and maintenance costs.
  - o **Quality Control:** AI-powered vision systems can inspect products for defects with high accuracy.

- **Transportation:**
  - o **Autonomous Vehicles:** Self-driving cars are being developed to improve road safety and reduce traffic congestion.
  - o **Traffic Optimization:** AI can optimize traffic flow by analyzing real-time data and adjusting traffic signals.

- **Entertainment:**
  - o **Recommendation Systems:** AI algorithms can suggest personalized content (movies, music, and books) based on user preferences.
  - o **Content Creation:** AI is being used to generate creative content, such as music, art, and even scripts.

Key Areas of AI Application

Let us understand the key areas of AI application.

- **Personalization:**

  AI enables personalized user experiences by analyzing data to understand individual preferences and behaviors. This is commonly used in e-commerce platforms for product recommendations and targeted marketing.

- **Automation:**

  AI automates repetitive tasks, improving efficiency and freeing up human resources for more strategic activities. Examples include chatbots for customer service and automated data entry.

- **Data Analysis and Insights:**

  AI processes large volumes of data to extract valuable insights, aiding in decision-making and strategy development. This is crucial in industries such as finance, healthcare, and logistics.

- **Natural Language Processing (NLP):**

  NLP allows applications to understand and respond to human language, enabling functionalities such as voice recognition, sentiment analysis, and language translation.

- **Predictive Analytics:**

  AI models predict future trends and behaviors based on historical data, helping businesses anticipate customer needs and optimize operations.

Benefits of AI in the MERN Ecosystem

Let us understand and analyze the benefits of AI in the MERN Ecosystem.

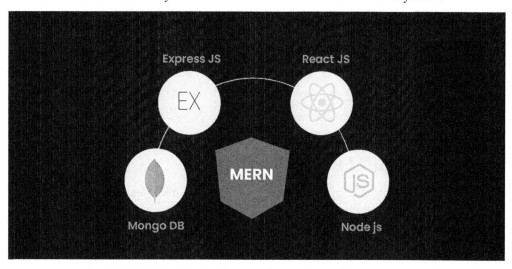

Figure 15.2: MERN Stack (Source - *https://api.reliasoftware.com/ uploads/mern_stack_e2cf626a69.webp*)

- **Scalability:**

  The MERN stack provides a scalable framework for deploying AI applications, allowing them to handle increased loads and user demands efficiently.

- **Flexibility:**

  The modular nature of the MERN stack enables seamless integration of AI features, allowing developers to choose the best tools and libraries for specific tasks.

- **Real-Time Processing:**

  AI applications built on the MERN stack can process data in real-time, providing immediate insights and responses to users.

- **Cost-Effectiveness:**

  By automating processes and optimizing resource usage, AI applications can reduce operational costs and increase profitability.

Challenges and Considerations

Let us check and understand the challenges and considerations of using AI.

- **Data Privacy and Security:**

  Ensuring the security and privacy of user data is paramount. AI applications must comply with regulations, such as GDPR, and implement robust security measures.

- **Ethical AI:**

  Developers must consider ethical implications, such as bias and fairness, when designing AI systems to ensure they are responsible and equitable.

- **Integration Complexity:**

  Integrating AI into existing systems can be complex. Developers need to ensure seamless communication between AI components and other parts of the application.

Challenges and Future Trends

While AI has made significant strides, it also faces challenges such as data privacy, bias, and ethical considerations. As AI continues to advance, we can expect to see even more innovative and impactful applications in the future.

By understanding the potential and challenges of AI applications within the MERN ecosystem, developers can create innovative solutions that enhance user experiences and drive business success. The following case studies will provide practical examples of how these concepts are applied in real-world projects.

Case Study 1: AI-Driven E-Commerce Platform

This case study explores the development of a dynamic e-commerce platform that leverages AI to provide personalized product recommendations. By integrating AI within the MERN stack, the platform enhances the user experience and drives sales through tailored suggestions.

Figure 15.3: *AI-Driven E-Commerce Platform (Source - https://common-blog -suffes.s3.us-east-2.amazonaws.com/1679570887641c37c7e9054.webp)*

Challenges Faced

Let us see the challenges faced by the aforementioned case study.

- **Data Management:**
  - ○ Handling large volumes of user data and product information efficiently.
  - ○ Ensuring data privacy and security while processing sensitive customer information.
- **Personalization:**

  Developing a recommendation engine that accurately predicts user preferences and delivers relevant product suggestions.
- **Scalability:**

  Designing the system to handle increasing user traffic and data loads without compromising performance.

Solutions Implemented

Let us understand the solutions implemented for the challenges faced by the aforementioned case study.

- **Technology Stack:**
  - o **MongoDB**: Used for storing user data, product information, and interaction logs. Its flexibility and scalability make it ideal for handling diverse data types.
  - o **Express.js**: Serves as the backend framework, managing server-side logic and API endpoints.
  - o **React**: Provides a responsive and dynamic user interface, allowing users to interact seamlessly with the platform.
  - o **Node.js**: Powers the backend development, enabling efficient handling of asynchronous operations.
- **AI Integration:**
  - o **TensorFlow.js**: Utilized to develop machine learning models for the recommendation engine. Models are trained on historical user data to predict preferences and suggest products.
  - o **Collaborative Filtering**: Implemented to analyze user behavior and identify patterns for personalized recommendations.
- **Scalability and Performance:**
  - o **Microservices Architecture**: Adopted to modularize the recommendation engine, allowing independent scaling and maintenance.
  - o **Caching with Redis**: Implemented to store frequently accessed data, reducing database load and improving response times.
  - o **Load Balancing**: Ensures even distribution of traffic across servers, thus maintaining performance during peak usage.

Outcomes Achieved

Let us understand the outcomes that can be achieved with ease.

- **Enhanced User Experience**:

  Users receive personalized product recommendations, increasing engagement and satisfaction.

- **Increased Sales**:

  The recommendation engine drives higher conversion rates by suggesting relevant products, boosting sales.

- **Efficient Resource Utilization:**

  The use of microservices and caching optimizes resource usage, ensuring the platform remains responsive and cost-effective.

- **Scalability:**

  The platform is designed to scale seamlessly with growing user demand, maintaining performance and reliability.

  This case study demonstrates the successful integration of AI within the MERN stack to create a powerful e-commerce platform. By leveraging advanced technologies and methodologies, the platform delivers a personalized shopping experience that meets the needs of modern consumers.

  Here are some code snippets illustrating key components, such as the recommendation engine using TensorFlow.js and server-side logic with Express.js.

TensorFlow.js for Recommendation Engine

Let us understand the key components, such as the recommendation engine, using TensorFlow.js.

```
const tf = require('@tensorflow/tfjs-node');

// Sample user-item interaction matrix
const userItemMatrix = tf.tensor2d([
  [5, 3, 0, 1],
  [4, 0, 0, 1],
  [1, 1, 0, 5],
  [0, 0, 5, 4],
  [0, 0, 4, 0],
]);

// Define a simple collaborative filtering model
const model = tf.sequential();
model.add(tf.layers.dense({ units: 4, activation: 'relu',
inputShape: [4] }));
model.add(tf.layers.dense({ units: 4, activation: 'sigmoid' }));

// Compile the model
model.compile({ optimizer: 'adam', loss: 'meanSquaredError' });

// Train the model
async function trainModel() {
  await model.fit(userItemMatrix, userItemMatrix, { epochs: 100
});
```

```
    console.log('Model training complete');
}

// Make predictions
async function makePrediction(userIndex) {
  const userVector = userItemMatrix.slice([userIndex, 0], [1,
4]);
  const prediction = model.predict(userVector);
  prediction.print();
}

trainModel().then(() => makePrediction(0));
```

Express.js Server Setup

Let us know the codes for the setup procedure for the Express.js server.

```
const express = require('express');
const app = express();
const port = 3000;

// Middleware for parsing JSON requests
app.use(express.json());

// Sample route for product recommendations
app.post('/recommend', (req, res) => {
  const userId = req.body.userId;
  // Logic to fetch and return recommendations for the user
  res.json({ recommendations: ['Product1', 'Product2', 'Prod-
uct3'] });
});

// Start the server
app.listen(port, () => {
  console.log(`Server running at http://localhost:${port}`);
});
```

React Component for Displaying Recommendations

Let us understand the react component for displaying recommendations.

```
import React, { useState, useEffect } from 'react';
import axios from 'axios';

function Recommendations({ userId }) {
```

```
      const [recommendations, setRecommendations] = useState([]);

    useEffect(() => {
      async function fetchRecommendations() {
        try {
          const response = await axios.post('/recommend', { userId
});
          setRecommendations(response.data.recommendations);
        } catch (error) {
          console.error('Error fetching recommendations:', error);
        }
      }

    fetchRecommendations();
  }, [userId]);

  return (
    <div>
      <h2>Recommended Products</h2>
      <ul>
        {recommendations.map((product, index) => (
          <li key={index}>{product}</li>
        ))}
      </ul>
    </div>
  );
}

export default Recommendations;
```

These code snippets demonstrate how to build a recommendation engine using TensorFlow.js, set up a server with Express.js, and create a React component to display product recommendations.

Case Study 2: Customer Service Chatbot

This case study focuses on the development of a customer service chatbot designed to enhance user engagement and automate responses. By integrating natural language processing (NLP) within the MERN stack, the chatbot provides efficient and personalized customer support.

Figure 15.4: *Customer Service Chatbot   (Source – https://support.cc/images/blog/ chatbot-customer-service.png?v=1682512742702523116)*

Challenges Faced

Let us list down the challenges faced by the preceding case study.

- **Understanding User Queries:**
  - ○ Accurately interpreting diverse user inputs and intents.
  - ○ Handling ambiguous or incomplete queries effectively.
- **Response Generation:**
  - ○ Providing relevant and context-aware responses.
  - ○ Ensuring the chatbot can handle a wide range of customer inquiries.
- **Scalability:**
  - ○ Designing the system to manage increasing user interactions without performance degradation.

Solutions Implemented

Let us understand the solutions that can be implemented easily.

- **Technology Stack:**
  - ○ **MongoDB**: Used for storing conversation logs and user data, enabling personalized interactions and insights.
  - ○ **Express.js**: Manages server-side logic and API endpoints, facilitating smooth communication between the chatbot and users.

- o **React**: Builds a responsive and interactive user interface, allowing users to engage with the chatbot seamlessly.
  - o **Node.js**: Powers the backend, handling asynchronous operations and integrating with NLP services.
- **NLP Integration:**
  - o **Dialogflow**: Utilized for natural language understanding, enabling the chatbot to comprehend user intents and entities.
  - o **Pre-trained Models**: Leveraged to improve the chatbot's ability to recognize and respond to common queries.
- **Scalability and Performance:**
  - o **Microservices Architecture**: Deployed to modularize the chatbot's components, allowing independent scaling and maintenance.
  - o **Load Balancing**: Ensures even distribution of user requests, maintaining responsiveness during peak usage.

Outcomes Achieved

Let us understand the outcomes that can be achieved in the aforementioned case study.

- **Improved Customer Engagement:**

  The chatbot provides instant responses, enhancing user satisfaction and engagement.

- **Operational Efficiency:**

  Automating routine inquiries reduces the workload on human agents, allowing them to focus on more complex issues.

- **Scalability:**

  The system is designed to scale seamlessly with growing user demand, ensuring consistent performance.

- **Data-Driven Insights:**

  Analyzing conversation logs provides valuable insights into customer needs and preferences, informing business strategies.

This case study demonstrates the successful integration of NLP within the MERN stack to create an effective customer service chatbot. By leveraging advanced technologies and methodologies, the chatbot delivers personalized support and enhances user experiences.

Here are some code snippets illustrating key components, such as integrating Dialogflow for natural language processing and setting up a basic Express.js server.

Dialogflow Integration

Let us understand the key components, such as Dialogflow integration for natural language processing.

```
const dialogflow = require('@google-cloud/dialogflow');
const uuid = require('uuid');

// Create a new session
const sessionId = uuid.v4();
const sessionClient = new dialogflow.SessionsClient();
const sessionPath = sessionClient.projectAgentSession-
Path('your-project-id', sessionId);

// Function to process user input
async function processInput(text) {
  const request = {
    session: sessionPath,
    queryInput: {
      text: {
        text: text,
        languageCode: 'en-US',
      },
    },
  };

  const responses = await sessionClient.detectIntent(request);
  const result = responses[0].queryResult;
  console.log(`Query: ${result.queryText}`);
  console.log(`Response: ${result.fulfillmentText}`);
  return result.fulfillmentText;
}

// Example usage
processInput('Hello, how can I help you?');
```

Express.js Server Setup

Let us understand the setup of the Express.js Server with ease.

```
const express = require('express');
const bodyParser = require('body-parser');
const { processInput } = require('./dialogflow'); // Import the
Dialogflow function

const app = express();
const port = 3000;
```

```
app.use(bodyParser.json());

// Endpoint to handle chatbot requests
app.post('/chat', async (req, res) => {
  const userMessage = req.body.message;
  const botResponse = await processInput(userMessage);
  res.json({ response: botResponse });
});

// Start the server
app.listen(port, () => {
  console.log(`Server running at http://localhost:${port}`);
});
```

React Component for Chat Interface

Let us analyze the code for the react component for Chat Interface.

```
import React, { useState } from 'react';
import axios from 'axios';

function Chatbot() {
  const [messages, setMessages] = useState([]);
  const [input, setInput] = useState('');

  const sendMessage = async () => {
    const userMessage = { text: input, sender: 'user' };
    setMessages([...messages, userMessage]);

    const response = await axios.post('/chat', { message: input
});
    const botMessage = { text: response.data.response, sender:
'bot' };
    setMessages([...messages, userMessage, botMessage]);

    setInput('');
  };

  return (
    <div>
      <h2>Chatbot</h2>
      <div>
        {messages.map((msg, index) => (
          <div key={index} className={msg.sender}>
            {msg.text}
          </div>
```

```
      ))}
    </div>
    <input
      type="text"
      value={input}
      onChange={(e) => setInput(e.target.value)}
      onKeyPress={(e) => e.key === 'Enter' && sendMessage()}
    />
    <button onClick={sendMessage}>Send</button>
  </div>
  );
}


export default Chatbot;
```

These snippets demonstrate how to set up a customer service chatbot using Dialogflow for NLP, Express.js for server-side logic, and React for the user interface.

Conclusion

This chapter provided an insightful exploration of how AI can be effectively integrated within the MERN ecosystem to solve real-world problems. Through the detailed examination of two compelling case studies, readers gain a practical understanding of the challenges, solutions, and outcomes associated with AI-driven projects. The first case study showcased an AI-driven e-commerce platform that used machine learning for personalized product recommendations, while the second focused on a customer service chatbot leveraging natural language processing to enhance user engagement. These examples illustrate the transformative potential of AI and MERN technologies, offering valuable lessons and inspiration for developers looking to embark on their own AI projects.

Multiple Choice Questions

1. What is the primary focus of the first case study in this chapter?

   a. Data encryption

   b. Personalized product recommendations

   c. User authentication

   d. Real-time data processing

2. Which technology is used for developing machine learning models in the e-commerce platform case study?

   a. PyTorch

   b. TensorFlow.js

    c. Scikit-learn

    d. Keras

3. What is the main goal of the customer service chatbot discussed in the second case study?

    a. Data mining

    b. Automating responses and enhancing user engagement

    c. Image recognition

    d. Financial forecasting

4. Which library is used for natural language processing in the chatbot case study?

    a. NLTK

    b. Dialogflow

    c. OpenCV

    d. TensorFlow

5. What role does MongoDB play in the AI-driven e-commerce platform?

    a. Frontend development

    b. Data storage

    c. User interface design

    d. Load balancing

6. How does the e-commerce platform improve user experience?

    a. By reducing server load

    b. By providing personalized product recommendations

    c. By enhancing data encryption

    d. By simplifying API design

7. What is a key benefit of using microservices architecture in the chatbot project?

    a. Increased data redundancy

    b. Independent scaling and maintenance

    c. Simplified frontend design

    d. Reduced computational power

8. Which framework is used for building the responsive UI in the e-commerce platform?

    a. Angular

    b. React

    c. Vue.js

    d. Svelte

9. What is the primary advantage of using Express.js in these case studies?

    a. Managing relational databases

    b. Handling server-side logic and API endpoints

    c. Designing user interfaces

    d. Encrypting data

10. What outcome is achieved by automating routine inquiries in the chatbot project?

    a. Increased server costs

    b. Reduced workload on human agents

    c. Enhanced data storage

    d. Simplified user authentication

Answers

1. b

2. b

3. b

4. b

5. b

6. b

7. b

8. b

9. b

10. b

Index

Printed in Great Britain
by Amazon

57402993R00242